A mes chers amis
André et Eva Mandel

"If a man does not keep pace with his companions, perhaps it is
because he hears a different drummer. Let him step to the music
which he hears, however measured or far away."
Henry David Thoreau

Contents

Acknowledgments

The author wishes to express his deep gratitude to Carol C. Kneeland, director and cofounder, with Theodore R. Kneeland, of the Language Retraining Program at Trinity-Pawling School, an independent boys boarding school in Pawling, New York. Her wisdom, counsel, and deep faith in the ability of all children to learn has helped make this a reliable reference that parents, teachers, and counselors can trust.

Special thanks are also due Susan Schwartz, senior editor, NTC/Contemporary Publishing Company, whose skills and objectivity brought order and reason to a most difficult work with far-reaching implications for untold numbers of learning-abled children.

Also instrumental in making this book possible were Edward W. Knappman, New England Publishing Associates, Inc., and Randy Ladenheim-Gil.

A Note to Parents

I believe this is the first book to expose as nothing more than normal learning differences what many practitioners of special education now call learning disabilities. The truth is that special education can often turn normal learning differences into disabilities. Many children now enrolled in special education do not need special education—they need good education tailored to their individual needs. The chances are that good education is all your child needs, too.

To make this book as practical and easy to use as possible for parents of school-age children, it is divided into two parts. The first explains the differences between true learning disabilities and normal learning differences. It shows you how to keep your child out of the special-education traps in childcare facilities, preschools, and elementary and secondary schools. It will show you how to help your child convert learning differences into learning advantages and prevent them from becoming liabilities or disabilities.

The second part of the book provides a step-by-step guide to infant education and intellectual development from the time your newborn comes home to the beginning of kindergarten. It shows how proper intellectual training of infants at home can prevent children from developing academic and intellectual problems many schools are quick to call learning disabilities.

All children have learning differences and what they usually need is good education, not special education. This book will show you how to assure your youngster will receive the good education every learning-abled child deserves. The appendixes provide lists of organizations and schools that can help. I hope that you will find the book useful and that it will help you keep your child out of the learning disability and special-education traps.

PART I

Chapter 1

Different but Not Disabled

If your child is bright but learning more slowly than other children you know, you may already be tempted to step into the learning disability trap. Every day, those two words—*learning disability*—are unnecessarily luring parents and their kids into an impenetrable web of devastating diagnoses, ineffective and unnecessary special education, or assorted drugs, vitamin supplements, and other remedies.

There is no need for you to get caught in that web. The overwhelming odds are that your child is just fine—perhaps different, but *not* learning disabled. As this book will show, your youngster can be different but still get on the right learning track in school and lead a happy, normal childhood—without either of you suffering any unnecessary emotional upheaval.

Inabilities and Disabilities

Most children do not have learning disabilities and do not need special education. They have learning abilities and inabilities, as we all do. But there is a big difference between a learning inability and a learning disability. A disability is an impairment or crippling condition; an inability is a normal incapacity resulting from inadequate resources.

All of us have inabilities to one degree or another. None of us is able to do or learn everything, and all of us do some things better or worse than others. That does not mean we are disabled—nor are our children.

The reason many children fail to learn as much as they could or should is that they lack proper resources. Either they simply have low aptitudes in certain areas and have more trouble learning certain things, or they have not been or are not being taught properly. In other words, parents, teachers, and schools are not fulfilling all their responsibilities to teach children properly.

That is why American children fare so poorly when tested against children from countries where education is a top priority. American kids finished thirteenth in mathematics proficiency in the world, behind such nations as Slovenia, and ninth in reading literacy, behind Iceland and just barely ahead of Singapore and Slovenia. American kids don't need special education; they need good education—and that's what this book is about.

This book is also about abilities, not disabilities, and how you can help your children develop their abilities and prevent their inabilities from becoming disabilities. You'll see how to find good teachers to give your youngster the resources to strengthen learning abilities, overcome learning weaknesses, and work around learning inabilities.

Creating an Epidemic

More than 88 percent of our children grow up to be perfectly normal adults. The vast majority of learning problems they develop in early childhood or at school are absolutely normal and not disabling, in any sense of the word. That may come as a happy surprise because you've undoubtedly seen distressing statistics to the contrary.

Indeed, the U.S. Department of Education reports that the number of children with learning disabilities in the United States soared 500 percent from 1975 to 1994, from fewer than eight hundred thousand to nearly four million, and the number has been increasing at near epidemic proportions ever since.

The official explanations for this epidemic range from environmental conditions to brain damage, and the costs to parents and taxpayers for various therapeutic programs have climbed to more than $10 billion a year. The most common programs include counseling, remediation, transfer to less demanding academic programs, and special education. There are many costlier, more extreme alternatives, however, including psychotherapy, hypnosis, drug therapy, or even institutionalization.

Some parents sacrifice all the joys of parenthood by dragging their children through an endless maze of counseling and treatment that leads to nothing but frustration and disappointment. They pursue an endless quest to learn why their children are only average—bright, but not gifted. Often, they refuse to accept the findings of skilled pediatricians and counselors and fall prey to fraudulent counselors and educational consultants.

Some parents are so disappointed in the averageness of their children that they simply give up. They decide nothing can be done to raise their children's achievement levels and they must accept the fact that their children are just different from other children, and perhaps a bit slower.

Unfortunately, there is limited, reliable help available in many areas of the United States for parents of bright children with learning problems. In smaller communities, there may be no help at all. Even those professionals who spend their lives teaching and counseling children know so little about learning problems they are often as overwhelmed and confused as parents by those frightening statistics.

Defining Learning Disability

What is now called a learning disability used to be called Minimal Brain Dysfunction, or MBD. MBD and what the modern world calls learning disabilities are still believed to be the result of some kind of faulty wiring in the brain—usually genetic in origin—that sends certain impulses along the wrong pathways. Physical injury to the brain before, during, or after birth can also cause learning disabilities, as can neurological disorders, premature birth, malnutrition, loss of hearing, vision, or speech, mental retardation, cerebral palsy, seizure disorders, autism, psychiatric or emotional disorders, a host of brain malfunctions, and any number of physical injuries to various parts of the body.

Only between 3 percent and 10 percent of American children are truly learning disabled, and almost all are enrolled in some form of special education, or retraining, by highly trained specialists who teach them new ways to learn. There is little question that children with such disabilities need special education. Most do learn successfully and often spectacularly.

Every child who has difficulty learning, however, does not necessarily have a learning disability, or we'd all qualify. This book is not about disabilities. It is about abilities and about hundreds of thousands of bright, learning-*abled* children—children like your own—who may have learning difficulties but are often mistakenly classed with truly disabled children as handicapped. Untold numbers of such children are normal in every respect. They are physically, mentally, and emotionally healthy, and often have above-normal intelligence.

Asking Tough Questions

Why then, if so little is known about learning disabilities, are they spreading so rapidly—and why can't something be done to halt the spread? A lot of skeptics are asking some tough questions:

◆ Do children today have more learning disabilities or are professionals more skilled at diagnosing a problem that used to be ignored?

◆ Are teachers misusing the learning disability label to rid classes of difficult students and shift responsibility away from their own faulty teaching methods?

◆ Are recent investigative reports correct in calling learning disabilities a racket that lets the special-education establishment and greedy parents and school administrators feed at the trough of federal funds for the handicapped?

The answers to all these questions are yes and no—and that is why most parents of children with normal, everyday learning problems are so confused. Let's try to clear up some of the confusion.

There are many reasons for the increase in the number of children diagnosed with learning disabilities. Some of these reasons are statistical, but others relate to the out-and-out deception, fraud, and profiteering that sometimes accompanies carelessly supervised federal- or state-funded programs.

Statistics

Statistical reasons for increased learning disability diagnoses include:

◆ *Increases in the school population.* As the general population has increased, so has the number of children, and therefore, the number of students with learning problems.

◆ *Broader base of students.* At the beginning of the twentieth century, only 10 percent of American kids went to high school. The rest went to work. Even in the late 1930s, before World War II, nearly one-third of American children went to work at fourteen—either because family circumstances required them to or because they had failed to perform academically and quit school or were expelled. Compulsory education laws now require all children to attend school well into their teenage years. Those laws have brought large numbers of deprived and disadvantaged children with language difficulties into public schools across America.

◆ *Increased numbers of non-English-speaking children.* Learning a new language often creates learning problems in every sector of education.

◆ *Increased awareness.* Improved medical technology and diagnostic procedures have uncovered a neurological basis for many learning disorders. Children who might have been called dumb or lazy several generations ago can now obtain special education and remediation that teaches them new ways to learn.

◆ *The federal Education for All Handicapped Children Act of 1975.* Amended in 1983, 1986, 1988, 1990 (and renamed the Individuals with Disabilities Education Act, or IDEA), 1991 (as the Individuals with Disabilities Act), and 1992, the act opened all public schools to handicapped children and added those diagnosed with learning disabilities to the category of the handicapped. Until then, an estimated eight million physically and mentally handicapped children were excluded from public schools and were languishing in institutions or at home. The act forced all public schools to guarantee "free and appropriate education" to all handicapped children, including the mentally retarded and emotionally disturbed—and children with learning disabilities.

The Law

Unfortunately, the politicians who wrote the Handicapped Children Act were no better able to agree on a definition of learning disabilities than experts and authors on the subject. The National Joint Committee on Learning Disabilities defines learning disabilities as "central nervous system dysfunctions . . . [that] are not the direct result of any external conditions or influences"—in other words, not the result of external trauma. That would limit the number of learning disabled kids to 10 percent of the student population at most, and perhaps as little as 3 percent.

Congress, however, broadened the definition to please all its constituents and opened the door for widespread abuses by greedy parents, teachers, counselors, school administrators, and school boards. The congressional definition called learning disabilities "a disorder in one or more of the basic psychological processes involved in understanding and using language, spoken or written, which may manifest itself in an imperfect ability to listen, think, speak, read, write, spell, and do mathematical calculations."

As if that weren't broad enough, Congress expanded the opportunity for greed still further, adding that students may be considered learning disabled if they do not achieve, at the proper age, ability levels in one or more of six skill areas in normal school subjects: oral comprehension, listening comprehension, written expression, basic reading skill, mathematics calculation, and mathematics reasoning.

The definition is so broad, however, that it is all but useless to educators or parents because it could include almost every child in America at one or another stage of life. And that, of course, is exactly why the number of kids tagged learning disabled has increased so dramatically. A lot of teachers and parents are using the term *learning disabled* as a catchall to explain normal, otherwise inexplicable steps backward that every child takes during the growing-up years.

A teacher or counselor who finds a child too troublesome to teach, or even disruptive, can recommend an evaluation to begin the process that may eventually assign the child to a special-education teacher or to a separate special-education classroom. Studies of many public-school systems have found that as many as one-third of the children in special-education classes probably do not belong there.

Why would usually well-meaning teachers or counselors mislabel normal kids as learning disabled? First, many public-school teachers and counselors have little understanding of learning problems, and the materials they read leave them so confused they often do not understand the differences between learning inabilities, low aptitudes, and learning disabilities. So, when they encounter normal learning difficulties they cannot handle, they often call children learning disabled to cover up inadequate, ineffective, and incompetent teaching.

The National Commission on Teaching set up by the Rockefeller Foundation and the Carnegie Corporation of New York found that more than 25 percent of newly hired public-school teachers enter their classrooms with inadequate teaching skills and are incapable of evaluating children's learning problems. The commission found fewer than half the nation's one thousand two hundred teacher's colleges met professional standards of accreditation and more than fifty thousand teachers who lacked training for their jobs had entered teaching.

By applying the learning disability label to children they are unable to teach, incompetent teachers and counselors can ascribe normal learning and behavioral problems to a medical condition for which neither the teacher nor the student can be held responsible. Little by little, teachers can use such special-education referrals to clear overcrowded classrooms of unruly, disruptive children who require individual attention, are difficult to teach, or are bored.

Unnecessary Referrals

The result is that many children are unnecessarily referred to special education. A normal, healthy, restless little boy who exasperates his teacher, for example, may be sent for counseling, and if his parents agree, eventually to special education with a diagnosis of Attention Deficit Disorder.

It is no coincidence that five to nine times as many boys are diagnosed by schools as having Attention Deficit Hyperactivity Disorder as girls. Every impartial study of this disorder has proved overwhelming teacher referral bias toward boys—especially boys who seem restless or act out, as normal boys tend to do more than girls. (Studies show girls tend to remain quiet and daydream when bored.)

Nor is it a coincidence that 34 percent of African-American students, many of whom speak a "Black English" that is incomprehensible to predominantly white teachers, have been identified as mentally retarded. (Nearly 90 percent of public elementary- and secondary-school teachers are white.)

Another reason for mislabeling normal children as learning disabled stems from the proliferation of confusing formulas for determining a learning disability. One such formula labels a child learning disabled when there is a two-year discrepancy between the child's age and school-achievement level as measured by classroom grades. A second formula narrows the discrepancy to one year, and a third declares a child learning disabled when there is a two-year discrepancy between I.Q. and achievement test scores.

All three can be valid formulas when used with average children, but they can be invalid for many other children. For example, the I.Q. formula correctly labels as learning disabled a mentally retarded ten-year-old with an I.Q. of 75 who functions at the level of a seven-year-old and shows a three-year discrepancy between I.Q. and achievement. But the same formula fails to identify the learning problems of the near-genius ten-year-old with an I.Q. of 145, who only functions at grade level when he or she should be functioning many grades higher.

The tragic result is that many normal, healthy children, with superior intelligence and ability end up drifting through school doing mediocre or substandard work in classes that often demand little intellectual achievement and produce even less. I hope you will not let this happen to your children.

Profit

Tragically, many public-school administrators and school boards are doing little to stop the growth of special education because each learning disabled child means increased subsidies from the federal and state governments—often as much as $7,000 per child. New York grants $4,000 to schools for each child they shift into special education—an incentive that has raised the cost of special education to 25 percent of the entire state budget for all education.

With little federal oversight of the kids schools call learning disabled—or how schools use government funds—some school administrators in sports-crazed communities misuse special-education funds for sports programs. In other schools, students who need remedial reading or math are sent to costly special education because the school can only get federal subsidies for special education and not remediation.

Except for students who are needlessly sent to special education and the taxpayers who pay for it, everyone profits from the Education for All Handicapped Children Act. Schools profit from government grants; classroom teachers profit by ridding their classes of children who are difficult to teach; out-of-work teachers profit with new part-time or full-time jobs tutoring, teaching special education, and even coaching football.

Even parents profit from their children's misery. Under the Supplemental Security Income Program, poor parents on Medicaid obtain an average of more than $5,000 a year in increased welfare payments for each child whose doctor certifies him or her as learning disabled. And all parents, rich and poor alike, are entitled to federal special-education funds to pay for costly private tutoring and private-school education if the public-school district is unable to provide the type of special education the child's doctor or parents approve.

Once a child is diagnosed as learning disabled, the local public-school district is required to provide a free and appropriate special-education program for that child. But the parent must approve the program. If the parent demands a program the school district cannot provide and can prove the child needs that program, in many instances the district must still pay for it, even if it means sending the child to a private school. The district must pay all costs, including tuition, transportation, books, student fees, and where required, room and board, school uniforms, or special dress clothing.

The LD Trap

While all the adults in their lives are profiting, however, many of the kids tagged "LD" are suffering tragic losses—in educational opportunity, self-respect, and eventual academic and intellectual achievement. They are labelled dumb or slow. Their friends know it, their teachers and relatives know it, and too soon, they know it and believe it.

For all too many of these unfortunate children, it simply is not true. As you read ahead, try to keep in mind that if, like all normal, healthy children, your child has a few learning difficulties, the overwhelming odds remain that your youngster is still learning-abled—with the same or perhaps even greater potential for learning success as any other child. I hope this book will help you help your child realize that potential.

Accepting Imperfections

The first thing to recognize is that it is normal to have imperfections of one sort or another. Imperfections and inabilities, however, are not necessarily disabling—which is why the term *learning disability* is so confusing that even some experts cannot agree entirely on a definition. As a result, the term has become cruelly misleading for many parents, teachers, and counselors of otherwise normal children.

The truth is that *learning disability* has become an ill-advised catchall phrase that is meaningless in the broad sense in which it is now used. Originally used to refer to brain-related dysfunctions that interfered with a person's ability to learn, it now refers to every conceivable intellectual and academic deficit and below-average aptitude.

The term should be abandoned because, as it is now used, the concept of learning disability poses a dilemma similar to that of whether a glass of water is half full or half empty. In the case of learning disability, the dilemma becomes whether none of us has a learning disability or whether all of us do. As with the glass of water, both statements are true because none of us, including your youngster, is perfect. When it comes to learning, all of us share these three imperfections:

1. None of us learns everything in exactly the same way as everyone else.

2. None of us learns everything at exactly the same age as everyone else.

3. None of us is able to learn all things that others try to teach us.

In other words, many imperfect learning skills, which some educational scaremongers are all too ready to call learning disabilities, are perfectly normal. They are not disabilities; they are learning differences, and there is no reason for them to disable us, either in school or in life.

A Personal Tale

My son, for example, learned to ride his first bicycle on his fifth birthday, with me huffing and puffing behind, steadying the rear of his bike for a few minutes until—Hooray!—he rode away on his own. My neighbor's son, who was born on the same day as my son, learned the same thing in a different way about six months later, with training wheels. He was smaller than my son and had not developed the same balancing skills and muscular coordination at the same time. Was he learning disabled?

Well, perhaps, in the broadest sense. For a while, at least, he could not learn what my son and other neighborhood kids had learned. But both boys eventually learned to ride equally well, and when they were old enough, they happily pedalled off to school together, displaying equal skills. Their differences had no effect on ultimate results, and it would be cruel—and inaccurate—to say my neighbor's son was disabled.

Like millions of other children who learn to ride bicycles, each of the boys learned the same thing in different ways at different ages—not because of any disabilities, but because of differences in the way each child developed, and in turn, the way each child learned.

Just as children's bodies mature at different rates, so do their brains. Few children speak their first words on the same day, or understand a particular abstract concept on the same day in ninth grade algebra class.

Unlike the rest of the body, the brain continues to mature until one's thirties, and no brain and no specific part of the brain matures at the same rate. In the case of my son and his friend, the part of the brain that controlled the coordination needed for bicycle-riding matured at slightly different rates in each child.

But let's say that neither my son nor my neighbor's boy mastered bicycle-riding—that the microscopic cells that control the needed coordination did not develop adequately. Well, so what? Neither would have been disabled in any realistic sense of that word, unless my neighbor and I traumatized the boys by humiliating them for their failures. They might have missed the fun of bicycle-riding, but that's hardly disabling over the course of a lifetime.

Similarly, in intellectual pursuits most of us have areas in which we excel and find it easy to learn, others in which we are average, and others in which we are below average and cannot seem to learn a thing. None of us can learn everything everyone tries to teach us, and the results are seldom disabling or critical to our abilities to lead normal, productive lives. The same principles are true for our children.

Redefining Learning Disabilities

Once again, the vast majority of healthy children with normal learning differences—even many who are now labelled "learning disabled"—are not disabled. That is why it may be helpful to use some new, more meaningful terms to describe normal variations in children's abilities to learn.

The British use the term *special needs*, which is far kinder and more appropriate and less pejorative than *learning disabilities* because it recognizes that all children have some special needs.

I prefer the terms *learning difference* and the more meaningful *learning impediment*, which I believe accurately reflect the normal variations in healthy children's abilities to learn at various stages of their development. An impediment is something someone may be able to jump over, get around, or push out of the way. A disability implies permanent crippling that destroys hope for too many children and parents.

To some, these distinctions may only be a question of semantics, but as a parent, I know how frightening a child's learning differences and impediments can be. There is no reason to add to that fright by using words that connote hopelessness when in fact, every child can learn to minimize the effects of virtually every type of learning difficulty.

Learning Differences

Although it may seem like a contradiction in terms, it is normal to be different. It is healthy and it is human. Every newborn infant's face is different from that of every other baby, even in so-called "identical" twins. Every baby develops differently and at a different rate from every other. Some are quicker than others to stand or walk, others quicker to talk, still others more nimble with their fingers. Some are bigger boned and husky, others thin and fragile. Some are agile, others clumsy; some quick to learn, others slow.

Regardless of such differences, the vast majority will grow up to be normal, happy, confident children and adults, able to accept and even laugh at their imperfections—if their parents love, accept, and enjoy them for what they are rather than fretting over what they lack. Children whose parents do not accept them because of imperfections invariably grow up discouraged about learning, not accepting themselves, and feeling imperfect. Sadly, the problem generating their failures is not theirs—it is their parents'.

Accepting the Unconventional

The vast majority of children can and usually will learn most (though not all) of the things most average children learn, but in different, perhaps even unconventional ways and at different times in their learning years. There are, as you know, many different ways of teaching children to read. Phonics teaches children to sound out letters and letter combinations; the whole-word approach teaches the child to see and learn the entire word and its meaning as a single entity.

The brightest, most gifted children often have the most unconventional ways of learning. Instead of multiplying, say, 23 × 46 on paper, some mathematically gifted children, with little effort, gradually incorporate in their memory multiplication tables of all double-digit numbers. Many instinctively see in their mind's eye the product of two-, three-, and even four-digit numbers and don't need to write out the problem in longhand. Ironically, instead of earning them praise, such shortcuts to learning often produce hostile responses from average-intelligence teachers and poor grades for getting the right answer in the wrong way.

Many teachers with large groups of students in their classes cannot or will not take time to provide individual students personal attention. Rather than confuse the group by attempting to explain the many ways to solve the same problem, they select the method they believe easiest for the most children.

The easiest method for the largest number of children, however, is not necessarily the easiest way for all children. Slower children invariably struggle to keep up, while gifted children are always a jump ahead and become bored.

The easiest way for most children to add double- or triple- or multiple-digit numbers, for example, is to add single numbers. Thus most average students learn to add, say, 43 + 22 by adding 3 + 2 in the right column to get 5, then 4 + 2 in the next column to get 6. But for other, perhaps more gifted children, an easier method would be to add 40 + 20 to get 60, then 3 to get 63, then 2 to get 65—all done in one's head, without the error-prone necessity of carrying over.

Too many students who fail to adopt a teacher's approach to solving problems, however, are labelled difficult, and therefore, prospective candidates for special education. But they are not difficult; they simply process information differently, much the same way different types of computers have different operating systems.

No sane person would expect every child to look like every other, and it is equally preposterous to believe that every child's brain operates and processes information the way every other child's brain does. Yet that is exactly what many parents and teachers insist upon. Indeed, far too many teachers and parents base their teaching methods on the premise that every child learns the same way. That is a faulty premise that can, in many instances, discourage a child's future efforts to learn successfully.

Keeping Perspective

I hope the terms *learning difference* and *learning impediment* will allow you to read this book with a new perspective of your child's learning processes. Try to keep in mind that your child is not learning disabled simply because he or she learns some things in different ways at different times from other children, or finds it difficult to learn some things other children seem to pick up easily. Your child cannot learn everything to the same degree as every other child, and it is unrealistic for you or any teacher to expect that.

The overwhelming odds are that your child is normal, healthy, and learning-abled, and any efforts to treat him or her otherwise may inflict psychological wounds that will leave your youngster with pervasive feelings of failure and unworthiness. Learning differences and impediments need not be disabling, but treating your child as disabled can be.

Critical and Noncritical Learning Impediments

Just because the term *learning disability* is overused and mis-applied does not mean there are no real learning disabilities—true physical or neurological impairments. Such impairments go beyond low aptitudes and actually prevent conventional learning.

Fortunately, most of them are noncritical because the skills they keep us from learning are nonessential—carrying a tune, for example, or seeing certain colors or developing the eye-hand coordination for fielding a ground ball on the baseball diamond. Such noncritical learning impediments have little consequence for the kind of learning needed for academic success in school or economic, emotional, and social success in adult life.

Critical learning impediments, on the other hand, prevent people from learning the language skills essential for competent functioning in school, in the workplace, and at home as capable and loving mates and parents. Critical learning impediments prevent a child from learning to read (*dyslexia*), write (*dysgraphia*), speak (*dysfluency*), listen (*distractibility, hyperactivity,* and *Attention Deficit Disorder*), calculate (*dyscalculia*), and perform other language functions that are essential for learning everything we need to learn in school and in life. Critical learning impediments require special-educational procedures described in Chapters 5 and 6.

Identifying Causes of Learning Impediments

Years of research have failed to identify all the causes of critical and noncritical learning impediments. Like many physical dysfunctions, many learning impediments probably result from any of a variety of genetic or environmental causes or a combination of both. Physical, psychological, emotional, social, cultural, and economic factors also have roles. It's often difficult to pinpoint which factors are most important in the case of any given child.

Genetics

For example, some studies have found that 25 percent to 40 percent of children with certain critical learning impediments have immediate relatives with similar impediments. Those studies would seem to indicate that learning impediments have genetic origins.

Environment

Other studies, however, provide equally convincing evidence of environmental causes of learning impediments. Children born in poverty, for example, with inadequate pre- and postnatal care, nutrition, and infant education, have higher rates of critical learning impediments than children born in better economic circumstances. But there is no way to be certain whether the learning impediments of children in the same poor family are the result of common genes or the consequences of poverty or both.

Similarly, adoptive children have five times the incidence of critical learning impediments of nonadoptive children—a statistic that may relate to either their genetic background or the high poverty rate among the birth families from which many adoptive children originate.

The factors that can come into play are virtually endless. Remembering that genetics and environment can play a role in almost every type of learning impediment, it is nevertheless possible to group the causes into two broad categories: learning impediments caused largely by internal factors such as physical impairment, and learning impediments caused by external factors such as educational deprivation.

Physical Problems

Physical impairments, whether genetic or environmental in origin, can cause both critical and noncritical learning impediments. Some noncritical learning impediments may have their genesis in a serious physical problem, while an apparently critical learning impediment may be the result of an easily correctable error that has nothing to do with neurological functions or the brain.

Thus difficulty learning to ride a bicycle might have its roots in a serious middle-ear problem affecting balance. But the serious inability of another child to write legibly might simply result from the way the youngster holds a pencil—an apparent learning disability that would only require a mechanical correction and a little practice.

Neurological Problems

On the other hand, many critical learning impediments such as dyslexia are believed to be the result of some kind of faulty wiring in the brain that sends certain impulses along the wrong pathways. If, for example, the wiring for certain visual impulses were tangled, a person's eyes might see the number *3*, but the person might think he or she saw the number *8* or the letter *E*.

We've all experienced the phenomenon when we've accidentally misread a number or word and could swear we saw something other than what was actually printed. For the person with a critical learning impediment, however, such misreading is constant, long-term, and not the result of accidentally reading something too quickly. No matter how slowly or carefully a child with dyslexia reads the number *3*, it still can appear to be an *8* or an *E*—just as a person who is color-blind invariably sees the spectrum in shades of grey.

As mentioned earlier, such faulty wiring may be inherited or may be the result of trauma—a physical injury—suffered in utero, at birth, or during infancy or childhood. The degree of physical injury does not necessarily produce a correspondingly severe learning impediment.

Learning Different Ways to Learn

Often, physical injury to the brain, spinal cord, or other part of the body only limits the number of ways a youngster can learn—just as an injury to a hand or foot might limit the ways a person can learn to write or walk. A person might require retraining to learn the use of other than the usual muscles to perform those operations. Drivers with color-blindness learn to differentiate green and red traffic lights by their positions—up and down or right and left.

Even serious physical trauma does not necessarily disable the learning process. It just makes it different, and sometimes more difficult, because it must follow a different path.

One of the most gripping stories of how retraining overcame serious learning difficulties is told in the touching film *My Left Foot*, which described how poet-artist Christy Brown was so crippled by cerebral palsy in infancy that he could not even talk. He eventually communicated by learning to write with the first and second toes of his left foot.

A better-known story is that of Helen Keller, who was rendered blind, deaf, and mute by an illness when she was eighteen months old. She learned to speak, read, and write, and not only graduated *cum laude* from Radcliffe College at Harvard University, but became a brilliant author, lecturer, and champion of education for the blind, deaf, and mute.

Though physically disabled, Helen Keller was far from learning disabled. In a less insightful and understanding family, however, her physical disabilities might have masked her learning abilities and potential, and in the era in which she lived, she might have been institutionalized. Instead, she remains the perfect example of why, for many, the term *learning disabilities* should be abandoned in favor of *learning differences* and *learning impediments*.

Developmental Impediments

Another internal factor that affects learning is the rate of a child's development. Many physically and neurologically induced learning impediments are developmental, or temporary, and the learning impediments they produce are also temporary. Most children experience and eventually outgrow them. An example is that of the six-year-old whose fingers cannot stretch across the eight keys of the piano to play an octave. The child's hands and fingers will probably grow and the inability to play an octave will fall into the huge category of temporary, developmental learning impediments we all encounter and outgrow.

There are, however, an almost endless number of less obvious, often worrisome developmental learning impediments to which many parents and teachers respond in inappropriate and sometimes harmful ways.

For example, many children go through stages when they write some letters backward or upside down or in incorrect sequences. They are not necessarily learning disabled.

Most boys go through periodic stages of restlessness during which they simply cannot sit still and find it difficult to concentrate on learning. They do not necessarily have Attention Deficit Hyperactivity Disorder (ADHD). Most girls go through stages when anything an adult says is "so boring" that they, too, find it difficult to learn—and they do not necessarily have Attention Deficit Disorder (ADD).

Among children who do have such critical learning impediments, about 15 percent to 20 percent eventually see their symptoms disappear. Even dyslexia, which most researchers consider neurological in origin, sometimes proves to be only a developmental aberration that disappears within a few years. One study at the Yale University School of Medicine found that only one of six in a group of four hundred Connecticut children with symptoms of dyslexia in the first grade continued to display those symptoms in the third grade. In other words, the symptoms of dyslexia disappeared within two years in five out of six first-graders.

Rushing to Judgment

Such temporary developmental learning impediments, therefore, do not require an anxiety-ridden dash to a psychologist for immediate testing, evaluation, and placement in special education. To infer that a child is disabled is to ensure that child's belief in his or her disability and inability. In other words, children who are told they cannot learn won't learn.

Developmental learning impediments require parent-teacher patience, not badgering, punishment, or forced repetition of exercises that only succeed in teaching a youngster he or she cannot succeed. Skilled piano teachers teach young children to practice success by playing pieces that do not require their tiny hands to play octaves.

The same teaching approach applies to every other type of developmental learning impediment. To force a child to try to learn what is impossible to learn at a given age is to force a child to fail. The more a child practices failure and associates it with learning, the less likely the child will try to learn in the future. An incompetent teacher or thoughtless parent can easily convert a temporary developmental learning impediment into a permanent one.

Controlling Environmental Factors

Although genetics unquestionably play a role in determining learning abilities and inabilities, home and school environments also affect a child's ability to learn and are responsible for many critical and noncritical learning impediments.

These environmental factors—external factors impinging on the child—are factors you as a parent can control. The choice of caregivers for preschool infants and the choice of preschools and schools can determine how well children learn the essential speaking, reading, and language skills needed to succeed academically and in adult life.

Even with no genetic history of critical learning impediments, a child who spends the first two to three years of life—the key years for developing language skills—in a linguistically pathological environment with poorly trained caregivers will inevitably develop learning impediments, possibly even critical ones.

Poor Infant Education

The first two to four years of a child's life are key language development years. Normal, healthy children who do not learn language skills at that age will seldom be able to learn them as well as they might have. A hungry or abused child cannot pay attention and will not learn, and a child will not learn in a home that provides no learning opportunities or does not emphasize learning.

There is little any school can do to help children catch up if parents fail to provide proper infant education by continuing conversation with and reading to their infants.

The government-sponsored Head Start preschools have been trying to help culturally deprived children in America's inner cities catch up since 1965, but children deprived of infant education before they enter preschool seldom acquire the language skills of children whose parents provided such education from birth.

In other words, parents themselves are responsible for creating many critical learning impediments that prevent a child from learning to read, write, or calculate adequately—by failing to provide infant education in a healthy environment in the years before schools and school teachers ever see the child. Chapter 2 discusses how you can prevent many learning impediments from developing.

Psychological Problems

Emotional or psychological problems can interfere with the learning process of children with the strongest intellects. A child with no speech difficulties at home might be unable to recite—or literally freeze—in public-speaking class. The origins of such shyness might be unconscious and unknown to the child, or they might be conscious, realistic fears of becoming the target of derision for having big ears or a squeaky voice.

Regardless of the origins, emotional and psychological problems frequently cause learning impediments. Although peer pressures can cause many problems, irrational demands of parents and teachers can also produce severe psychological problems that interfere in a child's ability to learn.

One of the most psychologically harmful parenting tendencies is what I like to call "the Little League syndrome." That is a phenomenon that sees parents (aided by teachers and peers) force a child to try to learn noncritical skills that others value but which the child is unable or unwilling to learn.

The result is often abject failure, public humiliation, and deep self-deprecation that can crush the normal intellectual risk-taking tendencies that make children want to learn. Forced by others to fail and absorb the hurt that accompanies failure, the child avoids the risking of future failures by not venturing into the intellectual unknown and risking rejection. In effect, a noncritical learning impediment can grow into a critical learning impediment in other unrelated, but far more essential areas.

Most healthy children test learning abilities in a variety of areas and instinctively give up activities in which they fail and pursue the rewards of success in areas of higher aptitude. Excessive parental or teacher focus on a child's learning inabilities can prevent the child from exploiting his or her abilities that could bring learning success.

Referral Bias

Still another externally imposed learning impediment is the referral bias mentioned earlier. By applying the learning-disability label to children they are unable to teach, teachers who are incompetent, impatient, or simply frazzled can effectively humiliate happy and healthy children with normal learning problems.

They do so by referring difficult children for testing, interviews, and evaluation for special education, which every child knows is reserved for "dumb kids." If formal evaluation identifies no specific learning disability, such children are often sent to general-education classes for slow or problem learners. Just the threat of such referrals is enough to frighten a child into questioning his or her ability and weaken the motivation to learn.

As mentioned earlier, school enrollment figures show as many as nine times as many boys with ADHD as girls. Studies of this disorder, however, prove that teacher referral bias against boys—especially boys who seem restless or act out—is responsible for the gender disparity.

Researchers believe there may be no gender difference in the occurrence of this learning impediment but that more girls than boys with ADD tend to withdraw, sit quietly, and daydream—displaying hypoactivity—while more boys than girls squirm in their seats and display hyperactivity. The tragic result is that fewer girls who need special education get the help they need and many boys who do not need special education are sent to such classes and lose the conventional academic instruction they need.

The tragic consequences for many children, with average, above average, and superior intelligence are years of drifting through school doing mediocre or substandard work in special-education, or worse, useless general-education classes, which demand little intellectual achievement and produce even less.

Expected to do less, students in such classes respond to those expectations and eventually stop trying to learn. In effect, the low expectations of teachers, who should have encouraged students, discouraged them and crushed their learning abilities. Such children do not start school unable to learn, but by the time they finish, many are unwilling even to try.

Special Education: A Growth Industry

Special education and general education have now grown into a multi-billion-dollar industry. Like many other federally funded programs that began with the best intentions, they are bilking American taxpayers and short-changing many youngsters the programs were designed to help. At its best—and that is usually in private schools—special education is indeed providing critical education for many children who would otherwise go through life truly learning disabled. At its worst, however, in many public-school systems, special education drains more than 25 percent of school funds from regular education and frightens parents into believing their kids are intellectual cripples. Ultimately, the process deprives many normal, healthy kids of the self-confidence and joy that learning and intellectual success instill.

I hope you won't let your child be lured into the learning disability and special-education traps.

Few of us have high aptitudes in every area of school and adult life. In most instances, a low aptitude is not a learning disability; it is a low aptitude, nothing more, nothing less. It is not disabling, and it does not need special education or warrant condemning a child to a slow academic track. Once again, most children need good education, not special education.

Identifying Noncritical Learning Impediments

Even if children fail to learn to play an instrument or sing on key, their world will not end, and as with children who never master bicycle-riding, they will not be disabled. Learning impediments such as tone-deafness are noncritical to the average person's eventual happiness, success, and ability to function in school or adult life. He or she may miss a few of the pleasures others enjoy, but will easily compensate with pleasures that accrue from learning other skills.

Not all of us can learn to draw, play an instrument, or sing, but such noncritical learning impediments are nondisruptive. They do not leave us intellectually dysfunctional or otherwise disable or disrupt our lives as successful, productive, and happy individuals—and they certainly do not warrant costly special education.

Although some duffers continue taking costly tennis or golf lessons for years (and I am still trying to learn to play the piano), most of us simply abandon efforts to learn those things we cannot learn, concentrate on learning what we can, and get on with our lives.

Similarly, just because your child runs into a learning impediment in one noncritical area does not mean he or she cannot function magnificently in many other areas. For your children's mental and intellectual health, it is far better to teach them to ignore or work around noncritical learning impediments and take full advantage of skills that they can easily and happily master.

If the school your child attends does not agree with this philosophy, or worse, suggests your child be evaluated for special education for a noncritical learning problem, try to find another school. If this is impractical or impossible, approach the appropriate teachers, school administrators, or school-board members and try to explain your point of view and the type of education you expect for your child. Become your child's advocate!

A child with a low aptitude in science who writes beautiful poetry or is a gifted dancer does not need special education to strengthen a weakness in science. There are far simpler, less disruptive choices, such as one-on-one tutoring, or even dropping science altogether after fulfilling the minimum requirements for graduation, and perhaps, admission to college.

The questions parents and children must answer about any learning impediment is when and whether to invest the time, effort, expense, and even heartache to try to overcome such problems. Once again, the answer usually depends on whether it is critical or noncritical to other essential learning.

Identifying Critical Learning Impediments

Unlike noncritical learning problems, critical learning impediments can be disabling if proper education is not provided. Some critical learning impediments may be the result of a neurological disability or dysfunction—the faulty wiring mentioned earlier—that makes learning seem virtually impossible in the critical areas of language skills. A youngster with dyslexia that has not disappeared by sixth grade may never see the letters and words in a sentence in the same shapes, sequences, and positions that nondyslexics do. Some sort of microscopic neurological connection is probably not functioning properly, and that is why dyslexia has been officially classified by the U.S. government as a disability.

A critical learning disability can seriously interfere with a youngster's ability to acquire such essential skills as reading, writing, calculating, and language functions needed to lead a normal, fulfilling life. Critical learning impediments are the only learning problems that can conceivably become learning disabilities and are the only ones for which parents should consider special education.

There is no question that, in today's world, the inability to read, write, or calculate is truly disabling and crippling in every sense—unless the person learns a way around the problem.

The *Encyclopedia of American Education* calls critical learning impediments "a broad spectrum of malfunctions of unknown causes that deter otherwise normal, healthy and intelligent individuals from understanding and acquiring language skills." The encyclopedia also points out that between 15 percent and 20 percent of children with such impediments outgrow them. In many cases, these otherwise disabling impediments are developmental. Although they do interfere with learning for a while, their long-term effects turn out to be minimal.

Finding Ways to Learn

Some children and adults with learning impediments find their own ways around them independently, either instinctively or with a teacher's or parent's help. Such children develop their own unique and different approaches to learning a particular skill.

Just consider some of the incredibly accomplished figures from the past and present with learning disabilities who found alternative ways to learn what they needed to succeed:

◆ Inventor Thomas Edison's difficulty writing complete sentences did not stand in the way of his inventing the incandescent light and illuminating New York City's streets.

◆ Woodrow Wilson couldn't read until he was eleven years old, but later graduated from Princeton University, became president of that university, governor of New Jersey, and president of the United States.

◆ Gen. George S. Patton couldn't read until he was twelve, but successfully led his U.S. troops up the Italian peninsula and across Europe to victory against the Nazis in World War II. Both Wilson's and Patton's parents read to their boys incessantly and instilled in them a love of reading that eventually helped them overcome their reading problems.

◆ Hans Christian Andersen, whose still-beguiling *Ugly Duckling* tale for children was a thinly disguised autobiography, had to dictate his stories because he never learned to write.

Other famous people who overcame learning difficulties include: French Emperor Napoleon, sculptor Auguste Rodin, French author Gustave Flaubert, Confederate President Jefferson Davis, author F. Scott Fitzgerald, King Olav of Norway, British Prime Minister Winston Churchill, New York Governor Nelson Rockefeller, New Jersey Governor Thomas H. Kean, artist Robert Rauschenberg, journalist-scholar Fred Friendly, singer-actor Harry Belafonte, actress-singer Cher, actor Tom Cruise.

In addition to the celebrities who had problems learning certain skills, there are untold thousands of doctors, lawyers, engineers, business men and women, teachers, nurses, computer operators, chefs, plumbers, actors, mechanics, barbers, firefighters, clerks, carpenters, postal workers, police officers, electricians, meat cutters, travel agents, dentists, artists, musicians, and authors with learning difficulties who are leading happy, fulfilling lives.

And we all have at least one thing in common with them: at one time or another, we all developed learning tricks—special ways to remember essential things that seemed impossible for us to learn but that others seemed to learn easily and in conventional ways.

I had a form of dysgraphia when I was eleven years old. My handwriting produced tiny, incomplete, telescoped letters that invariably climbed uphill as they traveled illegibly across the page. Not only couldn't my teacher read my handwriting, neither could I. So I learned to type. The typewriter solved my problem then, as the word processor now does for thousands of other adults and children with the same learning problem.

Taking Responsibility

Parents and teachers, however, cannot routinely ignore critical learning impediments and expect children to develop learning tricks of their own or find ways around such impediments as dysgraphics have done with word processors. Such children need special education.

Neurological disabilities do not make learning impossible. Some 90 percent of dyslexics can and do learn to read and write correctly, although not as easily as nondyslexics—just as tone-deaf children can learn to play the piano and even to sing, although not as easily as children with relative or perfect pitch.

In reality, then, even critical learning impediments need not have any long-lasting disabling effects. They may limit the ways a child can learn, but they don't prevent learning. Children with critical learning impediments usually only need the guidance and instruction of caring, highly trained adults to develop alternative ways of learning to overcome those difficulties and function effectively.

Developing alternative ways of learning—ways that are not instinctive and that most children would almost never discover on their own—is one of the greatest challenges for parents, teachers, and the children in their care.

These alternative processes are often the result of formal and informal teaching processes that identify effective techniques children with critical impediments such as dyslexia can use to learn effectively.

The thrust of this special education is not just to help a child get through school by passing tests, but to counter and minimize the effects of each child's learning impediment. Such special education effectively retrains children to function as independent people at their full potential.

Along with the concepts of learning differences and learning impediments, I urge you to keep the concept of retraining in the forefront of your mind as you read this book. All three concepts are essential to your child's educational success and happiness.

Hearing a Different Drummer

Anyone who has ever told a friend or loved one, "I'm so ashamed I never learned to . . ." knows the pain and humiliation of critical learning impediments. Just as you and I had our share of learning differences and impediments, your children and mine have their share. This book will show you how to help your children convert those learning differences and impediments into exciting triumphs.

Long before the term *learning disability* was invented, the American philosopher Henry David Thoreau may have presaged the concepts of learning differences, learning impediments, and retraining when he wrote these beautiful thoughts in his classic work *Walden*:

"If a man does not keep pace with his companions, perhaps it is because he hears a different drummer. Let him step to the music which he hears, however measured or far away."

The child some are so quick to call "learning disabled" because he does not keep pace with his companions simply hears a different drummer and may be learning in a different way at a different rate.

Eventually, most children can learn what they need to know to function as healthy individuals, but in their own way and at their own speed. And the things they don't learn or are unable to learn are often unimportant in helping them develop rewarding lives. Helping them develop the abilities they have is of far greater importance than focusing on their inabilities.

Ultimately, the abilities of children to learn and the ways parents and teachers nurture those abilities determine how joyful their learning years will be and whether their experiences as youngsters will encourage further learning throughout their lives. One of the worst problems children with learning differences and impediments face are the cruel and discouraging efforts of friends, teachers, and parents who try to force them to learn everything everyone else does, in the same way and at the same time.

If your child hears a different drummer, you as a caring parent, must listen for and try to hear that different beat so you can offer appropriate guidance and encouragement to help your child step to the music he or she hears and learn effectively. And you must find skilled teachers who will do the same. I hope this book will help you in those tasks.

Summary

Learning differences are normal. None of us learns everything in exactly the same way as everyone else, none of us learns everything at exactly the same age as every one else, and none of us is able to learn all things others try to teach us.

Genetic and environmental factors can turn learning differences into learning impediments. There are two types of learning impediments:

1. Critical learning impediments interfere in the acquisition of language skills necessary for learning in school and in the workplace—and require either one-on-one tutoring, remedial education, or special education.

2. Noncritical learning impediments are poor aptitudes in areas of nonessential skills. Children can try to improve with either one-on-one tutoring or remedial work. Or, they can simply ignore their noncritical impediments

and concentrate on activities where they demonstrate higher aptitudes. They do not require special education.

Parents cannot do anything about genetic factors, but with good infant education and careful selection of child-care workers, schools, and teachers, they can eliminate many environmental factors that produce learning impediments.

Chapter 2

Preventing Learning Impediments

The best and simplest way to deal with problems of all kinds, including learning problems, is to prevent them from developing. Alcohol, caffeine, drugs, nicotine, malnutrition, improper nutrition, poor hygiene, inadequate pre- and postnatal care, reckless driving, and other reckless behavior prior to and during pregnancy can injure your baby and produce learning impediments and serious physical and neurological disabilities. Cigarette, cigar, and pipe smoke can harm your newborn and children of any age forced to breathe smoke-filled air. Do not permit smoking of any kind in your house.

After your child is born and throughout his or her childhood, there are many steps you can take to prevent and overcome learning impediments and keep your child out of the learning disabilities trap. You've undoubtedly learned from parenting books how to protect your child's physical health, but most of them offer little help for protecting your child's intellectual health and ensuring proper development of essential language skills.

These skills are the foundation of your child's academic and professional future. They include conversing, memorizing, listening, understanding, responding, reading, writing, calculating, and developing other linguistic tools necessary for successful learning. The optimal time for learning these skills comes only once in each child's lifetime, usually during infancy, and often for a relatively short period.

Part II of this book is a step-by-step guide to infant education, with a timetable of intellectual skills development from earliest infancy to five years when formal schooling begins at the kindergarten level. Even if your child is already in school, you may find the guide helpful because many teaching techniques to prevent development of learning impediments can be used to help older children overcome such impediments.

Windows of Learning Opportunity

The windows of learning opportunity open at different times for every child. And while they never close entirely, they open widest at specific periods in every child's life and remain open for a limited time. It is during those moments that a child is most receptive to learning specific intellectual skills.

If you miss one of those optimal moments and fail to help your child learn an appropriate skill to the best of his or her ability, your child may find it almost impossible to learn that skill to the same degree later on. It is never too late to start learning, but keep in mind that it is difficult and sometimes impossible to play catch-up in the game of learning.

Nowhere are the difficulties of trying to learn too late more evident than in America's inner cities, where millions of educationally deprived children, through no fault of their own, emerge with inadequate speaking, reading, writing, and calculating skills. When, as late adolescents or as adults, they realize their deficiencies, many find time has passed them by and made it all but impossible to raise their skill levels to those required by the workplace. Anger is the inevitable result of intellectual impotence, and there is little question that much of the violence in American inner cities is directly related to poor education and illiteracy—and the unwillingness of Americans to invest adequately in the education of their young.

Understanding Language Disorders

A one-year-old who is constantly alone and ignored will never acquire adequate language skills. A six-year-old illiterate can learn to read, but that child's reading skills will almost never match those of a child who acquired word-recognition skills and learned the rudiments of writing and reading at three or four.

The government launched the massive Head Start program in 1965 to bring preschool education to three- and four-year-old inner-city children who would otherwise enter kindergarten and first grade illiterate and innumerate, with massive language disorders few would overcome.

There are two types of language disorders: receptive language disorders that interfere with understanding language and expressive language disorders that interfere with production of language. Environmental deprivation—word deprivation during infancy—is the most common cause of language disorders.

Although Head Start has helped millions of poor youngsters improve their reading skills, it has failed to raise their overall language skills to appropriate grade levels because of their cultural deprivation during infancy. More than half of all inner-city children are born to largely illiterate or semiliterate single parents who are unable to converse with or read to their children enough for adequate development of language skills.

By the time such children reach Head Start preschools or public-school kindergarten, the window of opportunity for acquiring complex language skills has narrowed considerably.

Millions of Americans in adult-education courses justifiably boast that you're never too old to learn, but they all sheepishly admit they don't seem to be able to learn as quickly or easily as they did when they were young.

Controlling Learning Environment

Clearly, the most effective way to prevent development of learning impediments is by teaching children critical intellectual skills when the windows of learning opportunity are open widest. The widths of these openings will vary for each child and for different skills, according to both genetic and environmental factors.

There is little you can do to control genetic factors, but there are many things you can do to control your child's learning environment to prevent the development of unnecessary learning impediments after birth. The key to such prevention is to give your child the best possible infant education in the years before preschool or kindergarten.

From the moment your child came home as a newborn, you and your spouse became your child's first and most important teachers. As such, you and your child's other caregivers must provide the education required for preventing learning impediments.

It's not enough just to be with your child. You must be your baby's teacher and mentor and remain in those roles throughout your youngster's childhood and adolescence. Always keep in mind that, during every stage of your child's development, he or she will learn and acquire almost all your emotional and intellectual habits and those of your spouse and the rest of the family.

Being a parent is not an easy job. It is hard work, and it carries enormous physical, emotional, and intellectual responsibilities—and most parents make many mistakes. It's impossible not to. It's never too late, however, to correct some mistakes of the past.

Remember, for example, that if you tend to be nervous or sullen, your child, regardless of age, will sense your disposition and tension. If you fret, your child will be fretful; if you're friendly and outgoing, your child, whether a baby or an older child, will sense that, too, and reflect your cheer and warmth. Eventually, your child will adapt to the environment you create and reflect that environment with a tense and sullen or sunny and friendly disposition. In other words, you are constantly teaching your child, passively or actively, whether you realize it or not and whether you want to or not. Your child is constantly learning from you.

Communicating with Your Child

The same holds true for language skills essential to learning. If you are silent around your child, your child will not learn to communicate. A child with whom no one communicates is likely to grow up with serious and perhaps irreversible language deficits—expressive language disorders that leave the child unable to speak and receptive disorders that affect understanding and make learning difficult.

That doesn't mean you must talk nonstop to your child. Talking too much or leaving the television or radio on does not help your child learn to communicate any better than silence. Such one-way, conversational overload never allows a child to respond and leaves a youngster feeling that what he or she has to say is unimportant and not worth saying.

Television and radio are dangerous ways to build a child's vocabulary because the words are not associated with any objects or facial expressions the child can see. The words project no human values. Children raised by TV or radio "babysitters" invariably grow up bonding more to electronic than human voices and learn to communicate in electronic cliches. Moreover, much of the language they learn is grammatically incorrect and often includes gutter talk.

The conversational environment you create will determine one of your child's most important linguistic skills: speaking, and in turn, writing and reading. In teaching these and other skills, remember that extreme approaches—too much talk or too little—will tend to be self-defeating and can produce serious learning impediments that will interfere with intellectual growth.

Intellectual growth begins the moment a child is born, and two-way conversation is one of the keys to enhancing that growth—even with newborns. Talk to your child frequently, regardless of his or her age, but make it a two-way conversation, much like you would with a friend. Never be too busy to talk to your child. Don't say or even think it or your child will soon grow too busy to talk to you.

Talk to, not at, your child. Look at your child when you talk, and give your child a chance to respond. Stop and listen while your child responds—and let your child finish saying whatever he or she has to say before responding. Don't interrupt your child with what you think are responsive or comforting words, and don't let others interrupt. Don't suddenly remember you have to make a call and pick up the telephone while your child is in midsentence. It not only diminishes your child, it discourages your child from practicing important language skills—and teaches bad manners.

Don't respond to your child with disinterested monosyllables such as *yes* or *right*. Respond with meaningful words— complete sentences that indicate to your child that words and feelings elicit significant, thoughtful, and caring responses from others.

And read and sing with and touch and hug your child, the way no radio or television can. Remember, when any window of learning opportunity is open, if you don't take full advantage, you will effectively reduce your child's ability to learn in the future.

Miseducation

From the moment a child is born, a parent's words, phrases, and sentences begin laying the foundation for the baby's eventual verbal or linguistic skills. During the early childhood years, youngsters develop essential linguistic skills by conversing. The window of learning opportunity for linguistic skills is open widest during the years before preschool. If children don't develop those skills then, they may never attain the same skill levels they might have.

Much of the time, especially during the first twelve months or so of a child's life, some parents may think their child is only babbling—responding with apparently meaningless sounds or non sequiturs to things they hear their parents say and initiating illogical, nonsensical conversations. The important thing for parents to do at that time is to keep talking.

Whether you realize it or not, when you talk to your child, you are gradually building your child's vocabulary and teaching the value of words, how to use them, and how to think and relate to others. And that process continues, throughout childhood and adolescence.

It's essential to remember that children are intellectual sponges, absorbing all you say. Whether or not you actively try to teach, your child is constantly learning from you. Almost all things you tell your youngster in the course of conversation— things you believe your child is ignoring—are being absorbed and learned.

Parents are invariably astounded when, after saying something aloud to another adult and believing their children do not understand, they later hear their youngsters repeat the words verbatim. A friend's five-year-old boy was about to enter kindergarten class and was doing his best to listen to his mother's endless instructions of things not to forget—"behave yourself, eat all your lunch, be polite to the teachers . . ." Finally, when he could take no more, the little chap put his hands on his hips in exasperation and said, "You're giving me such a headache!" The point is that your child is always learning.

Linguistic Skills

Linguistic skills are the most important intellectual skills in the learning process and the basis of all learning throughout life. Linguistic skills differentiate humans from other animals and differentiate each of us from our fellow humans. They eventually permit us to read, write, and calculate and to communicate in complex ways with others. That is why it is so important for parents to talk *with* rather than *at* their children, regardless of their ages, if they are to avoid developing learning impediments.

While building your child's vocabulary and conversational skills, however, it's important to bear in mind at all times that your child is *not* a small adult. Children do not think or learn the way adults do. They are children, and they think and function in radically different, often irrational, ways.

For one thing, they need a lot of hugs and kisses as they learn—to know their parents love them and that they are pleasing their parents by learning. They must know that learning is as much fun for parents as it is for them.

The Right Words

When conversing with your child, be sure to use real words—not "baby talk" or popular street or teen talk—and to speak in complete sentences. There is no reason real words and complete sentences cannot be uttered to a newborn, with as much joy, warmth, and love as gibberish and slang.

Every principle of learning and child-rearing substantiates that frequency of exposure relates directly to learning, and the longer a baby hears gibberish, the older it will be before it learns to speak English. Surely, no loving parent can possibly have any serious objection to using real words. Exactly who benefits when mature adults utter incomprehensible, preliterate coos and grunts that mean nothing to either the baby or the adult? The practice is ludicrous and can delay a baby's ability to learn critical linguistic skills—possibly beyond the time when the baby is most able to acquire those skills.

And there is never a reason for a parent to try to sound "cool" when speaking to an older child by using slang words, phrases, and other speech that reinforces poor speaking habits and abdicates your responsibility to help your child grow into a literate adult. Your child will not learn proper speech later. The time to teach your child to speak properly and develop conversational skills is now!

Learning to Teach

The secret to all good teaching is to tailor instruction to each individual child's needs and abilities, and that means building an inventory of different training and teaching approaches adapted to your child's unique ways of learning.

First, however, you must discover how your child learns. To borrow once again the insights of Thoreau, if a child hears a "different drummer," you must let your child "step to the music which he hears, however measured or far away."

Your ability to do that requires a certain mind-set, based on the realization that your child is not your clone or that of your spouse, regardless of any similarities to both of you. Your child is different from both of you and may have to learn many things in different ways from you. In the end, it is of little consequence how your child solves a problem as long as the problem gets solved. The old ways of doing things are not necessarily the best ways. If they were, thousands of companies driven out of business by smarter competitors would still be operating.

From earliest infancy, every child is an individual who will necessarily be different from its parents. Yes, the child has some of your genes and those of your spouse, but also the genes of four grandparents, eight great-grandparents, and hundreds of unknown ancestors.

How often have you heard a parent say, "I don't know where he (or she) got that? It's not from either of us." In other words, each infant is a unique individual with genes from many forebears other than its parents. Any effort to mold that infant into parental fantasies of the ideal child are doomed to fail.

Don't think of your child's mind as clay to be molded. Instead, think of a magnificent rock to be sculpted, but with an individual, unique inner structure whose surface can be shaped but whose core will shatter under inappropriate handling.

No child will learn everything its parents want and most certainly will not learn all things the way its parents learned them. If your child succeeds by doing things differently from you or your spouse or from other children, it's essential to praise your child—and be grateful your child has learned.

Nothing is more discouraging to a child's learning efforts than the do-it-my-way syndrome, whereby parents or teachers say, "That's the right answer, but the wrong way to do it." Every child is different from its parents and other children and must learn many things in different ways.

An Inventory of Teaching Techniques

As a parent-teacher, your responsibility is to determine how your child learns if you want your teaching to be effective.

Keep a careful list of what works and what doesn't and build an inventory of teaching techniques that will effectively facilitate your child's learning. Keep track, too, of your child's learning strengths and weaknesses, aptitudes and ineptitudes, what your child does and how well he or she does it.

One method is to examine closely the games and activities your child most likes and convert aspects of these into vehicles for teaching academic skills. Does your daughter like cooking? Let her help you. Having her read the recipes aloud will strengthen reading and speaking skills, and there is no better vehicle than cooking for teaching mathematics and many aspects of elementary chemistry and physics.

Do your children like gardening? The yield must be calculated from the number of seeds and plants, planting directions must be studied carefully, rows must be neatly labeled, and so on. If you didn't start doing this when your child was younger, start doing it now. It is never too late to begin helping your child learn more effectively.

Watch to see how your child learns when left alone. A child's instinctive approaches to learning—stacking and moving blocks, for example—can give you many clues about specific learning differences and help you adapt the way you teach to fit in with the ways your child learns.

Providing Subject-Centered Education

Like every school teacher, you will often have to choose between subject-centered and child-centered approaches to teaching. The choice becomes most difficult when trying to teach something that provokes anxiety, such as potty-training often does.

Under the subject-centered approach, many parents arbitrarily select a specific age to train their child. They place the infant on the potty and insist it remain there until it meets the parent's definition of success. The hysteria and anger that often result invariably inhibit learning. As often as not, the child eventually leaves the potty without a successful bowel movement, only to soil its diapers a few minutes later and infuriate its parents.

Nevertheless, parents trapped by a subject-centered teaching approach and the do-it-my-way syndrome often repeat such lessons day after day, month after month, until the child eventually learns—albeit unhappily and with many psychological scars.

Some parents adopt this approach with twelve-month-old infants who have little or no control over their physical functions and have even less intellectual understanding of what the parents want. All baby knows is that its parents are very angry and dissatisfied. Success with this type approach—if and when it comes—is largely the result of physical and intellectual development, but by that time, the child will have suffered weeks of failure and parental disapproval.

Providing Child-Centered Education

At the other extreme of the teaching gamut is the child-centered approach that permits a child to learn when it's ready—everything from toileting to the disadvantages of torturing the family dog. The parents provide the child with virtually no formal potty-training until the youngster consciously appreciates the benefits of using the toilet and decides to use it voluntarily.

Pure, child-centered learning inappropriately places responsibility for deciding when and whether to learn on the child. No child—not even an adolescent—is mature enough to shoulder a broad responsibility that should be based on worldly knowledge not available to children. In effect, child-centered learning demonstrates that parents do not really care enough to fulfill their teaching responsibilities and have abandoned the child and left it on its own in the world.

Pure child-centered teaching is obviously as ineffective and psychologically damaging as pure subject-centered teaching. Both methods teach children to abhor learning.

The use of coercion teaches children to associate learning with fear, anxiety, and pain. It teaches children that learning is not fun.

Allowing children to learn entirely on their own, on the other hand, teaches them that learning isn't very important because adults don't seem to care whether they learn or not. Such children often develop a self-destructive arrogance that they need not respond to anyone or anything until they're good and ready. Many retain that attitude throughout their lives.

Inflexible teaching approaches fail to take into account the needs, aptitudes, developmental level, and learning differences of the child. Tragically, when such methods fail, the child is usually blamed for failing to learn—at home as well as at school.

Creating Balance in Teaching

Skilled teachers try to combine elements of many approaches in most lessons and vary the relative use of each technique according to what is being taught and the learning differences of each youngster. Unfortunately, most parents, like most teachers, bring their own mind-sets into the teaching process. They have preconceived notions about the best way for a child to learn a specific lesson.

There is an almost endless number of gradations between teaching extremes. As your child's first and most influential teacher, it's important that you discover as early as possible in your child's life the teaching approaches that most effectively facilitate learning.

The same approach will not necessarily work with every type of lesson. As you teach your child everything from toileting to tic-tac-toe to multiplication, try always to remember the three basic reasons your child may be slow or fail to learn a specific lesson:

1. *Development*. Your child has not developed adequately physically, intellectually, or emotionally and is simply not ready to learn that particular lesson. After praising your child for the effort, abandon the activity for a few days or weeks and try again another time.

   If the skill or activity is essential for future learning activities, you may want to discuss the problem with your pediatrician if your child fails to progress after a reasonable time beyond the appropriate age for such learning. Keep in mind, however, the huge variations in age range for various types of physical and intellectual development. Some enuretics, for example, do not acquire nighttime bladder control until their early teens.

2. *Aptitude*. Your child may have a low (or no) aptitude or possibly a learning impediment in the particular activity you're trying to teach. If that's the case, and assuming it is a noncritical skill or activity, be certain to let your child know it's all right to be different and imperfect. Praise your child for the effort and laughingly demonstrate your own incompetence in a similar activity.

3. *Ineffective teaching*. You may not have discovered the appropriate teaching method for your child's normal learning differences. Abandon the approach immediately—before your child gets discouraged and says, "I don't want to do this anymore." Wait a few days or weeks before casually returning to the activity with a new and different approach, saying, for example, "You know that puzzle we tried to solve yesterday? Well, I don't know if this will work, but I found a different way of trying to do it—it makes it easy and a lot of fun."

Getting Discouraged

It is most important that you not get discouraged when your teaching approach fails. Remember, human parents do not harbor the same infallible instincts for raising their children that animals do. Many of us, including professional teachers, tend to use the same teaching techniques that helped us learn successfully. Some of us don't even know another way to teach. Unfortunately, the way we learned may fail to teach our children and finding a different teaching method that works can often be difficult and frustrating.

One obvious place to search for other training and teaching methods is in the standard child-care and parenting books. Unfortunately, you may find yourself nodding in agreement with many of the suggestions in such books, but be unable to apply them, either because you forget them or because you simply do not have the emotional makeup to apply them.

It's one thing to read about appropriate responses to your infant repeatedly throwing a plateful of spaghetti from the high chair. It's quite another always to remain calm—especially when you're also preparing dinner for guests and your other children are demanding more to eat and the dog is barking and the telephone is ringing . . . and . . . and . . . and . . . !

Finding Time to Teach

In infant and child education, as with many other elements of child rearing, it's essential that you keep in mind the importance of time segmentation. It's impossible to teach a child two or three or more things at the same time, and it's impossible to teach if the length of the lesson extends beyond a child's attention span.

The kitchen scene I described is simply not the appropriate environment for teaching an infant not to throw eating utensils from the high chair—or teaching older children to say please or teaching the dog not to bark. No parent can possibly teach so much to so many at the same time.

Most effective teaching requires special moments of quiet time—a period your youngster knows you have reserved especially for him or her and during which you will not tolerate interruptions except for emergencies. By reserving teaching time in this way, you not only tell your child tacitly that he or she is important to you, but that learning is important.

Such teaching time bears no relationship to classroom instruction. The foremost purposes of teaching time at home are to love and support your child, to explore your child's mind and heart, and to learn the depth of your child's understanding and how your child goes about learning things. One secret to good teaching is to be a good listener and let your child teach you—about himself or herself, about his or her fears, difficulties, and limitations, which you can then try to help your child overcome. Teaching time should be the equivalent of "rap sessions" between friends—a time for getting to know each other, and in so doing, instructing each other. It's also a chance to reveal your own mind and heart—and your intellectual and moral priorities.

Making Learning Fun

Although all education involves learning real lessons, it does not have to seem like two or three lessons crammed into one—especially when the teacher is a loving parent. When teaching your child, beware of overload. Inject as much fun and excitement as possible into each activity so home does not seem like an extension of school.

Remember that play can be one of the most enjoyable and effective teaching tools. There are endless enjoyable, educational board and card games, for example, to enhance mathematic and vocabulary skills. Home should be a safe, happy haven from the cares of school. Learning can and should go on, but it must take place under far different circumstances from school.

So make learning at home a joyful experience for yourself and your child without, however, forgetting a few basic principles that underlie every good teacher's approach to education:

- ◆ *Planning.* Decide exactly what you expect your child to learn from a particular activity and never stray too far from that goal. When you take your child to the zoo to teach about animals, don't get sidetracked into explaining the rules of baseball. To avoid overload, each lesson should be simple—for example, animal locomotion (fish swim, birds fly, etc.) on one trip and animal camouflage on another. Know when to stop. Make your child an active learner by letting his or her instincts and curiosity determine which subjects to investigate.

- ◆ *Managing instruction.* Know the material and be as prepared for "why?" as possible. Prepare your child for what you're going to see, do, and learn before getting there. Each instructional element should be kept short. Set appropriate goals. Make a point and quickly return to laughter and having fun, unless your child demands to know more. Let your child's curiosity dictate the length of each inquiry. Remember to use all the teaching tools at your disposal: studying maps on trips, reading menus and checking addition on bills at restaurants, getting change at ticket windows and stores, reading nutrition labels on food packages at the supermarket, keeping track of the budget when shopping, and so forth. Every activity in your daily life can expand your child's ability to speak, read, calculate, and make decisions—if you make your child a partner and make these activities seem like fun.

Fun and love must be central to each learning activity, even reading a story; instruction, though important, should appear incidental.

Involve your child in every element of instruction, joyfully asking questions that elicit responses. Don't try to instruct in the face of distractions. If, for example, some friends and their children show up unexpectedly at a museum, end the lesson on extinct reptiles and pick it up later or repeat the visit another time. Windows of learning opportunity don't close overnight.

◆ *Delivering instruction.* A good teacher must be enthusiastic about each new fact she or he introduces. If teachers or parents do not love to learn and show it, the children they teach will never love to learn. Use positive reinforcement as much as possible, reminding your child of similar, previous activities and seeing what your child remembers.

◆ *Evaluating instruction.* It's important to monitor your child's progress without making it sound like testing or checking up. Ask your child to repeat some of the lessons learned from time to time as a way of reminiscing about a wonderful time shared together. "Do you remember the dinosaurs we saw at the Museum of Natural History?" may sound trite, but it is a typical form of monitoring that can be followed by naming the animals and drawing and coloring some of them.

Child Care

For a variety of reasons, not the least of which is the need to work, many parents are forced to trust the care of their child during the critical learning years to hired workers. Child care, however, can be a learning disability trap for children whose parents place them in the care of low-paid, unskilled workers instead of hiring well-paid, well-trained, certified, or licensed nannies and child-care workers.

The investment you make in infant education and child care is unquestionably the most important educational investment you can possibly make for your children—more important than preschool, elementary or secondary school, and far more important than college.

Setting Proper Priorities

Many American parents place college at the top of the list of educational priorities for their children instead of at the bottom. College is nothing more than the icing on the educational cake. The cake itself is baked in elementary and high school, and the ingredients are selected and mixed from infancy to age three or four, at home, before a child begins preschool.

If the educational ingredients are not the best and if they are not mixed in the right proportions during those early years, the cake will not bake properly in elementary school. It will emerge from high school a misshapen brick, and no amount of icing at college will turn it into a wedding cake.

I hope the analogy is clear. The basis of all learning skills are formed at home during a child's first three or four years of life. They are the most important learning years and they warrant the largest investment in your child's education, with preschool and elementary school the next most important, middle school and high school next, and college the least important.

A bright academically motivated youngster can obtain as good an education at any state university as he or she can at a private Ivy League college. High-quality higher education is there for the taking at any accredited college or university. The same books can be found at every one of America's fine colleges and universities if a student wants to read them.

So college does not warrant the financial priorities American parents tend to give it. Indeed, college can be a waste of time for students with too many learning impediments. Right now, about 50 percent to 55 percent of all students at four-year colleges drop out without completing their education. There are many reasons for this disgracefully high statistic, but one of them is the large number of students with learning impediments that block academic success.

The vast majority of those students could have and should have learned to overcome those impediments in elementary school, and many would never have developed impediments at all had their parents invested in their education at home, during the formative years of infancy and before preschool.

I urge you to invest unstintingly in the best child care and infant education from the minute you bring your baby home from the hospital. You cannot do anything to prevent the genetic learning impediments your child brought into the world, but you can certainly prevent your child from suffering intellectual deprivation that produces other impediments by ensuring proper at-home infant education.

Finding Qualified Caregivers

Unqualified caregivers—even part-time caregivers—can leave children from even the most culturally advantaged homes with serious, perhaps critical, learning impediments. Some experts on learning disabilities maintain that semiliterate day-care workers and nannies who care for infants during the critical language-development years may, along with television and radio, be one of the most serious and pervasive causes of learning impediments among American school children.

Across the nation, babies and pre-preschoolers are left— long hours, day after day, during critical language-development years—to listen to semiliterate child-care workers who cripple the language skills of the children in their charge.

Investing in Infant Education

Educators throughout history have agreed that the first few years of life are the critical period in human intellectual development. As a parent, you have total control over the early education that will shape the adult your child will become. Do not give the responsibility of your child's early education at home to a stranger without a great deal of planning and investigation.

Almost all parents are guilty to a certain extent of exposing their children during their formative years to less-than-literate, noncommunicative baby-sitters. Nothing can be more detrimental to an infant's education than the continual presence of a teenager who sits in silence, or staring at a television screen, or who chats in meaningless slang on the telephone while the youngsters in their care are deprived of the language training they desperately need.

Few parents, of course, can spend twenty-four hours a day with their children. All parents need a break from child care—for their own mental health. Many parents also need to work to support their children. In any case, no parent can protect children entirely from learning words and other things they would rather their children not know.

What parents can do, however, is recognize that whenever they leave their infants and young children in the care of people other than themselves, their children will learn from those other people. Placing any infant or young child in someone else's care is fraught with dangers to the child's intellectual, emotional, and physical health.

Evaluating Your Child's Caregivers

You probably already know most of the qualifications to look for to ensure your child's physical and emotional health when you take on a child-care worker: references, age, experience, health history, personal habits, availability, training, child-care philosophy, knowledge of hygiene and first aid, etc. Just as important, however, are the qualifications needed to ensure your child's intellectual health and growth, including the caregiver's level of literacy and formal education.

Your Child's Needs

Immediately after your baby is born, you have the option to choose whether your child will have below-average, average, or above-average language skills and the equivalent academic and intellectual skills language skills produce. But you only have that choice once—during the first three years of your baby's life. After that, it will be too late.

It's not essential that child-caregivers have university degrees in education or child development, but they should have the following minimum qualifications:

- *Literacy and numeracy.* Any caregiver should be a high-school graduate who is literate, numerate, and well trained in child care and development, if you expect your child to reach his or her intellectual potential with a minimum of learning impediments.

- *Clear, correct enunciation.* If you want your child to speak English clearly and correctly, your caregiver must be able to do the same.

- *Language skills.* If you want your child to be able to read, your caregiver must be able to read to your child and teach your child letters, syllables, sounds, words, and phrases.

- *Mathematical skills.* If you want your child to learn the meaning and relationship of numbers, to count and calculate, your caregiver must have the same skills.

- *Education.* Your caregiver should have a rich vocabulary and broad enough formal education to know the names of foods, plants, flowers, animals, and other animate and inanimate objects that every normal child encounters. Your caregiver also should know enough mathematics, natural history, science, astronomy, music, art, and other topics to give your child reasonably intelligent answers to the endless questions every youngster inevitably begins asking at age two or three.

In short, your caregiver must be have all the parent-teacher skills outlined in Part II under infant education. Do not settle for anyone without such skills.

Qualified Caregivers

There are innumerable ways of finding skilled child-caregivers. Avoid most conventional employment agencies that advertise workers specializing in housekeeping or child care. Such applicants are seldom skilled enough to provide superior infant education. Most workers willing to do housekeeping are unskilled and perhaps even semiliterate. A well-trained nanny is not an unskilled worker and will not usually do housework outside the nursery.

Instead, try to find one or more agencies that specialize in finding and placing trained nannies. There are more than a dozen in New York City, and the telephone directories of most major cities have listings with toll-free numbers. Appendix A lists professional groups that can help you find qualified nannies in your area. In addition, many parents' groups, pediatricians, churches, synagogues, schools, nursing agencies and registries, and hospitals may also be helpful in finding trained personnel.

England, Ireland, and Germany have well-known nanny schools that require students to apprentice or intern before they can graduate and receive certificates or licenses. London newspapers such as the *Times* and several newspapers published in the United States that serve the Irish and German communities print classified advertisements for nannies and nanny agencies.

Still another source of trained child-caregivers are preschool or elementary-school teachers who often seek part-time work in private homes.

The Interview

When considering applicants to care for your child, interview them more than once—the first time privately, away from your child. Although it may be politically incorrect, it is not wise to consider male nannies. Here is a checklist of what to look for and discuss at such interviews:

- *Personal qualities.* Check her punctuality, grooming, physical appearance, dress, orderliness (watch her handbag when she has to find references), patience, and interest.

- *Professional skills.* Outline the kind of care you expect for your child and the range of knowledge you want the candidate to introduce to your child—reading, arithmetic, music, drawing, natural history, science, and so on. Her responses will show you the range of her educational and cultural background as well as her experience caring for children of various ages.

- *Previous experience.* Get a resume and make sure she has cared for other children your child's age and has experience providing first aid or nursing care. Find out how long she stayed at each previous job and why she left. Don't consider anyone who did not consistently remain at each job two or three years. Ask her if she has any questions and note carefully the type questions she asks to see if they display more concern for her welfare than the baby's.

- *Health and physical condition.* Be certain to get evidence of a complete health checkup, including negative tests for drugs, tuberculosis, AIDS, or other diseases. Does she appear strong enough to handle your child?

◆ *Verification.* Follow up your meeting with a *thorough* check of every reference and every significant aspect of the candidate's life to that point. Do not consider a candidate who proves untruthful either in person or on paper or who omits details about a significant period of time (six months or more) in her life.

A Second Interview

Assuming you're pleased with a candidate—your comfort level with her is an important consideration—have a follow-up interview with your child present to see how the two interact physically, emotionally, and intellectually.

Does she seem comfortable and enthusiastic holding your infant or toddler? Is she warm and affectionate in her tone of voice and touch? Does she speak to your child with words or babble in baby talk?

If you're pleased after this second visit, ask the nanny to come for an afternoon, or if she is to live in, for a weekend with pay to demonstrate whether she is capable of giving your child the level of care you demand. Depending on how pleased you are, the visit will also give you an opportunity to provide some training.

A Trial Engagement

If you hire her, be certain you hire on a trial basis for two, three, or four weeks to see if she and your family, including your child, get along. A trial engagement will allow you to check your child's mood and diapers when you get home to see if nanny has kept the child happy and clean. Check your baby for any marks or bruising, and watch your baby's mood carefully. Long, unexplained periods of crying, unusual fatigue, or chronic crankiness are signals of trouble. Come home unexpectedly from time to time and ask friends or relatives to drop in unannounced to check on your baby when you're not there.

Stability

In addition to language skills, you must ensure stability in your infant's life by finding a caregiver you can be certain will remain for at least two, three, or more years. Even the youngest infants need continuity and stability if they are to grow up without serious learning impediments. They quickly bond to and grow to love and depend on those who provide the majority of their care. And they just as quickly grow depressed when they lose someone who provides a significant amount of their daily care and security.

The best evidence of such depression can be seen among infants who are transferred to multiple foster homes. They almost invariably lose their appetite, their tendency to smile, and their natural curiosity in new objects and people. They have difficulty eating and stare blankly when a new toy or a new face appears. They often grow up with diminished learning skills, and sadly, little capacity to love or trust others.

Even if you remain your infant's primary caregiver but hire someone to assist you regularly, avoid sudden departures by either of you from the life of your baby. If, for example, you're planning to go away for a week or even a long weekend, begin preparing your infant at least a week earlier. Spend a little less time with baby each day, progressively allowing your caregiver to spend more time with the child.

Similarly, if your caregiver plans to go on vacation or leave your employ, make the departure as gradual as possible, over a period of several weeks, with the caregiver spending a little less time with the child each day. If possible, hire a replacement while the departing caregiver is still in your employ so the substitute can gradually take over without interrupting or disrupting your baby's education.

Day-Care Services

Some parents turn to group day-care services to complement or substitute for at-home caregivers. On average, group day-care centers are not healthy places for babies and many such centers are learning disability traps. Individual care and scheduling flexibility are difficult to obtain. Employee turnover is high and rates of infection can reach life-threatening proportions. Even the most conscientious workers cannot ensure that toys, teething rings, or pacifiers won't pass from one baby's hands to another without being sanitized.

Although most states require day-care facilities to be licensed, such licenses only reflect compliance with general sanitation and safety regulations—whatever they happen to be. The fire and health regulations in some states, however, are so minimal they border on criminal negligence. Moreover, even the strictest licensing standards cannot, in the absence of state inspectors, ensure that:

- employees wash their hands after changing diapers, helping children at the toilet, or wiping children's mouths and noses

- employees dispose of diapers in covered containers out of reach of children

- every infant's immunizations are up to date

- no baby with a rash, stomach or intestinal disorder, fever, or infectious or contagious disease is brought into the facility

- food utensils are properly sterilized and food is prepared under sanitary conditions

Do not underestimate the danger of disease transmission to your baby or through your baby to you, your other children, or even to your fetus if you're pregnant.

Finding Good Facilities

Now that doesn't mean there are no excellent group day-care facilities. There are, but even the best facilities cannot give your child continual individual care. And if your baby is already beginning to put everything in its mouth, you must expect your baby to have a much higher number of illnesses than if he or she had been cared for at home.

If you have no choice but to leave your baby at such a facility, make certain it meets the highest standards and that it is licensed by the state. Check that the teachers and those who handle the children have college or university degrees in early childhood education and child development and that they are trained in first aid and know CPR.

Do not place your baby in a facility staffed by unqualified workers who simply "love to work with babies." The low pay at day-care facilities inevitably attracts workers who are unqualified for higher paying jobs and are unqualified to teach your baby.

In addition to educational qualifications, ask to see health reports on each worker, including evidence of negative tests for drugs, tuberculosis, AIDS, and other contagious or infectious diseases. Be certain the center has conducted background checks on each worker for criminal behavior or severe mental illness. Here are other obvious and less obvious things to check:

- ◆ *Staff ratio*. Check that there are no more than three babies per worker and that babies are separated by age.

- ◆ *Safety*. Be certain the place is safe for crawling babies and that there are no small objects that can be swallowed, no poisonous products, no sharp objects, no open doors or windows, no exposed radiators or electrical outlets, no cleaning materials or medications within reach. Make sure the floor is clear so a worker doesn't trip while carrying a baby.

- ◆ *Sanitation*. See that there are ample covered containers to dispose of tissues and diapers and that there are liquid soap dispensers at all sinks. Check the cleanliness of bathroom fixtures, toys, and other materials.

◆ *Conformity with the law.* Verify that the facility conforms to state licensing regulations. See if there are ample first-aid materials, smoke alarms, working fire extinguishers and fire exits that are clearly marked and free of obstructions. Check on the date of the last safety inspection by state regulatory agencies and call the local health department to see if there is a history of complaints against the facility or any outstanding violations.

◆ *Quality of infant education.* Babies should have ample age-appropriate toys, manipulatives, books, scribbling and drawing supplies, and a variety of things to handle. Babies should have constant physical and linguistic contacts, with workers continually conversing, reading, or singing to the babies in their care. Babies should have ample opportunity to hear music and play outside if the weather permits.

To reassure yourself about the quality of the facility, drop in unannounced in the middle or toward the end of the day when babies tend to get cranky. Do not consider any facility that does not allow such visits or does not invite parental involvement in daily activities.

Finding Alternatives

There are three viable alternatives to conventional group day-care:

1. *Home day-care.* Parents who fear the dangers of conventional group day-care facilities sometimes opt for group day-care in private homes where a mother, often of one of the babies, cares for a few others. These can and do

offer many advantages. Costs are lower; the environment is warmer; scheduling is far more flexible, usually allowing for early drop-offs, late pickups and even holiday care; there are far fewer children, and therefore, less exposure to infection; and there is more individual care.

Sound too good to be true? It is. Here are the negatives:

◆ Most home day-care facilities are unlicensed and do not meet local or state fire, safety, and sanitation codes required for public facilities. Most private homes are fire traps, and if the mother is less than obsessive-compulsive about sanitation, infections of one child quickly infect the entire group.

◆ The mother or caregiver is usually untrained, with no degree in child development or early child education and no professional experience in either field. Indeed, she may be barely literate.

◆ If the caregiver or her baby is ill, parents of the other babies are left with no alternative.

2. *Corporate day-care.* Long a fixture at major corporations in Europe, corporate day-care offers by far the best type of infant education and all-around baby care available. Staffed by trained professionals and magnificently equipped, they are designed and operated with the infant's best interests in mind, usually offering the finest infant education in a safe, healthy environment.

Obviously, no socially conscious corporation wants to risk the displeasure of its employees. Apart from the dangers of lawsuits and strikes, the costs of worried mothers or fathers racing back and forth from their posts to check on the status of their babies would be too much for any company to bear.

Parents do indeed visit their babies throughout the day at corporate facilities, including visits for breast-feeding. Because of the high quality of corporate care, however, most parents find themselves better able to concentrate on their work and limit visits to lunchtime.

3. *Office care.* Depending on your company's policy, your working conditions, and the type work you do, an alternative to group day-care is to take your baby with you to the office. Good office care is only possible, however, if you have a private office and it is big enough for a playpen or crib and all the playthings your baby needs. Office care, of course, is perfect if you're breast-feeding. Otherwise, you'll need facilities to prepare your baby's formula or food.

Remember, though, your baby is not a pet that will sit or lie quietly while you concentrate on your work. When your baby's not napping, it will require the same type of active infant education in the office that was described earlier for baby at home. If, for example, you're a writer, you may be able to provide that kind of education and pursue your work successfully, but there are very few types of work that combine easily with active infant education.

Preschools

Depending on a child's social development and experiences, he or she will be ready for preschool between two and four years of age. Chapter 3 will give you more details and guidelines for selecting the right schools for your child. Before beginning the school-selection process, however, the question most parents must answer is whether their child is ready for and needs preschool or should wait to begin academics in kindergarten.

A three-year-old who is mature enough for preschool should speak relatively rapidly, clearly, and fluently, in complete, varied, and often interesting, thoughtful sentences. He or she should ask questions to obtain information, not to get attention.

With a few outstanding exceptions, most preschools are not essential to the development of either social or academic skills. If a parent can provide the same training at home and the child has a rich social life, there may be no need for preschool.

If the home harbors a warm, loving extended family and is filled with kids all the time, the preschool experience might actually be detrimental if it proves to be a less enriching environment. Most preschools are usually only geared to teach kids how to cooperate with each other, take turns, help with chores, obey rules, make appropriate independent decisions, and get along with everyone. If that learning is now taking place at home, there's no reason to change.

If, on the other hand, a child is alone much of the time with a parent or adult caregiver and has few or no daily contacts with other children of the same age range, the social benefits of preschool can be invaluable and may be essential for the child's development. In small towns, it's essential to find out what percentage of children attend preschool. If the figure is close to 100 percent, it may be essential for a child's social happiness to attend. Not only will the child have no playmates if they're all attending preschool, the child may be left out of the social groups the children are forming.

Selecting Preschools

The problems of selecting a preschool, however, are much the same as those described for choosing a day-care facility. Like day-care facilities, most preschools are independently operated and many are learning disability traps because of the caregivers employed. Few are ranked and they don't need professional accreditation to open.

However, some respected and accredited public and private schools also operate preschools that feed youngsters into the regular K–12 academic program. These are the exceptional pre-schools referred to earlier. The quality of such feeder programs are geared to and usually match the quality of each school's regular operations. Most offer considerable advantages over independent preschools.

A good preschool should be more than simple day-care. It should be a developmental kindergarten or organized educational play group in which play is used to teach social, physical, behavioral, and academic skills essential for smooth functioning in full-time school. A good preschool is what kindergarten used to be, but the best kindergartens have now evolved into pre–first grades that concentrate on basic academic skills such as reading, writing, and calculating.

Many four-year-olds may have all the academic skills of a potential kindergartner, but not the ability to work with others or respond to authority or participate in rough-and-tumble physical play. Good preschools try to bring them up to grade nonintellectually as well as intellectually so they all can start at the same level when they begin kindergarten.

To work with a child with learning differences or learning impediments, preschool teachers should have academic credentials in remedial education and special education as well as conventional education and child development.

The school should not assign more than five children to each teacher and teaching assistant, each of whom can provide continual one-on-one tutoring and remedial education. The school and the teachers must be able to adapt to the child's individual needs rather than trying to force the child into a universal mold.

Visiting Preschools

Spend three or four mornings or afternoons at any preschool you consider, with at least two of the visits unannounced. Any good preschool will welcome your visit at any time of the

school day. In addition to all the criteria mentioned for selecting day-care centers (safety, sanitation, and so on), look for
academically oriented toys and activities. Check to see that cor-
ners are set aside for quiet, solitary activities and that there is
adequate space for children to play together in groups.

Watch the attitude of teachers to see whether they continually address the entire group, whether they seem harried,
and whether they focus on tidying up instead of working with,
teaching, encouraging, and comforting individual children. See
if the children are relaxed or tense, whining, or snapping at each
other. Do teachers have to shout to gain the children's
attention?

As noted earlier, these are the most critical years in the
development of your child's intellect. You should be prepared
to invest far more proportionately in preschool education than
college or university.

A good preschool can help transform your child into an
articulate youngster, able to read simple stories, write letters,
words, and numbers (though they may write many backward).
These are essential skills that will determine your child's ability to learn in the future. Superior skills developed now will
be superior learning skills for the rest of your child's life.
Learning those skills later when the window of opportunity
has narrowed could prove a struggle.

A good preschool will also teach your child to sing, dance,
act, and show an understanding of the aesthetic, mathematical,
scientific, and historic aspects of everyday life, including money,
food, kitchen appliances, events and when they took place (yesterday, today).

The Montessori Method

In selecting a preschool, it's well to remember that all good,
modern preschools use some aspects of the famed *Montessori
Method*, which uses normal child's play to educate three- and

four-year-olds socially, academically, and intellectually. Developed in Rome in 1907 by Maria Montessori, a physician, psychiatrist, and educator, the Montessori Method requires teachers "to stimulate life—leaving it then free to develop, to unfold . . . ."

Montessori worked with hundreds of young children and concluded that they learn mainly by themselves and absorb spoken language directly from their surroundings with remarkable ease and rapidity. Her method recognized and exalted learning differences as strengths rather than weaknesses. It allowed children to learn by themselves in their own way at their own pace.

A school using Montessori's method, which she originally designed for deprived orphans, can be the perfect place for many children with learning differences, although other such children may well need a far more structured learning environment.

The primary function of Montessori teachers is to prepare the environment to make it easy for children to learn on their own, with teachers intervening only to facilitate such autoeducation.

Montessori helped open thousands of preschools throughout the Western world. Her schools were the first to be equipped with functional, child-size furniture. They based their curricula on learning games that entertained while allowing children to absorb new knowledge and skills.

Montessori divided education into three parts: motor, sensory, and intellectual (language and education). She developed a large variety of sensory teaching materials that required gradually increasing skills and maturity to manipulate. They were constructed of wood, metal, cloth, cardboard, and other materials of all colors, sizes, shapes, weights, and textures. Some made sounds or had scents. Children could see, touch, smell, hear, speak to, or manipulate them by cutting, shaping, tying, building, and so on.

Little Explorers

Montessori called young children "little explorers" who must have freedom to make discoveries in their environment. To capture each child's interest and encourage concentration, she made educational materials attractive and challenging. Flexible time periods allowed children to spend as little or as long as they wanted to pursue any tasks they chose, using whatever materials they found most appealing.

Children had access to several different rooms, each with a different activity. They were allowed to work alone or in groups, but not allowed to intrude on the work of others. To discourage intrusion, each child had an individual piece of carpet on which to work—a kind of private property whose clearly visible boundaries were not to be crossed except by invitation.

Montessori fostered motor education with what she called "exercises of practical life"—care of one's person and of the environment, moving and arranging furniture, preparing meals, setting the table with china and flatware that was collected and cleaned afterward. Exercise included gymnastics, dance, and rhythmic games in which children learned good posture, proper speech, and graceful movements.

As children matured, the prepared learning environment grew more complex, with sensory experiences expanded to musical sounds, sandpaper letters, and wooden alphabets that could be manipulated to encourage reading and writing.

Learning Differences

At each stage of development, Montessori and her teachers took advantage of learning differences and of each child's particular receptivity to specific types of learning. She noted some preschoolers were word-lovers who demanded names for everything and took pride in learning even the most difficult words. She took advantage of each child's tendency at certain stages to order and number things. She gave them bead chains, number rods, and other devices that helped them learn mathematical concepts.

Although teachers were present at all times, children selected materials that most interested them and were allowed to learn through trial and error. The teacher mediated but did not instruct unless absolutely necessary to further each student's progress.

Designed to encourage independence and self-development, the Montessori Method avoids almost all forms of collective activities and discipline and the lockstep learning of public schools that turn children's learning differences into learning disabilities.

When properly applied, the Montessori Method is one of the most effective ways of teaching children with learning differences because it incorporates the learning of practical academic skills—reading, writing, speaking, and calculating—in a child's favorite activity: play.

Montessori Certification

Before you race to enroll your child in the nearest Montessori preschool, however, be aware that the vast majority of the more than four thousand preschools in the United States that call themselves Montessori schools *are not* certified Montessori schools. That's because the name Montessori is now in the public domain and any school can call itself a Montessori school and profit from the prestige the name carries.

Although thousands of schools use elements of the Montessori Method, only about eight hundred are certified by the American Montessori Society. The society requires that all teachers be specially trained and certified and that the schools themselves adhere strictly to its methods and standards. Before enrolling your child in a Montessori school, check that the school is certified by contacting the American Montessori Society: 150 Fifth Avenue, New York, NY 10010. Telephone: 212-924-3209.

That does not mean a noncertified school that claims to use the Montessori Method may not be a good preschool. It may well be, but you'll have to check it out carefully to see that all teachers are properly trained and qualified.

Kindergarten

If your child is not attending a preschool affiliated with an elementary school by the time he or she is four and a half, you should begin going together for occasional visits to kindergartens and explaining what schools for big boys and girls are all about.

Chapter 3 will give you more details on the school-selection process, including some of the things to look for when selecting a kindergarten. Remember, however, that kindergarten is a bridge between preschool and elementary school and the guidelines for selecting kindergartens are somewhat different from those for selecting preschools and elementary schools.

Kindergarten can easily become a learning disability trap if you pick the wrong school for your child. In selecting kindergartens, do not consider one that is not a full-day program, operating five days a week. Half-day programs leave too little time for learning between the lengthy process of getting five-year-olds settled when they arrive and ready when it's time to leave. If your child cannot handle a full-day program, he or she may not be mature enough for kindergarten and may need to take an additional year of preschool.

A good kindergarten is not a play school. To pick one that is a play school is to put your child in a learning disability trap by postponing his or her intellectual development at a time when the window of learning opportunity is open widest for many skills. Kindergarten should be a pre–first grade—an elementary-school preparatory program that uses some play as an effective teaching tool but that is academically oriented. In addition to play, a good kindergarten uses conventional instructional methods to teach kids to read, write, and calculate as well as the basics of music and art. Kindergarten also is designed to teach youngsters good learning habits and a variety of social skills, including proper behavior in and out of school and how to build good relationships with teachers and other students.

An effective kindergarten should teach these basic skills:

◆ the alphabet and combined sounds

◆ sight recognition of several hundred words

◆ the mechanics of handling and reading a book

◆ basic story form and the ability to relate the sequential events of a story

◆ the ability to express opinions, discuss stories, and connect external events or events in a story to his or her own life

◆ the ability to write many words phonetically (Because of limited motor development, your child will not enjoy the physical act of writing but should enjoy dictating stories.)

◆ counting up to twenty and an understanding of mathematical relationships—that two apples are more than one apple, for example, and less than three

In addition, kindergartners should learn to calculate with concrete materials and understand that adding another apple to one apple in a bowl produces a total of two apples and that taking one away leaves only one. (Abstract mathematics, including the concept of $2 + 2 = 4$, with numbers unconnected to concrete objects, may remain beyond the understanding of some, but not all, kindergartners at the end of the year.)

Although effective kindergartens stress academics, they also recognize the importance of social development for five-year-olds. As you evaluate kindergartens for your child, listen carefully to the principal and teachers you interview to determine the relative emphasis they place on each of the important aspects of education your child will need during the critical kindergarten year.

Summary

Parents can do little about preventing genetic causes of learning impediments, but they can prevent environmental causes of both critical and noncritical learning impediments by providing a rich language education.

Infant education is the most important educational investment you can make and should take precedence over college. In terms of investment, infant education and day-care should have the highest priority, followed, respectively, by preschool, kindergarten, elementary school, middle school, high school, and college, with college the least important.

Infant education should begin the moment the child is born. Parents should converse with their baby as they would with a friend, using real words, not baby talk that forces the child to learn every word twice. Build your baby's vocabulary while the window of learning opportunity is open widest. Failure to teach language skills during the first three years of a baby's life is the most frequent cause of expressive and receptive language disorders.

When investing in child care, hire fine, well-trained, literate, well-educated, English-speaking nannies who will ensure your baby is learning essential language skills. Then, invest in the finest preschools and kindergartens.

When selecting a preschool, find one whose teachers have academic credentials in remedial education and special education as well as conventional education and child development. A preschool should not assign more than five children to each teacher and teaching assistant, each of whom can provide one-on-one tutoring, and if necessary, remedial education. School and teachers must be able to adapt to the child's individual needs.

In selecting a kindergarten, choose full-day programs with pre–first grade academic programs that teach reading, writing, calculation skills, the basics of music and art, and basic social skills.

Chapter 3

Selecting the Right School for Your Child

Imagine being six again, walking into your first-grade class-room on the first day of school, and being asked to find your seat by reading the name cards on each desk. You and all your classmates are equally adept at reading. To your frustration, however, all you see on the cards are unintelligible words: *yllaS*, *drahciR*, *enirehtaC*, *nhoJ*, and *lelliH*.

As you and your classmates mill around in confusion trying to decipher the name cards, one boy quickly finds his desk and sits down. That boy is an Israeli youngster named Hillel. Like other Israelis, he learned to spell from right to left in his native Hebrew. Leonardo da Vinci might not have had any problem finding his name either because he was not only able to write his name backward and forward, he wrote his voluminous scientific notebooks in mirror script to make them difficult to decipher.

But Sally, Richard, Catherine, John, and the other American first-graders who learned to read from left to right would probably find it all but impossible to read their name cards with the spellings reversed.

The point is that all children learn different skills in different ways and at different ages. Your child does, too. By the time American children enter school, they have learned to read from left to right, and Israeli youngsters have learned to read in the opposite direction. Although many children playfully learn to spell and say their own names backward, most do not develop that skill to the extent Leonardo da Vinci did.

Suppose for a moment the children entered a classroom where the teacher did insist they spell from right to left. Some of the class would adapt to the teacher's method and eventually learn reverse spelling. But many, if not most, would have difficulties, and some would find it impossible because they simply cannot process the information the way the teacher wants—for a variety of reasons.

A few may have a genetic predisposition to process information from left to right. A more likely reason, however, is that by the time they enter school most have been conditioned to process information from left to right. All the information they've ever seen—in books and periodicals, on television screens, food packages, and roadside and store signs—has been presented left to right.

The Do-It-My-Way Syndrome

As absurd as it may seem for an American teacher to insist that children process letters and words from right to left, many teachers do the equivalent every day of the school year in classrooms across the United States. That's because they are in the almost inescapable grip of the do-it-my-way syndrome. That syndrome not only closes the minds of many teachers and parents, it makes learning more difficult, and even impossible, for many children. It should not be astonishing, then, that many American youngsters are discouraged with school and emerge with negative feelings about the learning process.

This is the problem you must confront as you consider preschools and other schools for your child. If your youngster is bright, the most certain way to discourage your child's natural interest in and love of learning is to force your child to march in lockstep with other children and to learn in a way that is unnatural for him or her.

Identifying Your Child's Needs

Before trying to select a school for your child, it's important to identify and define his or her needs—not your ambitions for your child, but your child's needs and the type of school that will best meet those needs. It is unimportant whether you, your spouse, and six generations of your families have attended a prestigious Ivy League college. It is important to recognize your child's strengths, weaknesses, and needs and to find a school that will build those strengths, shore up or overcome the weaknesses, and fill the needs.

Remember, primary- and secondary-school education form the foundations of intellect. College-level education is the icing on the educational cake, and a bright, academically motivated youngster can get as good an undergraduate education at a state university as he or she can at a private Ivy League college.

So don't let the prestige of the decal on your car window determine the choice of school for your child. Obviously, academic needs should be one determinant. How strong is your child in academics? How interested? In which areas?

Draw up a list of your child's intellectual, emotional, and social qualities, weaknesses as well as strengths. Does your child function better alone, in small groups or large—or equally well in all three? Is your child a loner? Rough-and-tumble or gentle? An avid reader or an audiovisual type?

Don't fantasize your child's strengths, and don't under any circumstances ask your child to define those strengths. All children want to please their parents by telling them what they want to hear. One ten-year-old I knew regaled his working parents with tales of his Little League baseball heroics. To surprise the boy, they left work early one afternoon to watch a game—only to find their son sitting alone, high atop the grandstand, in his school clothes. He had never even made the team.

Most children tell their parents what their parents want to hear, and most parents tend to see and remember only what they want to about their children. Don't write anything from memory. Watch your child and note everything he or she does at the time it happens.

How long is his or her attention span? Time your child to determine this. Does your child finish projects or leave them unfinished? Does your child enjoy puzzles? Building and making things? Listening to you read aloud? Devote considerable time to observing your child's activities and skills, or lack of skills. Keep a diary.

Getting to Know Your Child

If your child needs individual attention, don't select a school with an average of twenty or thirty students per class. If your child needs structure, don't pick a school with an open-classroom arrangement. One of the worst mistakes parents of overactive children make is to believe their children will be happier in schools that allow children to wander from class to class at will. That is a formula for disaster. Overactive children desperately need structure and discipline. Only the self-disciplined child can thrive in an open-classroom situation.

If your child is gifted or has special talents, be absolutely certain the school you select has a broad-based program for gifted children.

Other important factors to consider in selecting your child's school is the quality of your family life. Is yours a one- or two-parent home? How does that affect your child and how can the school compensate for the lack of one parent? If you have a two-parent home, do you and your spouse both work? Who is raising your child? Does a housekeeper or child-caregiver serve as a surrogate parent? Is your child left alone a lot of the time? Do you have an extended family? How large? Where does your child fit into relationships at home with brothers, sisters, or other family members? Family dynamics are important influences and will affect your child's school life.

Do you take many family trips? What kind of things do you do with your child: picnics? sports? concerts? museum visits? Do you read to your child? How often? What kinds of stories or books? What rules do you have at home? How does your child relate to other children?

Observe your child carefully with other children—and take extensive notes. Does your child share easily, snatch things from others, or let others snatch his or her things? Does your child listen and absorb what others say or interrupt incessantly and demand to be heard? It's important to document your child's behavior because what you consider cute may actually be immature behavior. What Dad describes as a boy who doesn't let others push him around may actually be an extremely disturbed, hostile, aggressive child who needs psychiatric help.

Similarly, a child whose lapses of memory you may have ignored as the absentmindedness of a true intellect may actually represent a serious learning disorder that should be evaluated by a learning specialist.

That is why it's so important to keep a diary—because it's more difficult to embellish documentary evidence with wishful interpretations. You simply won't be able to dismiss as the absentmindedness of a budding scholar eight or ten entries a day that begin, "Forgot to. . . ."

Similarly, written notations that document your child repeatedly slapping another child at play cannot be interpreted as the sign of a "real boy." Clearly, that's a sick boy, but most parents who love their children tend to overlook, excuse, or forget a lot of the behavior they don't like and remember only their children's positive behavior.

Evaluating Your Child

To evaluate your child as objectively as possible for purposes of selecting a school, take careful, accurate, and complete notes while observing your child alone and interacting with the family or other children. Assuming you don't ignore the obvious, you may find your notes portray a different child than the one in your fantasies. Nevertheless, they will serve you well in selecting a school.

Once you've identified your child's needs, the next step is to determine appropriate goals. Again, write them down and study them objectively to see if they are indeed appropriate. Don't use meaningless adjectives such as *happy*, *successful*, or *nice*—as in, "I want [my child] to be a nice person." Don't let college or career goals enter your mind unless your child is truly a prodigy—or thirty-five years old and still unemployed.

What do you want your child to learn? What does your child need to learn? Academics? Writing skills? Athletic skills? Concert piano? Extracurricular activities? Social behavior? Ethics? Religious values? Be specific and set your goals on paper before you start evaluating schools, so you can match them to the stated goals of each school you consider, and eventually, select an appropriate school that will meet your child's needs.

Why Public Schools Fail

Often patterned after the military, many public schools offer inflexible curricula, teaching methods, and class schedules, fixed limits on class time, and ability-grouping. Instead of opening the doors of knowledge and permitting children to explore and succeed by being different and learning in ways that facilitate knowledge absorption, many public schools actually limit children's access to learning—sometimes inadvertently, sometimes purposely. Here's how:

1. *Overcrowded classrooms.* Public schools pack an average of more than eighteen students into each classroom—twice the number of students in the average private-school classroom. Some public-school classrooms have thirty, forty, or more students, leaving teachers with too little time to give students individual attention.

2. *Time limitations for learning.* The National Commission on Excellence in Education found that the average U.S. public school provides an average of only twenty-two hours of actual instruction a week and that students spend only 70 percent of their school time on academic activities. They spend the rest of their time getting ready for class, checking attendance, listening to loudspeaker announcements, watching messengers run in and out of class, cleaning up, participating in extracurricular activities, and watching discipline of disruptive students. The average public-school student does less than one hour of homework a night, compared to 2.14 hours for private-school students.

3. *Limited learning opportunities.* Only 21.5 percent of public middle schools have laboratory facilities in science courses, compared to 50 percent of private junior high schools. Public schools spend a mere $36.54 per pupil for library facilities—half the average spent by private schools. Many public schools teach only one foreign language; some teach none. Many do not teach physics.

4. *Low academic requirements for graduation.* With graduation credits available for a wide variety of personal-improvement courses such as cooking, baby care, and "kindness to domestic pets," relatively few children have any incentive to struggle with academically demanding courses.

5. *Poor-quality teaching.* More than half the public-school teachers in America "come from the bottom half of their

[college] classes," according to a Carnegie Foundation study, and often do not hold degrees in the courses they teach. Recent estimates indicate that 30 percent of public-school English, math, and science teachers were unqualified to teach those subjects, and less than one-third of high-school physics courses are taught by qualified teachers.

6. *Ability-grouping.* The most effective way public-school education limits learning is with the vicious and cynical ability-grouping system, or academic tracking, that groups students according to academic achievement. Despite its name, ability-grouping has little or nothing to do with ability. Regardless of their ability to learn, children with the highest grades are placed in classes offering the best instruction and most-advanced and complex learning materials.

Often, however, high grades are awarded for effort and classroom behavior rather than learning ability. Meanwhile, children with lower grades attend classes with poor instruction and simpler learning materials that leave them further and further behind as each year progresses.

Falling into the General-Education Trap

Far from giving each youngster equal educational opportunities, ability-grouping gives the least instruction to children who need the most. The less the child knows, the less he is taught, and of course, the less he knows. It is a self-defeating, Kafkaesque system that has proved disastrous for American public-school education and has cruelly deprived millions of bright American youngsters of educational opportunity.

General education is the worst learning disabilities trap in the entire American educational system because it turns tens of thousands of intellectually healthy youngsters into learning disabled adults who are unable to read, write, or calculate adequately.

"The high school general education program," says Dale Parnell, longtime president of the American Association of Community and Junior Colleges and one of the most respected educators in the United States, "is the academic and vocational desert of American education. [It] relates to nothing, leads to nothing, and prepares for nothing."

Each year, more than 40 percent of American public-school children are dumped onto the slow elementary-school academic track and the general-studies track in high school, and they perform accordingly.

Nearly one-fourth of all students with critical learning impediments—the kids schools call learning disabled—are in general studies, which is essentially a custodial service.

Academics in general education are largely limited to personal-improvement courses. English courses assign any paperback novels the children choose from drugstore racks. General science courses often study nothing more than popular science-fiction films.

Sensing the uselessness of such classes, almost two-thirds of the youngsters in general education drop out without getting their high-school diplomas. More than one-third remain unemployed for at least a year after leaving school, and those who do find work earn an average of about $112 a week, or less than $6,000 a year.

Many such youngsters have the potential to be academic achievers, but because of learning differences that make many of them more difficult to teach for overburdened teachers, they are shunted out of the academic mainstream into classes that keep them occupied, but teach them nothing.

In effect, general-education programs represent wholesale child neglect and abuse of a public trust.

If your youngster is in or considering public school and is having learning difficulties, I urge you to avoid the slow-track or general-education "solutions" public-school teachers and guidance counselors may suggest. (See Chapter 6 for a discussion of your legal rights.)

Drifting Through School

The tragedy of some public-school education for children with learning differences is that the majority of teachers and administrators are convinced conditions in their schools are ideal for learning. And because such conditions make teaching easier, they have no inclination to change their current approach to teaching.

Some children do thrive in the traditional public-school setting—probably as many as 25 percent who are intellectually aggressive, command teacher attention with probing questions, and do above-average work in honors classes. There is another segment of the class that also commands teacher attention—namely, the disruptive students.

All but forgotten in the mob scene of many public schools, however, is the silent majority of students—those quiet, unassuming, average kids who are left to drift through school. Year after year, these students sit quietly in class, listening, trying to understand as much as they can without ever probing aggressively for the in-depth explanations that gifted children demand.

In effect, these students plod through their academic life, bored, learning little, earning only mediocre grades from sympathetic teachers who grade them as much for their passive, nondisruptive classroom behavior as for their actual academic performance.

Neither the students nor their parents demand better education. Like the teachers, they assume schools provide the right conditions for learning and that children who do not learn are responsible for their own failures—either because they are intellectually incapable or because they are lazy. That simply is not true.

The vast majority of children who fail to learn do so because they are not being taught properly in ways that take into account their individual learning differences.

Children of all ages sense what adults expect from them and think of them. It is the rare child who fails to meet adult expectations, whether those expectations are expressed or not. When teachers and parents expect a child to succeed, that child usually succeeds. When teachers and parents expect a child cannot or will not learn, that child usually responds accordingly—by not learning. A child who is told a concept is too difficult to understand usually agrees meekly, "I'll never get it."

As a result, students who start each year at the top, middle, and bottom of their public-school classes almost invariably remain in the same positions at the end of the year and at the end of their school careers.

Aware of the phenomenon of the self-fulfilling prophecy, good teachers and good schools do not let children fall behind or fail. They challenge every child. When it is necessary, they provide extra help such as one-on-one tutoring, remedial instruction, or whatever else it takes to help a child learn. Such teachers realize the purpose of their life's work—to help children learn.

In doing their work, teachers try to determine how each particular child learns. They then set up instructional programs that allow each child to learn the way he or she learns best—in Thoreau's words, to "step to the music which he hears." Appendix E provides a directory of private schools in each state with specific remedial and special-education programs for children with learning differences and impediments.

An Important Study

More than thirty years ago, the great University of Chicago psychology professor and educator Benjamin Bloom conducted a research program in which he proved that when conditions are right, all children can learn more than they do in conventional school settings.

By providing a group of children from all levels of the academic spectrum with one-on-one teaching and instruction tailored to each child's needs, Bloom found that 80 percent of his group achieved at a level reached by only 20 percent of the students who remained in conventional classrooms. Bloom thus disproved the theory that because a few children succeed in the conventional public-school setting, conditions in such schools allow all children to succeed and those who do not are themselves to blame.[1]

Bloom's findings are important for all children, but especially for children with learning differences and learning impediments. First and foremost, Bloom's research proved beyond any doubt the value of small classes and individual attention in education—an approach to education found more often in private than public schools.

Private Versus Public Schools

There are many wonderful public schools with small classes and highly trained teachers who will give your child the individual

---

[1]Benjamin S. Bloom *All Our Children Learning: A Primer for Parents, Teachers and Other Educators* (New York: McGraw-Hill, 1982).

attention he or she deserves and needs to thrive. And there are some private schools that are absolutely terrible.

Some states and cities have outstanding public magnet schools with rigorous admissions standards for gifted students. Many are specialized, such as New York's High School of Music and Art or High School of Science. Others, such as Stuyvesant High School, offer broad academic programs.

So don't dismiss public schools. Evaluate them as carefully as you do private schools. You may be surprised to find a wonderful public school near your doorstep that your child can attend free of charge, with none of the tuition costs of private schools nor the extra costs for transportation, lunch, trips, books, and dress clothing or uniforms.

But on average, every statistic proves beyond any doubt that children get more individual attention, secure a better education, and perform better academically in private schools than they do in public schools. A child with noticeable learning differences or learning impediments does not, in my opinion, belong in the average public school—especially a large public school where children are expected to learn in lockstep and where being different can often invite the neglect of teachers and the scorn and hostility of other students.

Considering Private Schools

Millions of American parents realize this, and six million of their kids—12 percent of the student population—now attend private schools. They are not necessarily rich. About 36 percent of families with children in private schools have incomes less than $50,000 a year, while another 21 percent have incomes between $50,000 and $75,000. As many as 40 percent of the students at private schools receive financial aid.

More than half the kids at private schools are from middle-income families who believe that, next to love, a good education is the most important gift they can give their children—and they're willing to sacrifice to make that gift. Moreover, millions more parents are actively campaigning for the right to obtain credits, or vouchers, for the tax dollars they now spend on inadequate public-school education and to spend those credits to give their kids the superior education of private schools.

As mentioned, private schools assign only about nine students per teacher, compared with more than eighteen in public schools. Teachers can give each student the individual attention needed to exploit rather than suppress learning differences. Private schools try not to admit disturbed, unruly children who monopolize teacher attention in public schools. The handful that slip through are expelled if they disrupt school routine or the lives of other children. Private-school teachers are thus free to devote their time to teaching instead of coping with disciplinary problems, and their students can concentrate on learning.

Academically, the philosophy of most private schools is that all students deserve the best possible education—if not to prepare them for college, at least to prepare them for effective citizenship in a society where they will be expected to govern themselves. Private schools require all children to study a core curriculum of college-preparatory English, mathematics, history, science, foreign language, music, and art, from kindergarten through high school.

Electives at the high-school level are limited to advanced courses in those disciplines, and children are not given the choice to veer away from the educational building blocks of civilization. All children remain on one educational track whether they are bound for college or carpentry. Good educators believe all children need a good education, regardless of career choice.

Excelling in Private School

The results are evident: Nationally, the U.S. Department of Education found that 68 percent of eighth-graders at independent schools achieved at the highest level of reading proficiency, compared with only 32 percent of public-school students. For mathematics, the study found 63 percent of independent-school eighth-graders functioning at the highest level of proficiency compared to a disgracefully low 18 percent of public-school students.

Now those results are not because private schools get the brightest kids. Private-school kids do better at school because their teachers and parents ask them to work harder. They do twice as much homework (eleven hours a week on average, compared to 5.4 hours in public schools), they read twice as much, and they watch one-third less television—fourteen hours a week, compared with nearly twenty-two hours a week for public-school kids.

The Right School for Your Child

In selecting a school for your child, remember there are no "best" schools, regardless of what your friends, neighbors, or local newspapers say. The school that's perfect for one child may not be perfect for another, even in the same family. If you've been deeply involved in your child's early education, you should know by now your child's intellectual, social, and emotional strengths and weaknesses—and needs. The school that is best for your child is the one that meets those needs.

Evaluating a School

There are eight key educational standards for evaluating a school and comparing it with other schools: accreditation, educational philosophy (or educational goals), faculty quality, teaching methods, academic strength, educational results, financial condition, and physical plant.

1. *Accreditation.* Any school you consider—whether public or private—should be accredited by a recognized state, regional, or national school-accreditation association. The major accreditation associations are listed in Appendix B. Certification *is not* the same as accreditation. Every state requires schools to be certified, which is nothing but a legal approval to operate and usually only means that the school conforms to fire and safety regulations. Accreditation, however, involves a complex examination conducted every one to ten years by teams of educators from other schools. They examine educational goals, educational results, faculty quality, quality of the school library and other educational facilities, student-teacher ratios, student achievement levels, curriculum, remedial instruction or special education, and many other educational factors and compare them with other schools.

In addition to conventional academic accreditation, schools with programs designed for students with critical learning impediments often have some affiliation with one of the major service organizations listed in Appendix C, such as the National Association of Private Schools for Exceptional Children, the Learning Disabilities Association, or the Orton Dyslexia Society.

2. *Educational philosophy and goals.* No school can obtain accreditation without a clear statement of educational philosophy and goals that you can then compare to those of other schools and the specific educational goals you have formulated for your child. Beware of vague, misleading puffery, such as *caring faculty, modern facilities,* and similarly meaningless terms. The goals should be specific.

For a bright youngster with learning differences, you'll want to look at teaching methods, the amount of individual attention the school gives its students, the type of students they teach, the rules and controls governing behavior, the relative emphasis on academics and athletics or other extracurricular activities, faculty training, and school facilities for underachieving children or children with learning differences.

Educational goals may also include preparation for college, the teaching of a traditional liberal arts and science curriculum, military or religious training, and other goals that may or may not match your own. For a youngster with learning differences, any school you consider should make it clear that a primary goal is to provide individual attention by specially trained teachers.

If your child has any critical or noncritical learning impediments as described in Chapter 1, it is important to determine whether the school's program forces students to try to overcome their impediments and achieve total intellectual independence, or simply teaches them to learn to live with their impediments. Chapter 5 will give you details on evaluating special-education programs for children with critical learning impediments.

If possible, try to visit one or two classrooms of any school you're considering to see the size of each class and whether teachers actually give students individual attention. For a child with significant learning differences, do not consider a school with an average of more than a dozen students per classroom.

Individual attention does not mean just giving each student a chance to answer a question or recite. It means devoting time to each student, focusing on the student's learning differences, and showing the student—and the class—the advantages and disadvantages of a particular approach to a problem. It should also mean one-on-one tutoring when needed.

3. *Faculty quality.* One measure of faculty quality is the number of teachers with master's degrees and doctor-

ates. At academically superior secondary schools, about half the faculty have master's degrees and 10 percent have doctorates. All the teachers at any level should have majored in or studied in great depth the subjects they teach. Check how many in the faculty have undergraduate or graduate degrees relating specifically to learning differences, child development, remediation, and special education—a critical factor for many children with learning differences.

4. *Teaching methods.* There are two broad approaches to teaching children, neither of which is valid by itself: subject-centered, with the lesson as primary, and child-centered, with the child's readiness to learn as primary.

In subject-centered teaching, the child's needs, interests, and development are secondary. The child is forced—even bullied—into learning. In child-centered teaching, the lesson is shaped to fit the needs, interests, and developmental stage of the individual. The contrast between the two can be extreme, and the educational world has been debating the benefits of each for generations.

In practical terms, a pure child-centered classroom seems in chaos, with wild undisciplined students doing whatever they choose. The emphasis is on self-expression. In contrast, the subject-centered classroom is quiet, with well-dressed, well-groomed children sitting silently at their desks, listening and responding obediently to their teacher and politely raising their hands when they wish to ask a question. The emphasis is on discipline, self-control, and listening.

Both systems are educational disasters because each is more concerned with student behavior than with learning. Academically successful schools do not subscribe to either extreme, but borrow the best of both. The child with learning differences and learning impediments cannot thrive in a disciplinary straitjacket or in chaos. On the other hand, an overactive or hyperactive child cannot function in a chaotic environment free of external disciplinary strictures.

In considering a school for your child, try to assess the proportion of each method used and what mix of child-centered and subject-centered education you believe will be of most value to your youngster. For a child with learning differences, it's especially important to determine that teaching methods include individual attention in and out of class, with one-on-one tutoring when needed and remediation or retraining in appropriately equipped classrooms.

5. *Academic strength.* Children cannot thrive academically if they are so far ahead of their classmates that they remain unchallenged—or if they are so far behind that they must constantly struggle to keep up. Many parents have the mistaken belief that the intellectual stimulation of an academically superior school will stimulate a less gifted youngster to succeed scholastically. That usually won't happen.

A more likely result is that the youngster will fall further and further behind, grow discouraged, and fail or quit. Such a youngster is far more likely to thrive in a school where he or she fits in comfortably and where individual teacher attention promotes improvement. Accredited schools publish so-called profiles of their student bodies, giving average student scores on entrance examinations and other standardized tests, with which you can compare your child's test scores.

Another measure of academic strength is the curriculum. A minimum acceptable elementary, middle, and high-school curriculum is outlined in Appendix D. Beware of soft course offerings such as social studies as substitutes for rigorous disciplines such as history, or language arts instead of English grammar, composition, and literature.

Academically strong schools offer required core curricula based on English, mathematics, science (general, biology, chemistry, and physics), history (ancient, medieval, modern, and American), one or more modern foreign languages, fine arts, and music. Do not consider a secondary school whose graduation requirements for nondyslexic students do not include at least four years of English and three years each of mathematics, science, history, and one foreign language. (Some outstanding secondary schools often waive the foreign language requirements for dyslexic students.)

6. *Educational results.* Any school you choose for your child should be able to prove it meets its educational goals. Standardized tests provide the simplest measure of educational results. You can compare student scores with scores of students at other schools. Test results should come as close as possible to matching the stated educational goals of each school. A school that calls itself a college-preparatory school but only sends half its graduates to college obviously has poor educational results that do not fulfill the stated educational goals.

In the area of learning differences, determine whether the school can document improved performance by students with specific learning differences and impediments. Ask to speak with a half dozen or more parents of current and former students with noncritical and critical learning differences.

7. *Financial condition.* Any school should be willing to disclose its financial condition. Do not consider a school that is in poor financial condition and in danger of closing. Home and school are the most stable worlds in a child's universe, and any child can be hurt badly by the collapse of either. Unfortunately, half the children in

America are now the victims of parental separation and divorce. Don't risk placing your children in a school that might close and force them to part with the teachers and friends they love.

8. *Physical plant.* In considering a school for your child, it's important to be certain that the physical plant includes facilities and state-of-the-art equipment that not only help youngsters grow academically, but leap ahead in areas where they are most gifted. A good school should be able to help your children build on their strengths, whether these are meteorology or field hockey. Check the playgrounds and sports facilities, the science laboratories, the classrooms. Does the school have computers for every student, audiovisual laboratories for teaching foreign languages, music rooms where students can practice, art studios, a fully equipped theater?

Looking at the Little Things

Besides the eight broad standards for evaluating schools, there are a number of specifics to check as you evaluate each school. No single criteria should rule out a particular school, but for a child with learning differences, they certainly will help give you an impression of each school that should enter into your final decision. Some of the following need no explanation.

◆ *Neighborhood safety.*

◆ *Condition of grounds and building.* Make certain all the playground equipment and athletic fields are safe and that neither the school grounds nor the building has been vandalized.

◆ *School interior.* Is the building clean and safe? Don't consider a school with graffiti on the walls. Look carefully at hallway displays to get a picture of what school administrators emphasize and what the school community considers most important. Children's art? Prize essays? Science achievements? Athletic trophies? Plans for the dance? Each says something different about school priorities.

◆ *Administration office.* Do not consider a school whose staff is not friendly, helpful, and open—and pleased to show you a variety of helpful materials about the school. They should be eager to arrange for you to tour the school, visit classes, and meet teachers and administrators. The principal or admissions director should be pleased to see you and answer any and all questions.

◆ *School catalogues.* All good schools have printed materials that clearly state the school's educational goals, rules, and regulations and give a profile of the student body and faculty.

◆ *School size and organization.* Even a large public school can operate fairly well academically if it has organized itself into what are variously called schools-within-a-school or academies. What such schools do is break down the student population into small, manageable units with, say, an entire grade restricted to one floor, which becomes the school within the confines of the larger school building.

One key to good education, however, is classroom size. Check that there are no more than about a dozen students per teacher. And the classroom routine should *never* be interrupted by loudspeaker or student announcements or by messengers running in and out.

◆ *Academic tracking or ability-grouping.* Do not consider any school that maintains a general-education track for students it deems incapable of handling traditional academic or vocational education.

◆ *Sports and extracurricular activities.* Although secondary to academics, a broad range of extracurricular activities and sports can teach untold numbers of skills that classrooms necessarily ignore. Such nonclassroom activities can be critical to successful growth and development and offer a child some of his or her happiest moments at school.

◆ *Administrative services.* Depending on your child's needs, a health office, transportation, after-school child care, homebound instruction, psychological services, and guidance services may be essential.

And don't forget to visit the school cafeteria. It may seem like a secondary consideration, but food, glorious food is of utmost importance to children of all ages and is important for their morale. Like the army that marches on its stomach, students generally study on theirs.

Visiting the Classroom

Do not consider selecting a school that does not eagerly invite you to visit classrooms and look in on, or at least listen to, part of an actual class your child will attend.

Here, in broadest terms, are things to look for when visiting classrooms in each grade and other school facilities:

◆ Kindergarten class should have an extensive in-class library—with a minimum of a dozen easily accessible books per child and ample, comfortable places for children to sit and thumb through books or read on their own. You should see plenty of blocks, educational toys (play is still the chief educational tool), manipulative rods and cubes to learn mathematics, art and writing supplies, plants, a few pet animals, and a mind-boggling array of other materials to learn reading, writing, arithmetic, the use of calculators and computers, science, music, art, and dramatic presentation. Some order to the chaos should be evident by grouping materials into learning centers or specialized areas that ring the room.

A lot of large, colorful signs should be posted to label various objects in the room. The words *Good Morning* might be written on the chalkboard or *Today is Wednesday*, or *It is raining*. Children's seats and desks should be appropriately sized and movable so children can move from one learning area to another or bring them together for storybook readings by the teacher.

The center of the room should look like a playroom, however, with no military-style rows of desks lined up in front of a chalkboard. The teacher and assistants should be working with or reading to individual students and small groups—not lecturing to a large, silent class. Five-year-olds don't need prolonged drills. Young children learn best by doing, and children should be busy doing in any kindergarten you consider for your child. Check the playground and gym to see if they are clean and safe, with all equipment in good repair.

◆ First- and second-grade classrooms should have fewer playthings and visibly expanded in-class libraries. The perimeter of the room should be organized into neat learning areas equipped appropriately with calculators, computers, and word processors, and there should be more evidence of schoolwork on display—wall charts, maps, and so on. Materials should be varied to match the varying needs of students.

Each child should have his or her own movable seat and desk, and as in kindergarten, teachers should be working with individuals or small groups—not lecturing to the entire class. All the children in the class should not be learning the same skills at the same time. Children should be eagerly involved in what they are doing, not fidgeting, wandering, leaving and entering the room, or fighting.

Check the quality of the reading program. The reading program should be tailored for each child's needs, and therefore, be slightly different for each child. If all students in class use the identical reading program, only the average child will do well. Children with low aptitudes will struggle to keep up and grow discouraged, frustrated, and angry. Children with high aptitudes will grow bored, frustrated, and angry. Both will invariably come home complaining about the school and their teachers and proclaim universally, "I hate to read."

- ◆ Third- and fourth-grade classrooms represent a dramatic metamorphosis from play to scholarship, with a radically different atmosphere and physical layout. By third grade, children in good elementary schools begin dividing their time between their homeroom and specially equipped classrooms where teacher-specialists now take over teaching art, music, science, and foreign languages, while the homeroom teacher concentrates on English, mathematics, and history. Computers are now an integral part of daily learning.

- ◆ In fifth grade and beyond all the classrooms will begin to look alike, and there are few things you can check other than the apparent quality of teaching, the amount of individual attention the teacher seems to give each student, and the number of children in each classroom. Check to see that there are abundant computers available for each grade. See if science laboratories are well equipped, that each workbench has functioning equipment, and that supply cabinets are filled with chemicals and other supplies. Watch the lab in action to see that the supplies are used and not just stocked for show.

Checking Other School Facilities

Other facilities to consider include:

- *Library.* Regardless of your child's age, ask to visit the school library. Good school libraries have separate areas for the youngest children, with card catalogues they can manipulate and understand easily. A key indicator of a good school is the care with which it adapts its facilities for each age group. Older students should have access to a computerized retrieval system that not only searches the library's shelves and stacks, but accesses data bases at other libraries and prints out a bibliography for virtually any topic the student might be studying. A well-equipped school library should have an average of fifty books per student and a wide variety of periodicals, over and above any materials and books in in-class libraries.

- *Writing center.* See whether the school has a writing center to ensure development of student writing skills. Writing centers are akin to science laboratories in that they supplement the work in English classes and allow students to apply what they've learned in class to the writing of essays, poetry, fiction and nonfiction stories, or anything else they choose to write.

- *Computer facilities.* Visit computer labs to see whether there is at least one computer for every two students and preferably one per student. Computer literacy is as essential today as language literacy.

- *The arts.* Visit the art, music, and drama areas to see how broad a cultural education the school offers its students. Check on the variety and number of musical instruments, music stands, backstage equipment, private practice rooms. Are any works in progress? Do you see and hear kids painting, playing instruments, singing, rehearsing play parts? All children, with or without learning impediments, thrive academically and culturally and get excited about learning in an atmosphere teeming with learning activities in which their friends and teachers are eagerly participating. If, as you walk around a school, you find yourself caught up in the enthusiasm and eager to jump in and learn, you know your child will, too. If the atmosphere is dull and dead, walk out and don't look back.

Talking to the Boss

Before making a final decision on any school, it's important to have an in-depth interview with the principal—ultimately, the boss at any good school. Study after study has found that a school's educational success is directly related to the principal's competence and authority over educational policy.

A basic reason private schools work better educationally than public schools is the autonomy of principals and teachers. Whenever elected politicians—local or state school boards— dictate educational policy, as they do in public schools, educational quality falls.

No profession in the United States other than teaching allows laypeople to dictate policies. Indeed, service on a school board or board of trustees and the right to dictate educational policy for your children does not even require a literacy test, let alone a high-school diploma or college degree. Probe deeply into the question of authority over educational policy. Is it in the hands of professional educators or amateur outsiders who may have their own agendas to promote? Find out who selects textbooks.

Be certain the principal is well educated and has under-graduate *and* graduate (at least an M.A.) credentials from recognized universities—and that he or she is not subservient to nonprofessionals in determining educational policies. Ask for a list of the members of the board of education, or board of trustees of a private school, to determine that they, too, are well educated and at least college graduates.

Have a list of specifics to ask the principal after you've finished with polite formalities. A good principal should be able to articulate the school's specific educational goals and demonstrate that the school has achieved those goals. See if those goals coincide with your own, and if not, see if you can reconcile the two sets of goals.

Choosing a school whose philosophy is different from your own will court educational disaster for your child.

Be specific in citing your child's needs and see if the principal has specific programs to meet those needs. Don't be satisfied with vague answers such as, "I'm sure [his or her] teacher will be able to work something out." That is not an acceptable response.

Ask the principal for a general assessment of the school—its strengths and weaknesses. What are the principal's major problems, important new programs, and vision for the future? If athletics are the major concern, cross the school off your list. Don't believe a principal who says a school has no weaknesses. Indeed, be wary of everything such a principal tells you.

Test the principal's awareness of the major problems and dangers children of all ages face today—for example, drugs, alcohol abuse, premature sexual encounters, racial hostility, and so forth. What is the school doing about them? Test the principal's knowledge about the specific problems your child is facing, and ask how the school handles such problems.

Ask about the frequency and ease of setting up parent-teacher and parent-principal conferences and the authority of teachers to solve problems on the spot. Some schools put students and parents through bureaucratic nightmares to solve every problem.

Ask about the difficulty of switching courses if your child cannot handle a particular subject or has been placed at a level that is too low or too high—and the difficulty of switching teachers if your child is dissatisfied or cannot get along with a particular instructor.

Find out, too, about one-on-one tutoring, remedial instruction, and special education and whether such academic help is routine or involves endless bureaucratic red tape. Seek well-detailed descriptions of each program. Before discussing special education, you may want to contact educational service organizations such as the National Center for Learning Disabilities, the Orton Dyslexia Society, the Council for Exceptional Children, and others listed in Appendix C. These provide parents and educators with the latest advances in research of learning-difference methods for teaching children with learning impediments. Make certain the principal is at least as aware as you are of the problems involved in learning impediments and that he or she receives materials from these organizations.

Evaluating the Curriculum

To give children freedom to choose their own courses and educate themselves is an abdication of adult responsibilities and borders on child neglect, if not abuse. Remember, American public schools send 13 percent of seventeen-year-olds to lives of unemployment and poverty as illiterates. That is child abuse, and any school that gives children a choice of what courses to study is failing them.

So in evaluating schools, the fewer electives the better. Elementary and middle schools should offer none. Good high schools should offer none to ninth and tenth graders and limit electives in eleventh and twelfth grades to no more than 50 percent of the curriculum—and only to students who have successfully completed the core curriculum in Appendix D. High-school electives should be limited to advanced academic courses for college-bound students and to business or vocational courses for students headed for community colleges, technical institutes or specific trades after high school.

If your child is ready to enter middle school or high school, do not consider a school that offers a cafeteria curriculum that allows children to graduate without the skills needed for college or the job market.

As the National Commission on Excellence in Education warned: "Secondary-school curricula have been homogenized, diluted, and diffused to the point that they no longer have a central purpose. In effect, we have a cafeteria-style curriculum in which the appetizers and desserts can easily be mistaken for the main courses."

In examining the curriculum, therefore, it's important to look at the quality as well as the quantity of courses. English courses, for example, should require progressively more skilled writing each year and be limited to serious literature, with little or no student choice. Weak schools often offer several dozen English courses that rely on audiovisual aids and allow students to pick their own readings from the racks of paperback romances and adventures at discount stores.

Reviewing Teaching Strategies

Ask the principal about teaching practices. Many top schools now use team-teaching and interdisciplinary education at almost every level of the curriculum, including the late elementary years. Instead of presenting each course independently, team-teaching relates each course to every other course in the curriculum, with instructors working as a team to coordinate their curriculum in a specific grade or class each week.

Thus, students in a history class studying ancient Egyptian history might move to math class to study the geometry of the pyramids, to science class to study the use of pulleys and levers for moving heavy blocks, to English class to learn the importance of hieroglyphics in the evolution of written language, and to art class to explore the absence of perspective in Egyptian art forms. A key member of such a team may well be a remedial or special-education teacher working with one or more students to assure their remaining in the mainstream.

Such interdisciplinary teaching can be an important indication of high-quality education because it turns control of the curriculum to professionals—namely, teachers.

Talking to the Teachers

After visiting with the principal, ask to interview one or two classroom teachers who will work with your child, and if appropriate, a remedial or special-education teacher. Although you'll want to repeat many of the questions you've already asked the principal—about school strengths, weaknesses, problems, and so on—it's important to discuss the specific strengths, weaknesses, and problems of your child to see if each teacher has specific teaching approaches that would be appropriate for your child. Make certain the teachers and the principal recognize the distinction between learning differences, difficulties that may require some short-term tutoring, and critical learning impediments such as dyslexia, which require special-educational resources.

Ask to see some textbooks. Check the dates of publication. You know something is wrong if they are more than five years old.

Be wary of a teacher who responds vaguely when you discuss your child's problems. Statements such as, "We can definitely work on that" or "A lot of our students have that problem" are not acceptable responses. If your child has a specific problem, a good teacher should have a specific solution, as in, "Here is how we teach the child to. . . ."

Probe deeply into the prevalence of social and academic problems of the school. You don't want to place your child in a school replete with social problems and classroom disturbances. Half the public-school teachers in America list disruptive student behavior, vandalism, student violence, drugs, and alcohol as their worst problems. Ask about these *before* you enroll your child.

Ask teachers about their educational backgrounds, including professional training in child development, and if appropriate, remedial and special education. Remember that elementary-school teachers should be generalists, with broad knowledge of English, math, history, geography, civics, science, music, and art. Fewer than 30 percent of public elementary-school teachers say they are qualified to teach science, and most others cannot teach music or art. If the teachers you interview cannot teach such courses, does the school provide specialists to fill the gaps?

Above all, as you interview teachers and the principal, keep looking into their eyes and at their facial expressions to see if they're happy guiding and teaching kids. If they do not exude deep satisfaction, love, excitement, and joy from their work at school, the children in their care won't either. The mood you see etched on their faces will be the mood your child will bring home from school. Make certain it is a joyful mood.

Special Programs for the Gifted

If your child is gifted in one or more areas, do not consider any school that does not routinely make special provisions to feed those talents.

Gifted children often develop different ways of solving the same problem and become bored and impatient with repetition and conventional approaches to instruction. Their memories seem boundless. They ask endless questions and prefer complex, challenging tasks and higher-level abstract thinking— which can often prove annoying to their less gifted peers and teachers. It is not endearing for a gifted youngster to display impatience and boredom while a teacher is desperately trying to teach the rest of the class for the sixth time why the concept of $2 + 2 + 2$ is the same as 3×2.

A mathematically gifted child who understands a basic concept automatically sees, without additional instruction, many ways to solve virtually all problems within the framework of that concept. In adding 38 and 43, for example, the gifted child would obviously see the conventional way of first adding $3 + 8$, carrying over the 1, then adding $1 + 3 + 4$. But such a child would also see at least a second way, namely adding $30 + 40$, then $8 + 3$. In adding long columns in one's head, the second method can be more efficient because it does not require the error-prone step of carrying over. Some mathematically gifted students have such well-developed memories they immediately know that $38 + 43 = 81$.

Learning Differences in the Gifted Child

As you can see from these examples, some learning differences speed learning. With an intelligence that often lifts them to genius or near-genius levels, gifted children display so many learning differences that they are often the most likely candidates in class to be misunderstood by teachers (and sometimes parents) with more average minds.

The gifted child can often see past the intermediate steps in problem-solving. Their minds leap directly to the solution or know how to obtain it more quickly and efficiently than most other children or adults.

That is largely because their extraordinary memories retain far more data than less gifted children. Once a gifted child has solved a type of problem, he or she usually remembers how to solve other problems of that type.

Gifted children also seem able to solve two problems at the same time—an ability that not only confounds most teachers, but also provokes suspicion that they may have cheated. Other characteristics of the gifted are higher-level abstract-thinking abilities, exceptional problem-solving abilities, quick wit, exceptional intensity and goal-directed orientation, and a high level of language development, with excellent listening skills and well-developed speaking vocabulary.

Discouraging Giftedness

Instead of being celebrated, however, gifted children often encounter enormous resentment and bigotry from those of lesser minds, regardless of age. It is no coincidence that the American public spends far more to educate retarded than gifted children. Fourteen states have no programs for gifted and talented children in their public schools. Taxpayers can apparently empathize more with disadvantaged than advantaged minds.

Indeed, there is ample evidence that schools actually discourage giftedness. A 1986 study found that the number of girls identified as gifted declines with age.[2] In attempting to explain the decline, the researchers found that intellectual behavior most necessary to giftedness—intellectual risk-taking, competitiveness, and independence—is the behavior that is least encouraged by adults who raise and teach girls.

Such behavior is also the least respected by most other children, and gifted children often respond by purposely doing badly in school so as not to be different from their peers.

In the average public-school classroom, gifted children tend

---

[2]R. J. Sternberg & J. E. Davidson, "Conceptions of Giftedness: A map of the Terrain," *Conceptions of Giftedness* (Cambridge: Cambridge University Press, 1986), pp. 3–18.

to be called on less because the teacher knows the gifted child already knows the answer. They are also the children most likely to encounter the do-it-my-way syndrome of public-school teachers. Faced with such challenges, a gifted child may seek to drop out of school entirely.

To discourage learning differences is to discourage and even crush intellectual giftedness, and you must not consider any school whose administration or teachers even whisper a belief that a school principal once shared with me: "There's a right way to do things and a wrong way," he said pompously. "We teach the right way."

There is, however, no one right way, and the gifted child offers the best evidence that there usually are a number of right ways to solve any problem. That is why, if your child is indeed gifted, you should probably limit the schools you consider either to magnet schools in the public-school sector, or to the most academically demanding private schools that limit enrollment to similarly gifted children.

Putting Gifted Children at Risk

Simply because gifted children boast extraordinarily high I.Q.'s does not mean they have no learning impediments. Indeed, it is not uncommon for geniuses or near-geniuses to have dyslexia— as we saw in the list of famed dyslexics in Chapter 1. It is, therefore, doubly important for you to probe deeply into the available educational resources of any school you consider for a gifted youngster.

It is all too easy for a child's intellectual gifts to go unnoticed or unexploited because the child is hampered by undiagnosed learning impediments. At the same time, it is just as easy for a gifted child with no learning impediments to be shunted into the special-education trap by mediocre teachers who cannot cope with intellectually aggressive children.

Do not consider any school that does not offer a challenging curriculum and a wide range of special learning resources and opportunities for gifted and talented children. You can get a lot of helpful information on evaluating school programs for gifted children by contacting the appropriate associations for the gifted listed in Appendix C.

Finding Schools for the Gifted

In evaluating a school for a gifted child, make certain the school has special space, such as music or art rooms, set aside where your child can practice or work to develop special talents to the maximum. Find out whether the school has teachers who are themselves gifted in the same intellectual or artistic area and whether there are enough other gifted students at the school to provide your child with a rich social life. Ask if the school permits outside specialists to come to the school to work with students.

A word of caution: the vast majority of American private and public schools *claim* to have programs for the gifted and talented. That is why no list of such schools has any validity. Most schools that make such claims do nothing more than "encourage gifted children to excel"—whatever that means.

Most do not offer specific programs with world-class instructors and opportunities to exploit the most advanced technology. Only a visit to each school in your area can identify those that do. Many schools that may have catered to gifted children in the past can easily fall behind, and some schools that did not do so in the past may have received special grants that permit them to do so now. Again, some of the national organizations in Appendix C can help.

In the public-school sector, schools for the gifted and talented are called magnet schools and they carefully restrict admission to students with records of extraordinary achievement. To gain admission to such schools, students must go through a rigorous battery of tests, auditions (in the case of the performing arts), and interviews and be able to demonstrate skills and talents that rank them among the nation's most talented students. Admission to private schools for gifted and talented children are equally rigorous.

It is fairly simple to check whether a private school does indeed cater primarily to gifted and talented students by asking to see average student scores on the Secondary School Admission Test and Scholastic Assessment Test. More than six hundred private schools use the tests to evaluate student applicants to sixth through twelfth grades. The Independent School Entrance Examination is a similar test used by more than fifty schools in the New York City area to test the same range of applicants.

At both private and public high schools, ask for a school profile that lists average student scores on the Scholastic Assessment Test required for admission to college—a test that will obviously mirror any high school's educational results. Gifted students, including students with learning impediments who take untimed examinations, invariably rank in the top 5 percent of the nation's students.

Of course, any public or private school with an average student body and a wide-ranging record of academic achievement may include one or more gifted and talented students. Someone finishes at the top of the class in every school in the United States. Simply because a child is gifted and talented does not mean that he or she cannot thrive and develop those gifts and talents to a maximum at an average school. But that's what your investigation of each school will have to determine.

Instead of holding gifted children back, good teachers and good schools encourage them to move ahead at a pace that best suits them. They show flexibility and adapt their curriculum to the needs of their students rather than the other way around. Such schools continually evaluate gifted children and let them test out of a course and move to more advanced levels—even to college-level courses at nearby colleges and universities.

Regardless of your child's age, ask whether the school provides alternative enrichment activities and independent projects and learning opportunities. Does the school work with other institutions—nearby colleges, for example—to permit students to take advanced courses in subject areas in which they demonstrate special talents?

If you are evaluating a high school, be certain it offers advanced placement courses—freshman college-level courses designed by the College Board for high-school students. And if your child is a prodigy, will the school arrange for special make-up periods and tests if your child must miss school to display his or her talents elsewhere?

Don't, however, confuse giftedness with the normal high aptitudes that most children display in one or more areas. Keep in mind that the most frequent cause of failure in the primary grades is overplacement—that is, promoting children to higher grade levels that are beyond their intellectual and social abilities.

Be very cautious about forcing or allowing your child to skip a grade. Someone has to be the best student in every class, and just because a child succeeds is no reason to force the child to skip a grade to the next highest class. Don't, in other words, punish your child for success with a promotion to a grade level that will produce academic and social discomfort or failure. A smart, successful student with high aptitudes in certain skill areas is not necessarily a genius who can speed ahead of his or her classmates and enroll in Harvard at fourteen.

As with every other aspect of your child's life, carefully list all your child's needs before evaluating a school, then see if the school can meet those needs. Don't try to work without written lists. You'll find you've forgotten an important requirement and constantly have to chase down school officials to ask questions later.

The Importance of Extracurriculars

Be sure to evaluate nonacademic facilities, regardless of their position on your personal list of priorities. They are or will be important to your child and his or her peers. Check the extent and condition of the athletic facilities. Be certain that those who work with children in the physical-education program are trained in physical education.

Check on the variety and depth of extracurricular activities, which can provide your child with a range of skills not available in the classroom. Such activities as the school newspaper and yearbooks teach writing, editing, design, photography, and other publishing skills. Various clubs teach chess, stamp collecting, and other worthwhile hobbies. And all such activities teach children the important social skill to work cooperatively with one's peers.

Finally, check on the guidance or student-advisory and counseling services available at school. Most children need an adult friend outside the family once in a while—usually a trusted teacher, a coach they admire, or an assigned counselor they like. Your child *will* find that friend, so be certain in advance the teachers and counselors at the schools you evaluate are trained to handle the task.

Summary

The school selection process begins by first evaluating your child's educational needs and setting appropriate near- and long-term goals. Choosing a school whose philosophy is different from your own will court educational disaster for your child. After carefully interviewing the school principal and teachers who will teach your child, use the following checklist for evaluating a school:

Physical Quality
Neighborhood
School grounds and building interiors

Administration
Atmosphere
Available published materials
    Educational goals
    Rules and regulations
Profiles of students, faculties
Interviews
    Principal
    Teachers

School Size and Organization
Schools-within-a-school or academies
Tracking (ability-grouping)
Tutoring, remediation, special education

Academics
Academic goals
Student achievement (academic results)
Classrooms (students per teacher)
Specialized classrooms (science labs, music rooms, etc.)
Library (media center)
Principal or teacher authority
Classroom interruptions

Curriculum
Open or restricted
Core curriculum
    English (reading, writing, speaking)
    Math
    History, civics, geography
    Science

        Foreign languages
        Fine arts
        Music
    Course quality
    Electives
    Teaching methods (team-teaching, tutoring, etc.)
    Textbooks (check dates of publication)
    Advanced placement
    Special facilities
        Programs for gifted students
        Programs for handicapped students
        Remedial education
        Special education

Nonclassroom facilities
    Extracurricular activities
    Athletics
    Guidance and counseling
    Parent-teacher conferences

Chapter 4

Helping Your Child Succeed in School

In 1977, the Swiss scientist Jean Piaget (1896–1980) published a broad and widely accepted graphic concept of how people absorb new knowledge. He used the image of a mental framework, which he called a scheme, to describe the totality of each person's existing knowledge, both instinctive and acquired.[1]

Newborn infants enter the world with such a mental scheme in which their limited, instinctive, genetically determined knowledge has been organized. As new knowledge is absorbed—as the scheme accommodates new information—the shape of the overall scheme changes to assimilate that new knowledge.

A person's scheme—the totality of one's knowledge and experience—permits the individual to solve problems never seen before, depending on whether he or she can connect the new problem to any past knowledge or experience his or her scheme has assimilated.

For example, almost any infant in a comfortable home with loving parents initially trusts all adults, assumes they are like

---

[1] Jean Piaget, *The Development of Thought: Equilibration of Cognitive Structures* (New York: The Viking Press, 1977).

Mom and Dad, and reaches out to hold and be held. When children learn not to speak to strangers, their schemes change and instead of reaching out, they shy away.

How Knowledge Accumulates

The Piaget scheme is only a device to help understand in broad terms how knowledge is absorbed. You can substitute any image—a sack, for example, with each bit of genetic or acquired knowledge shaped like a small child's block.

As each new block is thrown into the sack, it will come to rest in a specific way against other blocks, changing their positions and ultimately changing the relative positions of the other blocks and the shape of the entire sack. And although identical blocks may be thrown into many children's sacks, each will come to rest in a different part of the pile and have a different effect on neighboring blocks and the shape of the sack.

As each individual ages, the sack fills, and each new bit of information has less impact on the overall scheme. Eventually, when the sack is filled, no new knowledge is assimilated and learning ceases.

By the time children enter preschool at age three or four and regular school at five or six, they each have a different mental scheme. Some bits of information they absorb will be identical, but many will vary to different degrees.

Even subtle differences in the way mothers transmit similar information—"Eat your spinach; it's good for you," for example, versus, "Eat your spinach; it's delicious"—can alter the shape of a child's scheme and the way the youngster assimilates future information. These different mealtime approaches certainly can alter a child's feelings toward spinach, and perhaps all leafy vegetables, by prompting one child to say enthusiastically, "I love spinach," and another to sneer, "Yuck."

The Child in School

Depending on the type and number of knowledge bits thrown in the sack during the child's infant education, the child will begin school with above-average, average, or below-average language skills and different learning abilities. A good school with good teachers can help each child function to the maximum of his or her abilities. Teachers can't do the job alone, however, and without your help, even the finest school with the finest teachers cannot assure your child's academic success.

In the end, you and your child's teachers must work as partners to educate your child. Even if your child's teachers provide maximum amounts of individual attention, only you are in a position to provide long-term, consistent, one-on-one tutoring that researchers have proved so effective in lifting student academic performance. In the end, only you can keep your child out of the many learning disability traps that lie hidden throughout the educational system.

When your child begins kindergarten and each grade in elementary school, it's important to share your knowledge of your child with your child's teachers. They'll need to know your child's strengths and weaknesses.

They'll also want to know about your child's low and high aptitudes and learning impediments that make it difficult for your child to learn certain things. They will want to know whether you have accumulated an inventory of teaching techniques that have proved effective for your child—assuming, of course, that you've picked a school with teachers willing and able to provide individual instruction.

Even with such individual attention, however, your child will not always fathom a teacher's approach to every lesson and will undoubtedly turn to you for help after school. If you don't already have an inventory of teaching techniques for your child, now is the time to begin studying how your child goes about trying to learn.

Making Learning Easy

In helping your child with schoolwork, try to understand his or her learning differences and approaches to problem-solving. See if they work and succeed in solving problems and producing understanding. It's important that your child's teachers do the same. Remember there are many ways to learn and to solve almost every problem, and it is essential that you understand the ones that work for your child. If your child succeeds by doing things differently from you, praise your child—and be happy and grateful your child has succeeded in learning.

That does not mean you should not try to show your child other, different ways to solve the same problem or learn the same thing. Mechanical and electronic devices such as calculators, computers, and appropriate software programs can serve as helpful tools for explaining different approaches to the same problem.

By serving as your child's teacher in this way, you and your youngster will avoid the learning disabilities trap that has condemned so many bright children to academic mediocrity and failure by labelling learning differences and low aptitudes as disabilities.

Teachers don't, of course, purposely set out to make learning difficult for their students. The vast majority are dedicated, caring people who genuinely want to impart knowledge to youngsters. Sometimes, they simply don't know any better. The way they teach is the way they learned, and it is the only way they know. Teacher education in America is, after all, substandard.

As mentioned earlier, a 1996 report by the National Commission on Teaching found that fewer than half the nation's twelve hundred teacher's colleges met professional standards of accreditation and that more than fifty thousand teachers who lacked training for their jobs had entered teaching in 1992 and 1993.

The report found that more than one-quarter of newly hired public-school teachers enter their classrooms with inadequate teaching skills or training in their subjects, and that more than 12 percent of new teachers—one in eight—have no training at all.

Under these circumstances, it's little wonder so many American public schools are unable to offer anything more than the most mediocre education to even the brightest, most gifted students.

Sometimes, of course, the school curriculum requires teachers to teach a subject in a specific way. And in still other instances, a teacher may have too many students to offer each one an individualized approach to problem-solving. The average public-school class has more than eighteen students per teacher, and many have thirty or more.

For most students in public schools, successful learning—especially if the student's approach to learning is different—can actually result in academic failure. The right answer is not enough; the student must arrive at the right answer in the right way—namely, the teacher's way.

Monitoring Your Child's School

Regardless of the care you used in selecting a school, teachers, programs, school officials, and policies change constantly. Sometimes the changes are subtle, other times drastic. In any case, it is important to monitor your child's school programs every year, along with your child academic and emotional responses.

Throughout the elementary-school years, teachers should instruct small groups that give each child time to participate. Different groups should be working on different skills, and teaching materials should be varied enough to match each student's needs.

Remember that any teaching program that makes every child learn the same skills in the same way at the same time will only serve an average group. Slower children will struggle to keep up and gifted children will be bored. Both will grow frustrated, angry, and begin rebelling against school.

In any successful program, most students are enthusiastic about each new skill they learn. You can tell your child is thriving in a first-grade reading program when he or she comes home by mid-autumn eager to demonstrate new skills—reading from schoolbooks, spotting and barking out words on signs, menus, newspapers, and packages, and asking questions about the meanings of unknown words. Your child should continue to look forward eagerly to hearing new, more complex stories at bedtime.

If by mid-autumn, however, your child's interest in learning declines noticeably and he or she comes home each afternoon with a long list of grievances about the teacher, the school, and its programs, you should investigate the teaching programs immediately and sit in on some classes.

If all students in a kindergarten or elementary-school classroom are using the same learning program and learning the same skills at the same time, you'll need to talk with the teacher. Without being antagonistic or confrontational, you'll have to point out your child's individual needs and ask how the teacher believes these needs can best be met.

You may find out the teacher was unaware of the problem and may change approaches or be willing to work with your child individually. The teacher may also suggest ways you can help your child at home.

Learning Impediments

Although there are many different ways to solve problems, there are even more ways that don't work, and some learning differences that consistently channel a child's thinking in those wrong directions can slow or impede learning.

Fortunately, the majority of such impediments are noncritical and do not interfere with learning essential to maturing into normal, functioning adults. We all have them. Some of them are developmental and disappear. Most of us learn to work around the others—just as the tone-deaf avoid singing careers and the color-blind generally find careers outside the graphic or fine arts.

The causes of these impediments can be genetic, environmental, neurological, physical trauma, or a variety of emotional or psychological difficulties.

Before embarking on any educational strategy to help your child with an apparent impediment, always be certain to have your pediatrician give the child a thorough physical examination. A persistent inability to learn the balancing skills required to ride a bicycle, for example, might well be symptomatic of a middle-ear problem. An apparent inability to read, write, or focus might be a signal your child is near- or farsighted. Don't put your child through endless hours of unnecessary tutoring when all that's needed for success is, for example, a simple pair of reading glasses.

Dealing with Developmental Learning Impediments

As discussed in Chapter 1, many of your child's learning impediments during the early years are developmental and nothing to worry about—as in the case of the child whose hands are too small to play octaves on the piano. Developmental learning impediments usually disappear by the time a child is eight, although some may persist into adolescence, just as enuresis and physical-development problems sometimes do.

Children with developmental learning impediments often grow extremely frustrated because they recognize they have the intellectual potential to learn and perform the task at hand, but through no fault of their own, they are not ready developmentally. Children with developmental learning impediments often grow angry and moody and become discouraged. Although growth and development will eventually help your child over-come such impediments, you must, in the meantime, bolster your child's self-esteem by praising learning successes.

The best responses to developmental learning activities are patience, understanding, acceptance, confidence in your child, love, and the skill to divert your child's attention to areas where he or she displays strong learning ability. Diversity of learning activities is a key to relieving the anxieties associated with developmental learning impediments. Instead of focusing on and practicing failure, your child can focus on success.

Anger, annoyance, badgering, and other negative responses will not only prolong your child's developmental learning impediment, they will discourage your child and almost certainly produce other learning impediments that could become critical and interfere with all learning. Equally destructive are unrealistic attempts to force your child to overcome a develop-mental learning impediment. There is no way to stretch a five-year-old's hand to reach an octave on the piano without breaking the child's fingers. To try to force a child to learn any skill or academic discipline before the child is ready develop-mentally will almost certainly damage his or her spirit and interest in learning. Children eventually outgrow—and usually forget about—their developmental learning impediments. You must understand that, and you must help your child understand it, too.

One of the best feel-good techniques to help a child under-stand developmental impediments is to read stories—or act them out with puppets—in which one character very much like your child faces similar circumstances, including having to wait to grow up and having to make waiting time more enjoyable.

Even if you've succeeded in making your child accept and feel comfortable about such developmental learning impedi-ments, his or her peers may be less understanding. Many teach-ers may automatically—and thoughtlessly—respond by sending your child to special education or placing your child in a slower academic track.

Again, you can avoid that eventuality. First, carefully select your child's school and teachers. Second, schedule a parent-teacher conference before the school year begins to discuss these learning impediments and how teachers can handle them to permit your child to progress normally in the learning process.

Dealing with Other Noncritical Learning Impediments

All of us have imperfect abilities we will not outgrow. They are forever a part of us—like tone-deafness or color-blindness. In today's environment, many are mislabelled "learning disabilities" and result in perfectly normal, bright children being sent into special-education or general-education classes and possible academic oblivion.

Most imperfect learning abilities are not disabling—any more than imperfect physical abilities are disabling. They may have some disadvantages, but they are hardly crippling, and it is cruel to call them that. The color-blind child has an inherited inability to distinguish different colors from each other, and the uncoordinated child may play basketball poorly. Neither is crippled.

Both children have noncritical learning impediments—one of them genetic, the other perhaps genetic, or perhaps environmental, as a result of not having had enough motor-skill training as an infant. Neither impediment, however, will interfere with a child's ability to go on with his or her life and become a successful, productive adult and a capable, loving mate and parent.

Similarly, imperfect intellectual abilities are not necessarily disabling as long as they are noncritical and do not interfere with a child's ability to learn essential skills such as speaking, reading, writing, and calculating and to live a successful, productive life. A child who thrives on history, for example, but who cannot fathom abstract concepts of physics or higher mathematics is not intellectually disabled. Nor is the tinkerer who works wonders in the physics lab but who cannot understand poetry.

Don't subscribe to the myth of the well-rounded student. Few of us can excel in all areas, and it is unfair to expect our children to do so. To attempt to force your child to become well rounded is to court intellectual and emotional disaster.

Help your child grow in areas where he or she displays high aptitudes and don't dwell unnecessarily in areas of low ability. Build on success; don't focus on failure.

Your child may not be able to draw or sing as well as other children or may be less coordinated or less interested in active playground games. It will be of little benefit—and could be detrimental to your child's emotional health—to concentrate on building skills in which your child lacks innate talent while failing to devote attention to areas where natural talents could carry him or her to success.

If, say, your child has a low aptitude for science, don't fill the house with chemistry sets and microscopes that will only serve as a humiliating reminder of your child's weakness. Discover, instead, your child's strengths. Perhaps your child loves poetry or art or is interested in military history. There are endless activities and experiences that will reinforce such intellectual strengths and can build up intellectual and emotional self-confidence.

Once a youngster begins thriving in areas of high aptitude, the child's overall performance usually improves to surprisingly high levels—even in areas of lower aptitude. That's because of the interconnection between academic disciplines.

A child with a low mathematics aptitude who has a high aptitude and love for history must eventually learn dates, time spans, battlefield dimensions, and military movements that require mathematical calculation. A history student thus acquires some mathematics skills as a necessary, coincidental tool to pursue a love of history—and may reach a level of achievement in mathematics that would not have been possible from the study of mathematics alone.

Avoiding Failure

Children usually sense instinctively the areas in which they have low aptitudes and quickly lose interest in those activities. Interest and aptitude go hand in hand. A good teacher can and should make every academic area as interesting as possible to students. But even the best teacher cannot force a youngster to achieve beyond a reasonable minimum in noncritical areas for which the child has demonstrated a low aptitude or learning impediment. Again, by noncritical areas I mean non-language areas, such as science and advanced mathematics, that are not essential for functional speaking, reading, writing, and calculating.

Gifted children often exhibit more noncritical learning impediments than their less gifted peers, although many are environmental. That's usually because the world—and too often, parents and teachers—expect students who are gifted in one area to be equally gifted in every academic area. That is rarely the case, and the tragic result for many gifted children is an endless stream of criticism and expressions of disappointment by parents, teachers, and others.

Gifted children usually excel and have extraordinarily high aptitudes in only one broad category of learning—the arts, for example, or mathematics, or science. Even the most gifted may have average or low aptitudes—or even learning impediments—in other categories of learning. If these low aptitudes or learning impediments are noncritical, it can be counterproductive to force a child to improve in weak areas while holding back the child's progress in areas of strength.

Differences That Slow Learning

There are some learning differences that can slow essential learning of critical language skills. Earlier, I cited my personal history of dysgraphia, a way I somehow learned to write as a child that left my script lettering so tiny, crowded, and sloping that it was illegible to the teacher—and to me. The result was that I knew how to solve mathematical problems but got the wrong answer, because I couldn't read my own handwriting and often transferred the wrong numbers to the next step. Clearly, this was a learning difference that was slowing my learning.

Fortunately, learning disabilities had not yet been "invented" when I was a child or I most certainly would have been sent into the endless special-education maze. Classroom teachers had to deal with such problems on their own if they had the time and skill—or let the child fail. My insightful tenth-grade geometry teacher had both the time and skill, although he knew nothing about special education or learning disabilities. He instinctively used a simple technique of good, not special, education called remedial compensation, which you as a parent can easily adapt in helping your child overcome obstructive learning differences.

First, he made me go back to printing letters and abandon script, which automatically ties letters together and makes it all too easy for a child to run letters into one another. Printing separated each character from the next. Second, he made me write my homework and tests on wide-dimension ruled paper, with instructions to leave every other line blank and write each letter and numeral large enough to touch the line above.

My handwriting immediately became so big and bold, so legible and straight that it became virtually impossible to make errors, and my grades soared from near failure to honors level. To help me improve even more, he urged me to speak the words and numbers aloud as I wrote them on my homework paper in the quiet of my room, thus adding the multisensory approach to learning.

Getting Remedial Compensation

Remedial compensation accomplishes two important things: First, it analyzes the error and develops a strategy that prevents repeating the error. Second, it brings into play as many of the child's faculties as possible.

Analyzing the child's learning error—the self-defeating learning difference—allows a teacher to teach the student to perform the same operation in a way that makes it impossible to make the same error again. Initially, there may be some difficulty adapting, but within a few days, most children adopt the compensatory technique as their own—especially when they see the results and enjoy the rewards of improved academic performance.

Bringing into play as many of the child's faculties as possible is called multisensory education. All good teachers recognize that the more senses and faculties a student uses, the greater his or her concentration and more successful the learning process. In addition to the sense of feel and the visual sense that came into play when I wrote large numbers and letters, saying the numbers and words aloud added two more senses—speaking and hearing. It's far easier to concentrate on the concept that two plus two equals four when a child speaks the words aloud and hears them rather than when a child simply thinks them while a television or stereo projects competing sounds.

Helping Your Child

Just as my teacher used remedial compensation for my illegible handwriting, you can develop similar techniques to compensate for any learning differences your child may have that are interfering with the learning process. The principles are the same: Teach your child to prevent the unwanted pattern by performing the operation in a different, usually opposite, way that makes it impossible to repeat the error. Then bring as many sensory faculties into play as possible.

If, for example, your child has some minor spelling difficulties, analyze the errors to find a pattern. Examine your child's handwriting. Are the letters too close together? If so, help your child spread them out. If the letters are too small, help your child increase their size with wide-spaced ruled paper. Then, to add more sensory dimensions, have your child say each word aloud, then say each letter while writing it.

To break a tendency to reverse letters—*cta* instead of *cat*, for example—teach your child to write enlarged letters and spread them out while saying them aloud. See if the letter-reversal pattern affects specific letter combinations or is random and generalized and requires more complex retraining. If it's a specific word or letter pattern, such as the *at* reversal in *cat*, focus on that pattern by producing a list of similarly spelled words—*cat, bat, hat, sat, fat*.

In teaching your child, try always to transform lessons into games instead of anxiety-provoking remediation. "I wonder how many words there are that rhyme with cat?" Games turn learning into enjoyable challenges. Children not only remember what they learn in games, they tend to practice such games on their own. As they look around, they automatically start seeing things that rhyme with cat and repeat them and their spelling as a challenge.

Taking the Multisensory Approach

As mentioned earlier, the multisensory approach is one of the most effective ways to teach reading and writing and prevent many spelling and other writing problems. In addition to seeing, saying, and hearing a letter or number, the child feels it by tracing its shape with a finger.

In arithmetic calculation, many students improve their performance by saying each number and the product of the calculation aloud as they write. A child who says aloud the words *four plus four is eight* while writing each numeral is less likely to write 4 + 4 = 9.

Multisensory study can improve any student's performance in almost any academic area at almost any age. Beginning readers who read aloud with their forefingers touching the page beneath each word invariably improve the accuracy with which they read. Later, underlining important elements of text in social studies, history, or science serves the same purpose as well as promoting good study habits by making it easier to find key facts for review. The student who not only underlines key data, but reads the lesson aloud and repeats the underlined material a second time increases the amount of material absorbed.

If you cannot come up with a compensatory technique or are in doubt about correcting minor obstructive learning impediments, contact the remedial-reading teacher at your local school. Such teachers usually know simple techniques that help eliminate minor obstructive learning differences.

Remember, however, that the techniques discussed here are designed to build aptitude and work around or compensate for minor, noncritical learning impediments. They are not designed for critical learning impediments that result from neurological dysfunctions. The latter require highly skilled special-education teachers to retrain a child's approach to learning.

Tutoring Your Child

Don't even think about working with your child if you are going to become impatient, frustrated, angry, or disappointed when your child does less than perfect work or occasionally lacks motivation. It takes endless patience, understanding, empathy, objectivity, and skill to teach a child—any child. When parental love enters the picture, objectivity often fades away.

Try to keep in mind, however, that school days are not necessarily the best years of your life and certainly not the easiest. They represent years of hard work. After putting in a full day's work at school, most children arrive home tired and in need of relaxation—then have to face doing their homework. It's important to recognize these feelings and give your child a break when he or she arrives home from school.

If you can bring the required patience and objectivity to the tutoring situation, you should, by all means, try to help your child overcome learning difficulties and impediments as much as possible. That *does not* mean doing your child's homework. It means showing your child how to do it and helpfully pointing out errors in a gentle way so your child can try again to improve the work alone.

Remember that in tutoring your child you must serve as your teacher's partner in learning. If you cannot be enthusiastic about and support the work and projects your child is doing at school and brings home, do not undermine your child's belief in the value of school and education. Instead, go to the school, discuss your doubts with the teacher or principal or both.

Clearly, though, you should have investigated the kind of work your child would be doing before enrollment when there was still time to select a different school. It is a disservice and will create new learning impediments to undermine your child's faith in the value of school or to transfer your child in the middle of the school year.

Basic Principles

Here are some basic principles for helping your child improve academic performance:

- *Identify learning problems.* You may want to confer with your child's teacher to obtain an exact picture of the gap between your child's level of achievement and the teacher's expectations. In that way, you don't bore your child by needless repetition of things already mastered. Ask the teacher for specific teaching and exercise materials covering areas in which your child is deficient.

♦ *Organize work area and study time.* Learning is a discipline, which like other disciplines, is impossible to practice in an atmosphere of chaos. Your child's work area should include a clean, neat, unclutered desk with ample work space, bookshelves, a separate computer space or table, and a storage area for supplies. If your child's room is messy, explain the importance of neatness and organization, then help your child clean it, dispose of unnecessary toys and clothes, and organize the room and work area so he or she can always find things. If necessary, create a separate work or play area in another room, but the work area must reflect an atmosphere of calm, ordered discipline.

Help your child set up a study schedule, beginning after a reasonable period of relaxation or physical fun and activities following his or her return from school. The time allotted for relaxation and work will vary considerably from age to age. For a ninth grader who arrives home at 3:00 in the afternoon, 4:30 or 5:00 would be a reasonable time to begin an hour's worth of homework. After a break for dinner, your child might begin again at 7:30 for an hour or hour and a half, depending on your child's age, the academic demands of school, and the amount of homework on any given night.

If your child attends an academically demanding school, you can determine the minimum number of homework minutes your child should spend each weekday night and on the weekend by multiplying your child's grade level by a factor of ten to fifteen. A sixth grader should spend at least sixty to ninety minutes six times a week. Break the total amount into short, manageable, productive work periods—three half-hour periods, with a ten- or fifteen-minute break between each. For younger children with too little homework to fill their evenings, you can substitute intellectually enriching activities, such as puzzles and games, that you can enjoy together.

◆ *Build attention span.* The appropriate time you allot for studying and relaxing will depend on your child's attention span and will vary as your child matures. Monitor your child's studying from time to time to determine attention span. If your child stops making progress after ten minutes, there's no point forcing him or her to continue sitting idly for an hour or two.

First try to determine what has blocked the progress and see if you can help your child solve the problem. If it is truly a question of attention difficulties, let your child take periodic breaks, but help your child extend working time with each succeeding return to the desk. Use anything that helps extend attention span—an alarm clock, for example.

Let's say your child has been breaking every ten minutes. Suggest extending the periods to twelve minutes for a week, then fifteen, explaining each time that fewer breaks and longer study periods mean getting homework finished sooner and having more time for other activities.

In addition to setting up a time schedule, help your child order the work. Children often don't know what to do first when they face a series of projects and tend to skip around without finishing anything. Set up a schedule that gets as many assignments out of the way as quickly as possible. These are usually the easiest assignments. Then when your child confronts the more difficult assignments, they are down to a more manageable number, say, one or two.

◆ *Keep it short.* If your child is having learning problems, breaking each learning unit into smaller, more manageable segments is a simple way of making it easier to learn.

Don't give your child more than four or five problems at a time, so he or she can achieve success quickly and you can relax and enjoy a triumph together before attacking new problems with renewed vigor.

Short teaching units provide your child with immediate feedback and help correct errors in smaller, less painful steps. After a break, your child can then apply new learning to the next group of problems.

Change the pace—three problems in one unit, four in another, and so on. Watch your child's eyes to see if they're alert. Let your child participate in setting a realistic pace and the direction of the instruction: "How many problems should we do now?" or "What should we do first, science or math?"

◆ *Use the senses.* Bring as many of your child's sensory faculties into play as possible, repeating the lessons aloud for your child to hear while he or she reads the material. Then have your child say the material aloud and write the material out, thus adding feel to eyesight, hearing, and speech.

◆ *Use technology and other available resources.* High-tech equipment designed for children—including calculators, computers, video and audio equipment—makes learning fun. The simple mastery of such equipment constitutes a triumph for most children and makes them eager to use it more, and as a result, learn more.

A host of companies, whose names and addresses your school can provide, produce marvelous instructional software. Among them are Apple Computer, Encyclopedia Britannica Educational Corporation, The Learning Company, McGraw-Hill School Division, Milton Bradley Educational Division, Random House School Division, Scott Foresman and Company, and many others.

In addition to high-tech materials, don't ignore the value of such low-tech equipment as audio- and videotapes, film strips, slides, charts, instructional aids (alphabet and syllable charts and multiplication tables), games that teach (*Scrabble*, for example, or geography games), projects involving creative art, music, chemistry, biology, physics, architecture, and construction, and so on. Illustrated books, graphic presentations, and attractive posters and illustrations your child can post in his or her room can be extremely instructive as well as entertaining.

Other helpful projects include keeping a diary and writing original stories or visiting museums, companies with interesting production facilities such as chocolate or ice cream factories, historic restorations, and other educative installations. Remember that play and entertainment remain the most valuable teaching tools for adolescents as well as younger children.

◆ *Praise your child.* Give your child appropriate levels of praise whenever possible. Don't be inappropriately effusive. Your child is aware of being the only child who did not understand that $2 \times 2 = 4$ was the same concept as $2 + 2 + 2$. When you finally succeed in teaching a concept, provide appropriate praise and recognize (as does your child) that the understanding involved is not comparable to discovering the Theory of Relativity. A loving pat on the back is all that's needed, along with the comment, "I'm so proud you've caught up. You should be proud, too."

In scanning the list of problems your child has solved, check off the correct ones first so you can begin each session with praise. By focusing on errors at the beginning of each lesson, you start with so much anxiety your child will grow hesitant to call on you for help.

Don't criticize your child for the wrong answers. Find out how math problems were done to see if your child misunderstood how to do them or simply made a careless error. Then ask your child to redo the problems. Whatever you do, show no anger or disappointment—either verbally or with body or facial language that implies disapproval. Don't make your child deal with the fear of losing a parent's love as well as the anxiety of learning adequate calculating or writing skills.

◆ *Teach your child independence.* Ultimately, your task as your child's teacher is not to teach reading, writing, and arithmetic, although you'll obviously have to help him or her learn certain specifics in many areas. Your primary task is to teach your child *how* to learn so he or she can eventually handle learning independently. Don't sit beside your child or look over your child's shoulder while he or she is doing homework. By doing so, you are building an unrealistic and crippling dependency that will not be supported at school or in later life. Children must learn to work on their own. It is part of growing up.

Essential Study Skills

To teach your child to learn and work independently, you must teach your child these essential study skills:

◆ *Focus.* Your child should study in total quiet, with no distractions from radio, television, telephone, or family members. You and the rest of the family must respect your child's right to do homework without distractions.

◆ *Neatness.* An essential for good work is a clean, uncluttered desk, devoted exclusively to school work, with supplies organized and easy to find. Homework papers should be written neatly and rewritten if there are too many erasures.

◆ *Organization.* You should teach your child to organize work into units, with appropriate breaks at various intervals. Your child should learn to work continuously during the agreed-upon work period and to cease all socializing when it's time to get back to work at the end of a break.

◆ *Multisensory study.* Some children learn better reading aloud—especially younger children. In addition, your child should underline key points as he or she reads or mark them with a vertical line or an essential reference note in the adjacent margin. *Do not* encourage your child to use highlighters because they cannot be used to write essential notes in the margins. Teach your child to work with an ordinary pencil and to underline.

◆ *Technology.* Keep an eye open for new (and old) mechanical and technological devices that will eliminate or reduce the drudgery of some aspects of nightly homework chores—word-processing equipment, for example, for a child with slow or incurably poor handwriting. There are also some wonderful spelling aids on the market, including a speaking dictionary, which pronounces each word and gives its definition.

No parent would withhold eyeglasses and force a nearsighted child to squint to read or do homework. Don't withhold other mechanical or high-tech study aids that can be critical to language success. That doesn't mean introducing a calculator before a child has learned to do basic calculations by rote. But after the child has clearly demonstrated maximum calculation skills, there is little point wasting time dividing huge numbers such as 3,647.23 by 76.42 in longhand. Let your child move ahead to learning new material.

◆ *Regular review.* Your child should review each of the evening's lessons once—just for good luck—to make sure he or she remembers all the material, and as many more times as required before each test or final examination.

In teaching your child study skills and independence, make it clear you are not abandoning your child. Explain that you are always ready to help in any way you can, from correcting home-work to attacking specific problems.

Learning Strategies

In addition to developing good personal habits, self-discipline, and study skills, every child needs to develop learning strategies to succeed academically. You can help teach your child many of these strategies.

Reading

There are many elements that make up the reading process, with techniques for strengthening each. Try to identify those elements that are most difficult for your child.

- *Sight-word recognition.* Ask your child to read aloud and mark every word he or she either mispronounces or hesitates and has to think about. Keep the reading unit short, and at the end of it, have your child make a list of every marked word—in large, bold handwriting, with letters spaced apart for easy recognition. Depending on your child's age, it can be fun to draw a picture to illustrate each word and provide a graphic, visual memory aide.

  Make a copy of the list for yourself, and at the end of the lesson, have your child read the words on the list aloud three or four times in succession, putting a check by each word that continues to produce difficulties. Grade your child with each reading, and of course, praise your child as improvement grows evident.

  Sometimes you can overcome persistent mispronunciations by using phonetic symbols to indicate long vowels and a slash mark to cross out silent letters—or by dividing words into separate syllables. An example is the word *believe*, which might be written in separate syllables (*be-lieve*), with phonetic symbols and slashes through the silent letters (*bēliēvé*) or both (*bē-liēvé*). Use any technique that helps your child compensate for the problem or impediment.

As a first-grader, my son had persistent problems pronouncing the *s* in words that began with an *s* followed by a consonant. He pronounced *specific* as *pacific*. A remedial-education teacher gave him some wonderfully amusing sentences we could practice (and laugh at) together no matter what we were doing. It is now more than twenty-five years since he made his first crayon illustration showing how "Sammy Snake slithered into the swamp to sleep."

When your child has obviously absorbed a list of words, have a "retirement" ceremony in which your child throws the list away—with praise and a hug from you.

Invest in mechanical aids to improve sight-word recognition. The Learning Company puts out some exciting computer software such as *Reader Rabbit* that children (and parents) usually love.

◆ *Comprehension.* To improve reading comprehension, remove all distractions. Turn off the radio and television and do not permit any interruptions. If the telephone rings, let your answering device pick up—just as you would if you were out shopping. It's important to show your child that, for these ten or twenty or thirty minutes (according to age and attention span), reading is the most important, exciting—and only—activity in your and your child's world.

Depending on your child's age, you may want to read the passage aloud first, then have your child read it back to you aloud. Then begin to probe the depth of your child's understanding, from the general to the specific.

Ask your child what the passage was about. Instead of an examination, you might turn the situation into dinner-table conversation by urging your child to tell your spouse about the interesting story you read when he or she came home from school. Who is the most important character? What happened to the main character? What did the character do? How did the story end?

Another effective approach is called *practice and present*. The child reads a story until the reading is clear enough to present it on tape for replay during car trips and other times when the child can read along to his or her own presentation. Teach your child to use different voices for each character and add dramatic emphasis to each. A variation of the practice-and-present approach is to ask different family members to play a character for the taping.

After a few days, as your child acquires the habit of concentrating and absorbing the overall story line, begin questioning your child about specifics, adding only one question at a time over a period of many days: Was it day or night? What kind of flowers were blooming? What color was the house? What time of year was it? What was the weather like? What kind of animals were in the yard?

Keep initial readings short so you can take turns rereading them aloud when your child isn't certain about the answers to the questions.

Add the tactile experience to the oral, aural, and visual by asking your child to underline the words that answer your questions correctly, to write some of the answers on a separate piece of paper—or to illustrate the answers in an original drawing. Suggest your child draw a picture of the house or the animals in the story.

Another interesting approach for some children is to rewrite the story themselves in a way they prefer to the original or to incorporate family, friends, or relatives in a rewritten version. As your child gets into the late elementary or middle-school grades, teach your child to underline key points in each paragraph or collate key elements in a neat notebook that will facilitate review for examinations.

◆ *Speed.* Once your child has mastered sight-word recognition and comprehension, take a familiar passage of fifty to one hundred words and time your child's reading aloud. Repeat the exercise a second and third time and see if the speed improves. Make it challenging. See if your child wants to try a fourth time to beat the "old world's record for our house." Repeat the reading once each night on successive nights until your child reads about one hundred words a minute, then move on to other passages.

◆ *Motivation and interest.* Buy stories that appeal to your child's interests and imagination. There are hundreds of thousands of books of all varieties for boys and girls of all ages. Ask teachers for suggestions, but these may tend to be bland and noncontroversial.

It's important for you, as your child's closest friend, to haunt the children's bookstores and find books that will most intrigue, excite, and engross your child. Read to your child each night for an hour, for example, instead of watching television. Use evening readings only for fun—no lessons, unless your child asks the meaning of a word.

Remember, too, that children are always capable of understanding and enjoying books they may not be capable of reading themselves or whose length is intimidating. So use the pleasure-reading time to expand your child's horizons with longer stories and books.

In addition to books, you can use other types of reading to enhance your child's interest and motivation. Read interesting stories from newspapers or magazines to your child and give your child cartoons to read. Clipping an interesting newspaper article you feel is important makes your child feel important, too—and very grown-up.

In restaurants, let your child read the menu and select his or her meal. In the kitchen, let your child read recipe instructions and help. The same holds true for assembling things you buy. As you buy games, let your child read and explain the rules. Not all reading has to be learned in books. Directions for model and craft kits, floor plans in museums, and to a distant cousin's home are all exciting ways for children to learn that you trust them and their skills.

When your child makes errors reading stories or recipes—stumbles on words, loses the place, and so on—don't halt the flow of the experience by turning it into an embarrassing lesson. Simply supply the word and keep your child reading happily. To insist that your child sound it out distracts the child from the fun of sharing a new and improving skill with you. If you see a pattern of mistakes, work on it at another appropriate lesson time, but let your child keep reading.

Don't give your child materials to read that are too adult. When you see your child struggling, admit that the book is difficult—even for you—and that there are plenty of better books to read.

Don't overlook comic books as entertaining, illustrated books for young readers, and by all means enroll in book clubs and subscribe to children's magazines that cover topics in which your child may be interested. Check to see whether your local library has regular story-reading programs for youngsters your child's age.

Speaking

You and your child have already been practicing reading aloud. You can use those reading exercises to improve your child's speaking skills. Don't make fun of or even repeat any of your child's errors in pronunciation. Simply repeat the word or phrase the correct way.

Don't be afraid to have fun. Take any good story or play your child can read and understand, choose roles, and with grand, flowing gestures, imitate the actors—but say the words slowly and correctly.

The gestures, by the way, add up to more than fun. They represent a multisensory approach that adds meaning to words by letting your child see and feel the action of each word. It helps your child remember the meaning of *squirm* if he or she says the word while squirming.

Word and action games such as charades are also enjoyable ways to build a child's vocabulary. Such games can be fun for children of all ages and give your child the feeling of being a partner in learning rather than being the only member of the family who doesn't know anything.

In playing such games, however, try to design them as specific learning experiences. Family members can, for example, take turns choosing an action to illustrate, such as standing in place, moving from place to place, moving legs and feet, making a face, shaking hands and arms, making a sound, and so on.

Each member of the family can invent a different game, listing all the things players must do for each activity, then taking turns asking the others to perform. A game called "Stand in One Place," for example, might ask participants to bend, sag, collapse, lean, shake, stretch, wiggle, and so on. "Make a Sound" might ask participants to call, crow, cry, giggle, hiccup, howl, hum, laugh, sneeze, snicker, sob, wheeze, whistle, and so on. The game can be played in reverse and called "What Am I Doing?"

More complex word games that require more complex sentence construction and extemporaneous speech include "What Comes Next?" in which participants finish or begin consecutive sentences of a story, or create an entire paragraph the next participant must continue with a creative paragraph of his or her own.

Listening

Participation in the speaking games I just mentioned require listening skills, and obviously such games are designed to help improve those skills. The more you can engage your child in joint activities of that kind, the more your child's listening skills will improve.

Listening-oriented activities can range from cooking or

building things together to playing word games that require back-and-forth speech and comprehension, not silent board games.

If your child enjoys them, riddles can be great training for listening, especially as you gradually extend their length and complexity. There are plenty of good riddle books, but be sure to give your child a chance to ask you some.

Other strategies for improving listening skills include those listed earlier, including elimination of distractions such as radio, television, and telephone. As with teaching reading skills, keep work units short, reward success, and take appropriate breaks.

Writing

One problem in trying to help any child overcome writing problems is that writing is both a skill and a craft. It is, therefore, difficult to teach at home unless you're a teacher or a practiced writer. You can, however, help your child overcome certain elementary writing difficulties we have all experienced, professionals and amateurs alike.

- ◆ *Handwriting.* One challenge is the physical act of writing letters, which requires manipulating a pen or pencil by tiny, sometimes uncoordinated fingers. Although children often enter kindergarten or first grade knowing how to print many capital letters, they often do so inefficiently, and you can be of significant help by teaching your child the correct strategies for shaping letters. It takes a lot of practice.

  On their own, some kids grip a pen or pencil with their fist, as if they were about to stab the paper. Even children who hold writing instruments correctly often use the wrong letter-forming strategies. In writing the letter *E* for example, many first draw the three horizontal strokes for the letter *E* and then the vertical stroke.

  When they enter school, of course, they have to learn a new way to write *E*. You can prevent your child from having to learn everything twice. Teach the correct way to hold writing instruments as soon as your child's fingers and muscular coordination permit, then teach the strategies of letter formation, which you can find in any first reader at a children's bookstore.

These strategies include grouping letters with related shapes such as *C*, *O*, and *S*, which incorporate partial or full circles drawn counterclockwise, or the letters *l* and *t*, which are formed with a downward stroke.

You can also buy special ruled paper with faint dots outlining each letter and arrows pointing in the correct direction for forming letters. The sandbox or the beach is also a good place to practice writing big letters and combine another tactile experience with learning and having fun. Also fun is to spread a pile of open newspapers on the floor and practice making huge letters such as *O* or *M* in free and easy motions with crayons or marking pens.

◆ *Spelling.* At some point during elementary-school years, your child will come home with spelling lists. The problem for many children is that such lists seem forbiddingly long, and they simply don't know how to attack them.

There are several strategies you can teach your child that will not only improve spelling, but make it fun. First, go down the list to find the easy words your child has no problem spelling. Then put each of the remaining words on individual flash cards your child can study, repeat aloud, copy, cover up, spell aloud, and so forth. For longer words, it can be helpful to break each word into syllables and write each syllable in a contrasting color.

You can turn these exercises into an entertaining quiz game by giving your child an equal chance with you to be quiz master. Even when you are the speller, your child will have to read the correctly spelled word, hear you repeat it, and ultimately, learn. Your child can improve spelling skills with a number of word-building games and electronic spelling toys available in toy stores, and with computer software designed for each level of spelling skill.

◆ *Creative writing.* I think in today's world, the computer or word processor is the most efficient way to help a child learn to enjoy writing. It eliminates so much of the disagreeable physical labor associated with handwriting—tearing up the paper and restarting, laborious erasing, disappointment at one's unattractive handwriting or word placement. A child can tell when his or her handwriting goes uphill and knows that the finished product is ugly. The computer allows the child to forget about the uncomfortable physical aspects of handwriting and concentrate on imagining and creating—things children instinctively love to do.

The computer also makes writing more fun by permitting the child to illustrate stories and expand the scope of his or her writing activities. Your child can easily keep a diary or journal, put together souvenir books from trips, write letters to friends about a trip or excursion, or write those disagreeable thank-you notes to friends.

Other interesting and entertaining projects that teach writing include publishing a home newspaper, writing poetry, silly rhymes, a novel, and many other works. The spell-check feature helps your child improve spelling, although it does not correct syntactical errors involving homophones such as *to, too,* and *two, their,* and *there,* or *its* and *it's.*

Grammar

Syntax and grammar are subjects you'll have to try to introduce and teach according to your child's age and ability. You can probably teach the difference between a noun (name) and verb (action word) to a kindergartner and most certainly to a first-grader. As your child progresses through elementary school, follow the concepts being taught and monitor your child's level of understanding.

Although schools no longer teach children to diagram (or parse) sentences, I still consider it the simplest and most graphic way to teach a child sentence structure and composition. Like so many other effective teaching methods, it is a multisensory approach that brings visual and tactile faculties to sentence construction. If you don't recall or never learned the technique, diagramming breaks a sentence into a subject and predicate (or verb and its modifiers and objects), then hangs each modifying adjective, adverb, or phrase from the word it modifies. Thus:

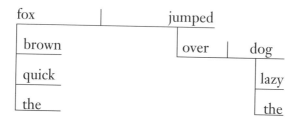

Another way to improve writing skills is to teach your child to proofread all papers twice—once silently for spelling, punctuation, and grammar errors, then a second time aloud to hear the texture and tone so it sounds more like a person talking than a person trying to write.

Mathematics

Your child should have learned many basic concepts of mathematics before entering kindergarten and certainly before entering first grade. These include *more than, less than, same as, and* (plus), *are* (equal), *take away* (subtract), and so forth. To help your child improve mathematics concepts and problem-solving skills, use and explain conceptual words such as *altogether, total,* and words associated with addition and subtraction, such as *spent, remainder, left over,* and *lost.*

As with every other area of study, there should be no distractions in the house when your child has to do arithmetic homework. No sounds of television or radio anywhere. Try to keep assignment units short. If a page has twenty problems that seem to overwhelm your child, copy five on another sheet and present only these before taking a break and returning to some of the others.

A chalkboard can be extremely helpful for a child who makes a lot of errors, and for a parent-teacher, because it permits easy correcting and helps the child practice what he or she might need to do in the school classroom.

To improve accuracy, let your child enjoy a succession of triumphs by repeating three or four times, one after another, a type of problem he or she knows how to do. On problems with errors, see if your child can find the error in three or fewer retries. To improve your child's grasp of basic mathematics, use manipulatives such as blocks or game chips.

Share everyday problems with your child to make mathematics meaningful and improve conceptual understanding and problem-solving skills. Play number card games and other games requiring simple arithmetic. Let your child keep score. Ask your child to accompany you to the store and help shop— and keep an eye on the family budget with a calculator and the family's health by reading the nutrition numbers.

Let your child add checks at restaurants, and when you travel and your child asks, "How much farther?" hand over the map and let your child figure it out. Let your child help measure when you need to buy things like rugs or curtains. You can also help improve your child's grasp of mathematics with any of the wide variety of toys, manual and electronic games, calculators, and computer software designed for children of all ages.

Summary

To help a child at school, it is important to monitor the work of the child's teacher as well as that of the child. Make certain not every child has to learn the same thing in the same way. A program that teaches only one way to learn leaves slower children struggling to catch up and faster children bored. See that teachers are giving each child an adequate share of individual attention.

At home, parents can most help their children by teaching youngsters good study habits that show students how to learn on their own. These include neat organization of the work area, careful allotment of study time, concentration, use of multi-sensory techniques that bring many faculties into play, access to technology, and careful review.

Chapter 5

Critical Learning Impediments

As I said at the beginning of this book, most children do not have learning disabilities and do not need special education. What they do have are abilities and inabilities or learning impediments. Good education, not special education, is all they usually need to take maximal advantage of their abilities, to minimize the effects of their inabilities, and to keep out of the special-education trap.

Despite all the efforts of their parents to provide the best possible education, however, some children are born with or develop critical learning impediments that interfere with the acquisition of certain language skills essential to all other learning. If the rate at which your child is acquiring key language skills seems to be slowing with each passing month, your child may have a critical learning impediment. Certain language skills are essential to learning: reading, writing, spelling, speaking, listening, reasoning, and calculating.

The U.S. Department of Education and school administrators use official jargon for the same terms: *basic reading skills, reading comprehension, written expression, oral expression, listening comprehension, math calculation,* and *math reasoning.*

Any impediment that blocks the acquisition of one or more of these language skills can block the gateway to all subsequent learning. Many critical learning impediments don't show up during infancy. Indeed, you may have provided your child with superb infant education and not seen a hint of any critical learning impediment before your child enrolled in kindergarten or even first, second, or third grade. Sometimes impediments may not show up until junior-high school.

One of the startling aspects of critical learning impediments is the frequency with which they show up in children of highest intelligence from the most economically, culturally, and socially advantaged families with no emotional problems. Many of these children may have scored notable academic successes in school without a sign of a learning impediment—which makes it even more difficult for parents and teachers to understand and identify the child's real problem: a critical learning impediment.

The Danger Signals

The first signs of a critical learning impediment may show up during the first few days or weeks of kindergarten or first grade. Some of these danger signals include persistent complaints about school and the teacher, along with a refusal to read or participate in reading-related activities.

If your preschooler, kindergartner, or first-grader never reads voluntarily and constantly complains, "I hate to read"—and seems genuinely pained when trying to do so—your child probably needs an evaluation.

For so young a child, however, move slowly and cautiously, though deliberately. First, evaluate the quality of the school's reading program (see Chapter 3). Your child's distaste for reading may simply reflect inadequate teaching or a poor choice of reading selections. If you're unsatisfied with the program and the books used, you might see if other parents feel the same way. If so, you might form a group to discuss the problem with the teacher and school principal to see how it might be improved.

If, on the other hand, you find the program is a good one, you should discuss your child's problems with the teacher to see if he or she can offer a solution. A little teaching trick or new approach can often remedy a lot of learning problems.

If the teacher has no solution, speak to a remedial teacher. They know far more teaching tricks and learning approaches than most teachers and can often help a child overcome learning problems with little fuss or bother. Usually they only need to spend an hour or two a week of one-to-one tutoring to produce spectacular results. If the remedial teacher cannot help and believes the problem requires more than individual tutoring, you should then consult your pediatrician.

Avoiding Misdiagnoses

Some parents and teachers of older youngsters with critical learning impediments conclude that their children are going through a phase of rebelliousness they will outgrow. There are, however, specific characteristics that, *when enough occur together*, distinguish serious learning disorders from normal childhood rebelliousness, if they persist long enough and occur too frequently.

The most evident academic danger signals are:

- a sharp decline in student grades from previous achievement levels for two or more successive quarters, *despite* great efforts to the contrary

- a slippage of achievement levels to at least one and perhaps two grades below the child's potential as measured by I.Q. tests

- inconsistent performance, with academic efforts that swing from triumphs to disasters; problems recalling information

- inability to follow oral directions, recall information, perform multipart tasks, and organize time

These academic symptoms are often accompanied by one or more uncharacteristic types of unacceptable behavior:

- changing markedly from an attitude of friendly cooperation to one of aggressive hostility

- reporting late or skipping class

- wandering aimlessly in school hallways during class time or reporting sick at the nurse's office

- handing in incomplete or no homework and test papers

- blaming others for his or her failures

- chronically lying

- angrily overreacting when others try to help

- bullying smaller children

- destroying property

- postponing or failing to do chores and schoolwork

- repeatedly forgetting to bring homework assignments home

- demonstrating consistent inability to get started with homework, leaving it until the last minute, taking an inappropriately long or short time to complete it, throwing it away in disgust; showing inability to translate ideas to paper

- being depressed and losing motivation; saying he or she is "dumb"

- often feeling too sick to go to school or claiming illness at school and returning home early; demonstrating school phobia

- constantly daydreaming in class and at home

- repeatedly speaking and acting impulsively in class and at home

- repeatedly interrupting others with non sequiturs or inappropriate actions

- showing inability to make or keep friends

- having prolonged sleep disturbances, including night anxieties or not waking when called after more than enough sleep

- having prolonged eating disturbances, including excessive eating or excessive dieting

- exhibiting marked mood changes

- demonstrating regressive behavior that is not appropriate for your child's age

In the face of one or more of these depressing symptoms, the most stunning characteristic of a child with a critical learning impediment is the lack of any evident cause—physical, social, emotional, cultural, economic, and so on.

All of us have suffered one or another of the many symptoms listed above—and probably a lot of others not listed. Yet most of us continued to function relatively smoothly in school. So it's easy to see why many caring parents and teachers might want to jump to the conclusion that such symptoms are merely a phase in the growing-up years.

Evaluating Symptoms

There are four keys to evaluating the seriousness of symptoms in a child with critical learning impediments:

1. *The number and frequency of occurrences.* In the previous list of symptoms, note the words *repeatedly* and *continually.*

2. *How long they've been in evidence.* Start worrying when the pattern is in evidence a month or two.

3. *The lack of any prior educational deprivation.* Your child's apparent impediment has developed despite the finest infant and early-childhood education as outlined in earlier chapters.

4. *A high level of intensity.* The symptoms are so intense they unquestionably prevent the child from learning essential academic skills such as reading, writing, speaking, listening, and calculating. In other words, your child is slipping further and further behind and will fail intellectually and academically unless you reach out and render help.

To get a better idea what a true critical learning impediment looks like, let's look at the first boy ever diagnosed with dyslexia.

A Short History

The first educator to recognize these symptoms as far more serious than a mere growth phase was Samuel T. Orton, M.D. (1879–1948), a neurologist, psychiatrist, and educator who studied brain disorders under Germany's famed Dr. A. Alzheimer.

In 1925, a school teacher brought a fourteen-year-old boy to Orton's mental-health clinic for an examination. The boy now immortalized in the scientific literature as "M.P.," was described by his teacher as "quite bright, does well in arithmetic . . . a very nice chap, of a good family," with no psychiatric or behavioral problems.

"Then what IS the problem?" asked the puzzled physician.

"That's what puzzles me," replied the teacher. "We just haven't been able to teach him to read."

After studying M.P. intensively for several weeks, Orton identified fourteen other, similarly bright, healthy children who were unable to read and eventually wrote his landmark paper, "Word Blindness in School Children," which he delivered to the annual meeting of the American Neurological Association, in Washington, D.C., in 1925.

Orton was thus the first scientist to identify what is now called dyslexia, which he appropriately named *strephosymbolia* (twisted symbols). His study opened up a new era for retraining dyslexic children who had hitherto been perceived as "feeble-minded"—a term even Orton used prior to meeting M.P.

Other Learning Impediments

Since Orton's discovery, pediatricians, psychiatrists, psychologists, social workers, and educators have discovered many other so-called "learning disabilities," critical learning impediments that block the acquisition of basic language learning skills. Just as M.P. saw twisted letters and could not learn to read, others cannot learn to write, and still others cannot learn to calculate.

The specific cause or combination of causes of such critical learning impediments, as well as the degree of criticality, determine the net effects on a child's learning ability and the type of special education or retraining that will help that child learn the most he or she possibly can.

Special Education

Successful special education teaches children strategies to work around critical learning impediments successfully. Special education does not cure learning disorders. It attempts to find new and different ways for children to learn to speak, read, write, or calculate successfully—ways that are designed specifically for each particular child to cope with a learning disorder and find different ways of learning that work when normal processes don't.

All of us have instinctively acquired our own individual strategies for overcoming some noncritical learning impediments that only interfere with learning nonessential skills. And we simply ignore all the other nonessential skills for which we obviously have little aptitude. Instead, we concentrate on learning skills in which we have higher aptitudes.

No one can afford to ignore critical learning impediments, however, because language skills are essential for functioning in school, college, and the world of work. Instincts usually don't help. Children with critical learning impediments need teachers trained in special education to teach them learning strategies so they can function on an equal intellectual level with their peers.

It's true that some critical learning impediments, including some dyslexias, may be developmental and disappear in a few years. In addition, some learning impediments seem to come and go, varying in consistency, severity, and duration. In the meantime, however, children with such impediments may lose valuable learning experiences without special education strategies for learning—and they may never catch up before the window of learning opportunity closes.

Evaluating Your Child

As you can see from the symptoms listed earlier, untended critical learning impediments can be disabling and prevent your child from acquiring key skills needed to learn in school and function as a productive person.

Any critical learning impediment that blocks your child's ability to acquire language skills requires evaluation by your pediatrician, and on your pediatrician's advice, a psychologist or psychiatrist.

Your pediatrician will first determine whether visual, hearing, speech, or other physical disorders may be causing the learning problem. Once these are eliminated, a psychologist or psychiatrist can evaluate whether the learning problem is a symptom of any underlying emotional, psychological, or psychiatric problems.

Once physical and psychological causes have been eliminated, it will be time for education specialists to determine the type and degree of learning impediment and the appropriate special education to help your child cope with or overcome it.

Getting a School Evaluation

The chances are that if your child's teachers are well trained, they will spot symptoms of a critical learning impediment before you do and either they or a school administrator will suggest an evaluation to assess your child's behavioral and academic performance. If an *experienced* teacher, with recognized credentials and training and years of working with kids, says your child is having learning or behavior problems, it's probably true. A public school must, by law (see Chapter 6), have your consent for such an evaluation, however, and you may prefer having a private evaluation.

If you let the public school proceed with the evaluation, your child's regular teacher and a special-education teacher will rate, often on a scale of one to five, your child's reading skills, reading comprehension, word-attack skills, sight-word vocabulary, computational skills, understanding of word problems, mathematical problem-solving skills, spelling skills, and handwriting skills. The teachers will also rate language skills such as use of vocabulary, fluency of expression, and quality of speech.

At the behavioral level, the teachers will rate such factors as reasoning skills, frustration tolerance, impulsivity, distractibility, and the abilities to listen, get along with classmates, cooperate with others, and follow rules—in games and in the classroom and hallways.

These ratings, combined with an evaluation by a physician and psychologist, will determine what kind of critical learning impediment may be interfering with your child's ability to function academically and socially.

Critical Impediments

There are five categories of impediments that affect, respectively, reading, writing, calculating, speaking, and listening impediments:

Reading Impediments

Commonly called dyslexia, reading impediments manifest themselves in many forms, and like most learning impediments, can vary in severity, consistency, and duration. The term Orton originally used, *strephosymbolia* (twisted symbols), is not inaccurate, but neither it nor any other term seems to go far enough to encompass the varieties of dyslexia.

Some dyslexic children, for example, hear or read a word correctly but only retain the sound or approximate sound, which then becomes the basis for the way they spell the word. Thus, *pencil* may become *pensl*, or *rough* respelled *ruff*. They see the correctly spelled word on the printed page but not in their minds when they need to reproduce it.

A type of remediation called phonic training slows the child's reading speed by spreading the letters of a word and teaching the child to sound out each letter or group of letters slowly, so that the word *pencil* assumes six sounds—*p e n c i l*—instead of the five in *pensl*.

On the other hand, equally intelligent children might be unable to pronounce letters or groups of letters. They hear and understand the meaning of every word the teacher dictates on a spelling test. But by the time the sounds are transmitted through the child's ears to the brain and converted into muscular impulses in the fingers, the spellings that emerge on paper are bizarre and bear no resemblance to the word the children actually heard and understood. Thus the word *cottage* might appear on the child's paper as *cogere*, or *fisherman* as *flabert*. Retraining such children teaches them to depend on rote—pure memorization of the letters in a word—rather than phonetics to learn new words.

There are, however, endless forms of dyslexia, which can affect a child's ability to read at any point in the sequence of reading-understanding-response. To understand the difficulties of dyslexic children and the training a special-education teacher must have, it's important to recognize the complexity of the language reception-and-transmission sequence.

The human mind is really nothing more than an information processing system. In reading, the eye picks up a group of symbols and transmits them through the optic nerve to the brain's memory center. There, the letters are assembled into a word in the mind's eye and the mind's ear, which either match it with an existing word the mind understands or implants it as a new bit of knowledge.

In writing, the memory system must disassemble the word and transmit each letter through dozens of nerves. The nerves trigger an explosion of controlled spasms in the muscles of the arm, hand, and fingers, which then push and pull a pen or pencil to reproduce the letters in correct order on paper.

A similarly complex process takes place during a spelling test. The child's ear must pick up speech sounds the brain converts into letters and assembles into words that are transmitted to the memory center for recognition. Then the brain must break the words down again into letters the child's hand reassembles on paper.

A microscopic failure along the huge number of neural and muscular connections can interrupt the entire process. One job of the special-education teacher is to identify the general areas involved in the breakdown—for example, visual or auditory—and find a way to teach the child to use open pathways that bypass nonfunctioning connections.

The breakdown can occur anywhere, and there are no mechanical devices to repair it. A child might see the phrase *see John run* as *seJohnrun* or any other combination of letters running into or over each other. Remediation must be designed for each individual's specific impediment—usually using a technique that counteracts or compensates for the malfunction.

When a child sees letters of two words running into each other in the phrase *see John run*, a special-education teacher may project the words on a screen, separating the letters enough so the child no longer sees them running into each other. Then as the child practices and gets used to seeing and reading the stretched-out characters and words correctly, the teacher can gradually close the gap between letters and words. Phonic drill cards are another commonly used teaching device to focus a child's attention on and promote better recognition of individual letters and sounds. One side of each card displays a letter or combination of letters that produce a single sound, for example, *f*, *ph*, *k*, *ck*, etc. The other side of the card shows a word that incorporates the letter or letter combination with diacritical marks to emphasize its pronunciation within the word.

In addition to reading impediments that block a child's ability to read letters and words, another form of dyslexia blocks comprehension. Children with this type of impediment may read and understand every letter and word and even short phrases and sentences. They may not, however, be able to connect the sentences into a unified whole that gives meaning to the entire text. Or having read the text, they may be unable to remember any of the elements they read about because the visual images did not register in the memory center.

Several strategies seem to bypass impediments to reading comprehension, including cutting textual material to a length that allows the child to understand it in its entirety—even down to one sentence. Once the material is shortened to a point that allows the youngster to understand the entire text, the length can gradually be extended over a period of time.

Tying textual materials to subjects of great interest to the child or to an overall theme the child may be studying also helps improve comprehension. As with basic reading instruction, a multisensory approach—namely reading the text aloud three or four times and rereading it aloud each successive day—helps many children improve comprehension. Programmed computer instruction also helps by presenting a short text with pictures and multiple-choice questions for the student to answer. Equally critical, however, is organizing the material into logical groupings that make it easier to understand and recall.

Other symptoms associated with dyslexia include a poor ability to associate sounds with corresponding letters, an inability to see entire sections of words, confused left-right or spatial orientation, losing one's place on the page or frequently skipping lines, having difficulty with jigsaw puzzles, and routinely forgetting words or stories that may have been read and studied intensively only the day before.

In addition to the actual reading impediment, dyslexic children also tend to exhibit some characteristics that may be evident in the preschool years before the child begins formal reading:

◆ inappropriate slowness naming objects in pictures

◆ inexplicable slowness reacting to auditory stimuli

◆ a tendency to ignore or respond with a blank stare to simple requests such as "please pass the corn flakes"

◆ difficulty understanding verbal directions and remembering sequential information

Writing Impediments

Dysgraphia represents a breakdown in the transmission of data from the brain to the motor system needed to reproduce it manually. Dysgraphia often shows up in painfully slow writing that may slope up or down or simply wander aimlessly over the page. Characters may be too small, misformed, or incompletely formed. Children with dysgraphia run words together, omit letters, reverse letters, or vary letter sizes inconsistently.

Some dysgraphics may also be dyslexic and make phonetically correct spelling errors (*graf* for *graph*) or phonetically incorrect spelling errors (*push* for *publish*). Dyslexic dysgraphics may also have difficulty breaking words into syllables, retaining auditory information, labeling objects in a picture correctly, and processing language effectively.

There is no question that dysgraphia is a critical learning impediment. But when it is limited to mechanical writing problems and does not affect language-processing skills, it is more a nuisance than anything else and can easily be overcome using mechanical devices. Indeed, desktop and laptop word processors and computers have made handwriting all but unnecessary, and even obsolete at times, in the practical world.

Training dysgraphics with mechanical writing problems to write legibly can be painfully slow since it involves forcing a child to print (no cursive or script is permitted) on ruled paper, stretching each letter vertically from one ruled line to the one above it. Concentrating on penmanship, however, inevitably distracts a child from focusing on content and can diminish creative skills at a time when children are most imaginative. The goal of good special education is not to aim for perfect calligraphy, but merely to improve the child's handwriting to a functional level.

The question for parents and the learning establishment is whether the time and retraining involved is truly worth the effort—especially since handwriting as a basic form of communicating is virtually obsolete. Because of typewriters, and more recently word processors, my own dysgraphia has not prevented me from spending a productive and rewarding lifetime as a journalist and author.

Mechanical devices have now converted mechanics-centered dysgraphia into a noncritical learning impediment. It is a waste of time for bright, creative minds to concentrate on practicing penmanship when a laptop word processor or computer will free them to learn things in which they may show far more promise—like nuclear physics, composing symphonies, or writing books about learning impediments.

Unfortunately, word processors are of no help to children with an extreme form of dysgraphia, a disability called agraphia. Agraphia is an inability to write because of a breakdown in neurological connections between the recognition of a number, letter, or word and the motor response needed to write it.

Although muscular paralysis can cause agraphia, it also occurs in people without paralysis who can perform other routine muscular tasks. In addition, agraphics may have no difficulty reading, speaking, hearing, or understanding numbers, letters, or words, but their agraphia prevents conversion into the muscular activity needed to write—with either pencil or word processor.

Some teachers, on the other hand, are all too quick to pin the dysgraphia label on children who seem unable to write compositions. Many of these children are perfect examples of kids who need good education rather than special education.

School teachers—including many English teachers—are notoriously inept writers who simply don't know how to teach good writing. What they do know is correct grammar, and they tend to make it central to writing instruction because they know so little about the craft and art of writing.

Many teachers expect their young, inexperienced students to generate ideas and when a child consistently says, "I don't know what to write about" or "I can't figure out what to write," they label the child dysgraphic instead of inspiring the child to write creatively.

Beware of this form of learning disabilities trap. If your child is faced with it, demand a new English teacher. There are many ways for good teachers and parents to inspire children who say, "I can't write":

◆ games that give each participant a chance to finish one sentence and create the beginning of the next sentence for the next player to finish ("The bear broke down the door and . . . "); variations might involve telling a story and asking the child to write another possible ending— or sequel or completely new version

◆ making souvenir albums using picture postcards from trips, but leaving space for the child to write about what he or she did or saw

◆ writing letters to famous people—television personalities, for example

◆ keeping a diary or journal or writing "The Story of My Life"

◆ starting a family or neighborhood newspaper, and becoming the star reporter, book reviewer, and editor

The list is endless, and any teacher who cannot stimulate the creative instincts of children should not be in the classroom. It is the teacher who is disabled in a classroom where children are not writing creatively—not the children.

Mathematical Impediments

Dyscalculia, or the inability to perform mathematical operations can manifest itself at different levels. The most serious is at the basic level of simple arithmetic—addition, subtraction, multiplication, and division—and the ability to apply it to everyday life.

This most basic form of dyscalculia can be an outgrowth of reading impediments that prevent the child from actually seeing the numbers clearly or in their correct order or spatial relationships.

A child may have difficulty keeping track of numbers in the same column or switch from one column to the next while adding or subtracting. A child who sees *38* as *83* is unlikely to obtain the right answer when adding it to or subtracting it from another number. Often, retraining directed at the reading impediment proves the solution to a child's dyscalculia.

Another form of dyscalculia unrelated to dyslexia reflects inadequate infant education before preschool. All early mathematics training involves two elements:

1. basic arithmetic—addition and subtraction—with concrete objects and manipulatives such as blocks, colored chips and other objects

2. abstract concepts and language-based facts such as *more than*, *less than*, and so on

Both aspects should first be taught during infancy training. Failure to do so can leave a child with serious learning impediments in the mathematics sectors.

In retraining young children during the earliest elementary years, special-education teachers use blocks, chips, and other objects to teach such concepts as adding, taking away (subtracting), how many do we have now? (total), how many do we have left? (remainder). As the child acquires an ability to use manipulatives, the teacher or parent can substitute real-life objects and money, along with such concepts as *buy, spend, money left over*. Retraining can involve setting up a classroom store, with students making their own "money," or depending on their age, using "checks."

The hand-held calculator is an essential tool for children with dyscalculia who cannot learn to perform calculations mentally and memorize basic arithmetic facts such as the multiplication tables. It is important for both teachers and parents to recognize when further attempts to teach mental calculations become counterproductive for a particular child.

As with all learning differences, the key to teaching a child with dyscalculia is to find any and every way that works and lets the child practice success rather than languish in failure and discouragement. If a calculator works for your child, use it.

Many students with dyscalculia never succeed in mastering any number of abstract areas of mathematics such as algebra, geometry, trigonometry, or calculus. Again, rather than forcing them to spend years languishing in academic failure, the best course is to concentrate on building skills in areas where they demonstrate higher aptitudes.

It's well to remember that few colleges require students to study any mathematics beyond the high-school level. Remember also how little algebra, geometry, or trigonometry most adults use or even remember. Calculators and computers have made personal mastery of such skills unnecessary.

Speech or Communications Impediments

There are four types of speech impediments, with varying degrees of criticality:

1. *Voice disorders.* Less common in children than in adults, and hardly critical, voice disorders include abnormal or inappropriate quality, loudness, or pitch. Examples include hoarseness, nasality, mumbling, and other qualities that may not be endearing but certainly do not interfere with learning.

   Therapy usually involves teaching the child exercises to increase breathing capacity and relaxation techniques.

2. *Articulation disorders.* The most common of the speech disorders among school-age children, articulation disorders include the omission of certain sounds, substitution of one sound for another, distortion of certain sounds, and addition of extra sounds not in the word the person is saying. A child with a severe articulation disorder, or

expressive language disorder, mispronounces too many words to be understood.

Although physical and neurological impairments can cause articulation disorders, many are the result of environmental deprivation. Regardless of the cause, they are usually critical learning impediments that prevent effective learning in school.

A widespread example of a massive articulation disorder is Black English, a vernacular that many African-American children learn in infancy but which bears little relationship in sound or syntax to the language they must eventually learn to read and write to function in American schools and the workplace.

A child who has learned only to "axe" a question during the first four years of life enters school with an articulation disorder that makes it difficult to learn to read, spell, understand, and pronounce the word *ask*.

In effect, the spellings and syntax of "Caucasian English," as many African Americans call Standard American English, are as foreign to many first-grade African-American children as those of any foreign language. The tragic result is that such children are seldom able to acquire the reading and writing skills of children who heard and learned to speak English correctly during infancy.

In 1992, the reading proficiency of African-American nine-year-olds was more than 15 percent below that of white students, and their writing proficiency more than 19 percent lower. Additional schooling and special education only narrows the proficiency gap slightly. The reading proficiency of thirteen-year-old African-American children was about 10.8 percent below that of white children and their writing proficiency 7.55 percent lower.

The effects of language deprivation are equally devastating for economically deprived Hispanic-American and other immigrant children whose infant education limits exposure to foreign vernaculars with no resemblance to English or the correct forms of their native languages. Ironically, as mentioned in Chapter 2, some parents turn their infants over to caregivers with speaking impediments they often pass on to the children in their charge.

Although prevention is the best cure for articulation disorders, speech therapists can usually retrain children with such impediments to speak correctly. Individually designed programs may involve at least three thirty-minute sessions a week in specially equipped resource rooms. Teachers use mirrors and tape recorders to permit children to monitor their speech production by watching the movements of facial muscles, lips, and tongue and listening to the sounds they make.

Speech therapy begins by retraining the child's articulation of the forty-five phonemes, or smallest pronounceable sounds, in the English language, then progresses to words, phrases, and sentences. Articulation therapy may be combined with teaching vocabulary, grammar, and syntax.

3. *Fluency disorders.* Uncomfortable, though somewhat less-than-critical impediments, fluency disorders result in stuttering, which blocks the smooth transition from one syllable to the next.

Stuttering occurs in three forms: abnormally long pauses or oral stoppages, prolongations of the previous sound, or repetitions of the same sound. Some speech therapists differentiate between stuttering, stammering, and cluttering, with the first referring to speech repetition, the second to speech blockage, and the third to garbling syllables.

Stuttering occurs in about 1 percent to 3 percent of preadolescent children and is often the result of emotions such as fear, embarrassment, hostility, and excitement. Most children outgrow stuttering, and any long-term continuation should be evaluated by a neurologist.

Although some stuttering is associated with neurological disorders, most children who stutter when talking to others do not stutter when talking to themselves, their toys, or their pets—an indication that most stuttering may relate to the timing of the muscular mechanisms involved in speech.

Therapies such as psychotherapy, drugs, relaxation techniques, and breath control have scored uneven successes. Most special education in school includes teaching the child to speak more slowly and prolong the sounds that are most difficult to produce. Tape recorders help children monitor their sounds, and metronomes operating at gradually increasing rates help them learn to speak rhythmically.

4. *Language disorders.* All-embracing speech disorders, language disorders are evident in two broad forms: expressive language disorder and receptive language disorder. Sometimes the result of environmental deprivation, expressive language disorder can be an extension of articulation disorders and unintelligibility to a child's entire range of speech—again, quite common among children who speak Black English and foreign vernaculars.

Receptive language disorder is the inability to understand spoken language—again, in much the same way deprived African-American children who grow up speaking Black English are unable to understand the traditional English of their elementary-school teachers, who are 89 percent white.

Language disorders are indeed critical learning impediments because they block acquisition of reading, writing and speaking skills in conventional Standard

American English, which is the language of schools, colleges, and the workplace.

Listening Impediments

A child who, for whatever reasons, cannot concentrate or is in perpetual motion cannot develop listening skills needed to acquire knowledge. These critical listening impediments are variously called Attention Deficit Disorders (ADD) or Attention Deficit Hyperactivity Disorders (ADHD), depending on the activity levels.

Children with ADHD tend to be hyperactive: they act out and either move about restlessly, speak or act impulsively, or behave in a disruptive fashion. Children with ADD tend to be hypoactive: they withdraw and daydream. More boys than girls are diagnosed with ADHD and more girls than boys are diagnosed with ADD. Tragically, many hypoactive boys with ADD go undiagnosed because they sit quietly and are not disruptive.

About 40 percent of children with other critical learning impediments also exhibit listening impediments, but there is no way to know which impediment precedes the other. Although the inability to read, write, spell, or speak properly may well discourage a child from listening, it is equally likely that an inability to listen might prevent a child from learning to read, write, spell, or speak properly.

ADD and ADHD have become the most controversial of all the critical learning impediments. Indeed, there is considerable disagreement whether they even represent a learning impediment. The problem stems from the nature of the symptoms, which every normal child displays from time to time. For normal children, however, the symptoms may result from a wide range of emotional, psychological, developmental, or even physical problems such as food allergies or visual or auditory problems. True ADD and ADHD, however, are the results of biochemical imbalances and almost always occur before a child reaches the age of seven.

The American Psychiatric Association (APA) defines true ADHD as educationally debilitating inattention, hyperactivity, and impulsivity lasting six months or more. In 1994, the APA updated its *Diagnostic and Statistical Manual for Mental Disorders* (DSM IV) and listed these basic characteristics:

1. *Inattention.* Six or more of the following symptoms of inattention have persisted at least six months to a degree that is maladaptive and inconsistent with development level:

   ◆ fails to give close attention to details or makes careless mistakes in schoolwork, work, or other activities
   ◆ has difficulty sustaining attention in tasks or play activities
   ◆ does not seem to listen when spoken to directly
   ◆ does not follow through on instruction and fails to finish schoolwork, chores, or duties in the workplace (not due to oppositional behavior or failure to understand instructions)
   ◆ has difficulty organizing tasks and activities
   ◆ avoids, dislikes, or is reluctant to engage in tasks that require sustained mental effort (such as schoolwork or homework)
   ◆ loses things necessary for tasks or activities (such as school assignments, pencils, books, or tools)
   ◆ is easily distracted by extraneous stimuli
   ◆ is forgetful in daily activities

2. *Hyperactivity and impulsivity.* Six or more of the following symptoms of hyperactivity-impulsivity have persisted at least six months to a degree that is maladaptive and inconsistent with developmental level:

   ◆ fidgets with hands or feet or squirms in seat
   ◆ leaves seat in classroom or in other situations in which remaining in seat is expected

- ◆ runs about or climbs excessively in situations in which such behavior is inappropriate (in adolescents or adults, may be limited to subjective feelings of restlessness)
- ◆ has difficulty playing or engaging in leisure activities quietly
- ◆ is often "on the go" or acts as if "driven by motor"
- ◆ talks excessively
- ◆ blurts out answers before questions have been completed
- ◆ has difficulty awaiting turn
- ◆ interrupts or intrudes on others (butts into conversations or games)

In addition, some of the hyperactive-impulsive or inattentive symptoms that caused impairment are present before age seven. Some impairment from the symptoms is present in two or more settings (for example, at school and at home). There is clear evidence of clinically significant impairment in social, academic, or occupational functioning.

What is most important to remember in applying the APA definition is that it represents a cluster of symptoms, large numbers of which must be present at the same time for at least six months or more to represent true ADHD. The two most frequently recommended treatments for ADHD are special education, which helps many ADHD youngsters, and medication, which slows them down but does not necessarily produce any improvement in academic performance or behavior.

Pseudo-ADD and ADHD

Unfortunately, ADD- and ADHD-like symptoms show up from time to time as developmental problems for many older children, who may be misdiagnosed by teachers and counselors. ADHD symptoms are most common among eight- to ten-year-old boys and disappear as quickly as they appeared. They bear no relation to true ADHD, but unfortunately, some of these normal, healthy youngsters are caught in the devastating special-education trap before they outgrow their problems.

The length and severity of each episode of ADD or ADHD symptoms, how they affect a child's long-term academic performance, and how adults respond to the child seem to be keys to treatment and resolution of these symptoms. ADHD symptoms, more than those of ADD, invariably draw immediate attention from teachers and parents, and troubled or neglected children may consciously or unconsciously display ADHD symptoms to gain such attention.

It is just as likely, however, that some children develop symptoms of ADD and ADHD from sheer frustration and boredom with inadequate education and incompetent teachers. The failure of public schools to tailor education to individual needs inevitably leaves many children too far behind or too far ahead of lockstep education geared for the average student.

Any healthy, academically motivated student will almost certainly tune out or explode with rage if forced to sit idly in a classroom where no learning takes place and where teachers fail to meet the child's intellectual needs, hour after hour, day after day, week after week.

For some children, inadequate schooling can amount to nothing less than a twelve-year prison sentence for the crimes of being slower or faster than average, having different aptitudes from other students, and learning things in different ways. Although they display many of the same symptoms as the ADHD child, they are not true ADHDs.

Regardless of the causes, there is little question that ADHD has become the most promiscuously overdiagnosed learning impediment among American children. A 1993 article by pediatric neurologist Fred Baughman in the *Journal of the American Medical Association* charged that many perfectly healthy children grow up believing "they have something wrong with their brains that makes it impossible to control themselves without using a pill. . . ."

True ADHD, with demonstrable biochemical imbalances, occurs in well under 10 percent of the student population, with the actual figure probably closer to 1 percent than to 10 percent.

After the Americans with Disabilities Act of 1990 was amended to include ADHD as a disability that qualified for generous federal grants to schools and parents, the number of claims in some areas soared to 33 percent of the school population.

There is little question that stimulating education would help stem the spread of restlessness and boredom many schools now label ADHD. If your child's teachers or school administrators have even hinted that your child might have a listening or attention problem or ADHD, have your pediatrician and skilled evaluators examine your child. If medication is recommended by a physician or evaluator you trust, by all means try it—but abandon it immediately if you see no dramatic results within one to four weeks.

The principles of special education for ADHD children are relatively simple, although they require patience. For all such children, it is essential to determine each child's intelligence level and aptitudes and to gear teaching to the child's abilities and interests.

Inattentiveness

Specific teaching techniques with inattentive children involve decreasing the length of each task to provide rewards for success as soon as possible. This means fewer words to spell, fewer math problems, shorter readings, and so on. Longer tasks are divided into smaller components.

To try to build attention span, teachers try to limit tasks to those that interest the child most and then gradually begin alternating low- and high-interest tasks. The longer the task, the more interest it should arouse. Audiovisual devices such as films are usually successful attention-builders. To build the child's social skills, the teacher designs tasks that allow the child to work with a partner or in small groups as well as on a one-to-one basis with the teacher.

Hyperactivity

For overactive children, the teacher's goal is to direct the child's activity into acceptable, academically beneficial, and rewarding activities of interest to the child and in which the child shows particular aptitude. The list of possibilities is endless: painting, sculpting, reading aloud, writing on the blackboard, speaking, asking and answering academically oriented questions, acting in plays, organizing the classroom for a project, running errands for teachers and school administrators, working part-time in the office, organizing and directing various academically oriented extracurricular activities such as class or school newspapers or a literary magazine.

None of these activities is designed to replace standard academic requirements, but a skilled special-education teacher can use these activities as both teaching vehicles and mechanisms to absorb a child's excessive energy—especially if the excess is due to boredom rather than true ADD or ADHD.

Impulsivity

Impulsivity is the most difficult of the three basic characteristics of ADHD for special-education teachers because it is unpredictable and therefore, difficult to prevent. More often than not, a special-education teacher must deal with impulsivity after the fact, and as all learning specialists know, it's difficult to teach any child not to do something that has already been done. It's akin to training a dog not to soil the carpet by rubbing its nose in its dirt after the fact. The dog has not the slightest idea why its master is angry because the punishment did not accompany the act and is not associated with it.

A child's impulsivity presents the same problem. To have any effect, special education must come at the time the impulse is developing, not afterward, but the timing of the event is unpredictable and there is seldom a special-education teacher around.

Although the child may be aware of the results of impulsive behavior, he or she may have no idea of the cause—or impulse. When asked, impulsive children invariably shrug their shoulders and say truthfully, "I don't know" or "I just felt like it" or "I thought it'd be cool." They really do not know.

Prevention is one key to controlling impulsivity. Some special-education teachers have taught impulsive children to a degree of success by using the equivalent of worry beads—an object such as a small rubber ball or Silly Putty to keep the child's hands active. Such devices allow the child to transfer disruptive impulses to the hand by squeezing the object as hard as possible. Doodling on paper or sculpting with pipe cleaners are other quiet distractions that sometimes help control impulsivity.

Another successful technique with some children is the careful mapping of behavior patterns and subsequent discussion with the child of how one type of event seems to provoke a particular response, and in turn, a specific consequence. Understanding and insight often produce a degree of voluntary control.

Impulsivity, however, is a problem that requires considerable insight and cooperation from classroom teachers and parents. Classroom teachers, especially, must monitor children with impulsivity disorders and provide a variety of alternative activities akin to those used to help overactive children.

Summary

The critical learning impediments are:

- *Reading impediments (dyslexia).* Broad-based inability to read, write, or spell correctly. May see or write letters backward, upside down, or in mirror image. Inability to associate sounds with letters or words or comprehend text. Confused left-right orientation, confused spatial orientation. Loses place on the page while reading, skips lines.

◆ *Writing impediments (dysgraphia)*. An inability to write legibly. Writes painfully slowly. Writing wanders across page. Characters small, malformed, or incompletely formed. Omits letters, reverses letters, varies letter size inconsistently, runs words together.

◆ *Mathematical impediments (dyscalculia)*. An inability to perform mathematical operations or comprehend the meaning of numbers enough to calculate.

◆ *Speech or communication impediments*. An inability to speak correctly that can manifest itself in four ways:

1. voice disorders—an abnormal or inappropriate quality, loudness, or pitch
2. articulation disorders—the omission of certain sounds, the substitution of one sound for another, the distortion of certain sounds, and the addition of extra sounds not in the word the person is saying
3. fluency disorders—stuttering, which blocks the smooth transition from one syllable to the next, and occurs in three forms: abnormally long pauses or oral stoppages, prolongations of the previous sound, or repetitions of the same sound; some speech therapists differentiate between stuttering, stammering, and cluttering, with the first referring to speech repetition, the second to speech blockage, and the third to garbling syllables
4. language disorders—disorders that occur in two broad forms: expressive language disorder, an inability to speak intelligibly, and receptive language disorder, an inability to understand spoken language

◆ *Listening impediments.* An inability to absorb information aurally, usually marked by an inability to concentrate or remain still for a reasonable amount of time. Usually called Attention Deficit Disorder (ADD) for children who tend to withdraw and daydream instead of concentrating, and Attention Deficit Hyperactivity Disorder (ADHD) for children who tend to speak or act impulsively, move about restlessly, or behave in a disruptive fashion.

Warning signs of critical learning impediments include:

◆ sharp decline in student grades for two or more successive quarters, despite great efforts to the contrary

◆ slippage of achievement levels to at least one and perhaps two grades below the child's potential, as measured by I.Q. tests

◆ inconsistent performance

◆ inability to follow oral directions, recall information, perform multipart tasks, and organize time

◆ unacceptable behavior—displays aggressive hostility, acts impulsively, interrupts others, comes late or skips class, produces incomplete or skips homework and tests, blames others for own failures, lies, bullies, vandalizes, postpones or fails to do chores and schoolwork, lacks motivation, acts depressed, constantly feels sick, daydreams, suffers sleep and eating disturbances, fails to make or keep friends, suffers marked mood changes, suffers bouts of regressive behavior

Chapter 6

Your Child's Choices and Legal Rights

If you and your pediatrician agree and strongly believe your child has a critical learning impediment, your child may need a neurological, psychological, and skills evaluation. Although a good evaluator can make it a relatively happy experience for most children, you should consider such an evaluation only if your child's impediment is critical and has lasted six months without showing any signs of improvement.

When Critical Is Not Critical

The key to a critical learning impediment is whether it indeed prevents learning to read, write, calculate, and reason at levels that will permit your child to function acceptably in school and in the workplace.

What you as a parent consider critical is immaterial. Some parents may deem eventual admission to Harvard critical. In my family, after four generations of physicians, my admission to medical school was critical—even in the face of my abysmally low aptitude and barely passing grades in science.

Low aptitudes, poor grades, and the inability to learn certain skills or understand certain concepts do not always represent critical learning impediments. They may not be critical to any child's success and happiness in school or adult life—unless parents, teachers, and peers interfere with the pursuit of that success and happiness.

Again, a learning impediment is only critical if it prevents a child from learning to read, write, calculate, and reason at an appropriate level for a particular age.

If your child has fallen six months or more behind his or her classmates in reading, writing, and calculating skills and is falling further behind with each passing day, you should by all means take your child for an evaluation.

Deciding on Evaluation

You can have your child evaluated privately or by your public-school system if your child is three years or older. Federal law requires every school district to evaluate every preschool or older child in its district on request by a parent, pediatrician, teacher, or school authority, if the parent consents in writing.

Beware, however: you get what you pay for, and a free evaluation by the school district can be costly if it traumatizes your child or yields a faulty result.

Before signing up for an evaluation, demand to see examples of workups from both private and public-school district evaluators and compare them. Workups should be specific, easy to understand, and logically outlined, on a test-by-test basis, with a specific, numbered result after each test. Reject any evaluator whose workup consists of nonspecific generalizations that are difficult to understand.

Evaluation consists of a wide variety of tests geared to your child's age and administered on an individual basis by psychologists and educators. In addition to psychological tests, these include tests of intelligence, language skills, perception, behavioral maturity, and reading, spelling, writing, arithmetic, and comprehensive academic skills.

Most of these tests are designed for children already in or about to enter school. That's because most critical learning impediments don't show up until then. Either they haven't developed yet or they simply haven't appeared. After all, children can hardly exhibit any serious writing impediments before they start doing any serious writing.

There are, however, some infant and early childhood assessment tests and even a few tests that claim to measure infant intelligence at three months. Most tests designed for infants younger than a year, however, measure neurological development rather than intelligence.

I cannot urge you enough, however, to defer to your pediatrician's judgment before putting your infant or preschooler through the testing ordeal. If your pediatrician tells you that you have a fine, healthy, normal infant, leave it at that and enjoy your child. Teach your baby all you can, and recognize that it will not learn all things as well as or at the same time or at the same pace as other babies.

Paranoid parents who fear the worst or expect miraculous prodigy-like behavior from their children damage their children immeasurably and implant learning impediments where none existed. Your infant, no matter how young, knows whether you love him or her or are disappointed—and he or she will behave accordingly.

Similarly, in the early childhood years before preschool, constant fretting over your child will wreak untold emotional, psychological, and intellectual damage. These are not the years to be dragged from office to office, to be poked constantly by pediatricians, and questioned and tested unmercifully by psychologists.

Going Through the Evaluation Process

If you decide to go ahead with an evaluation, your child will first undergo the teacher evaluations described in Chapter 5. The next step is a battery of intelligence and skills tests to determine your child's functional skill levels in basic reading, writing, speaking, listening, reasoning, comprehension, and calculating.

Once your child completes all the tests and interviews, a team of trained evaluators determines whether your child's skills are appropriate for his or her age, and if not, they try to identify your child's specific learning impediment and educational needs.

The team then prepares a list of realistic short- and long-term goals for your child and designs an education program to help your child achieve them. Again, look for specifics. An Individual Education Program (IEP) should detail the techniques the school plans to use—for example, phonics to improve reading. Reject any IEP with meaningless goal-oriented generalizations such as raising of reading comprehension to 80 percent of grade level. Ask for specifics; ask *how* the school intends improving reading comprehension.

Such programs, if they are any good, should have accomplished most long-term educational goals by the end of two years, although your youngster may encounter setbacks from time to time for years thereafter and even into adulthood.

Such programs, however, should teach your child the learning strategies to acquire the basic reading, writing, listening, speaking, reasoning, and calculating skills to complete his or her schooling successfully, including college and graduate school if aptitude and intelligence permit.

This chapter could end here quite happily if evaluation and special education were that simple. They aren't. What I've given you is an ideal overview; now we'll explore some specifics.

Public-School Evaluations

The first signs of long-lasting, critical learning impediments often don't begin to show up until a child enters school, and a teacher brings the child's problem to the attention of the parent. If your child is in private school, the school will recommend a private evaluation, and the process will be fairly clear-cut, as previously described.

If your child is in public school, however, the process is completely different. By law, public schools have to provide the evaluation at no cost to you, if you give your consent. The school official in charge of the evaluation must consult you at every step of the public-school evaluation process, and you must approve each succeeding step for the process to continue.

If you oppose evaluation, you may opt for an independent, outside evaluation at school expense, or you may refuse evaluation entirely. Although the school can override your refusal, you may appeal the school decision at an impartial hearing and even appeal the decision of the impartial hearing officer to the review officer of the state education department.

The reason for this public largesse is the federal Education for All Handicapped Children Act of 1975. The law ordered every public school district to provide free, appropriate, public education for all students between the ages of three and twenty-one with disabilities.

The law has been amended several times, but as now written, it includes among its definitions of disabilities "a disorder in one or more of the basic psychological processes involved in understanding or using language, spoken or written, that may manifest itself in imperfect ability to listen, think, speak, read, write, spell, or to do mathematical calculations. This term includes such conditions as . . . dyslexia. . . ."

Unfortunately for taxpayers and a lot of healthy, normal kids, it also includes all the critical learning disabilities described in Chapter 5—and some that are not described because they are not critical to anything or anybody.

So like it or not, children with dyslexia and other critical and noncritical learning impediments are, by legal definition at least, disabled. As such, federal law entitles almost any child who has an imperfect ability to a host of free evaluations and special-education services, and in some cases, direct government subsidies.

Unfortunately, the law does not define or set standards for the quality of the evaluation or educational services. The education department doesn't help matters. It specifies only that a team of professionals must evaluate and assess the child's educational needs.

The Child-Study Team

The child-study team usually includes a psychologist, social worker, physician, the child's regular teacher, and a second teacher trained in special education. If appropriate, however, the parent can insist on a vocational or rehabilitation counselor, or if the child's native tongue is not English, a teacher fluent in that language—and anyone else needed to protect the child's interests, including a lawyer. Here's what happens next:

- A licensed school psychologist does a psychological evaluation to determine the child's intelligence, instructional needs, learning strengths and weaknesses, and social and emotional dynamics.

- A social worker takes a complete social history of the child and the family.

- A physician performs a complete physical examination.

- The child is placed under careful observation in the classroom by the regular teacher and a special-education teacher temporarily assigned to the classroom for that purpose. Each fills out elaborate forms that rate the child on dozens of academic and behavioral factors.

Identifying the Learning Disabled

To identify a child as learning disabled and eligible for special education, all members of the child-study team must agree on at least three things:

1. The child exhibits discrepancies between the tests of intellectual ability (I.Q.) and actual achievement or academic performance.

2. The discrepancies are great enough to warrant special education in one or more of these areas: listening comprehension, oral expression, written expression, basic reading skills, reading comprehension, mathematics calculation, or mathematics reasoning.

3. The child's behavior is incompatible with successful academic performance.

Unfortunately, these determinations vary widely from state to state, school district to school district, and even school to school.

In some states, the child is assigned to special education if the discrepancy between intelligence and achievement is one grade level or more. In other states the discrepancy must be two or more grade levels. Still other states use point differentials on scores to determine whether a child should be placed in a special-education class, while other states allow schools to decide arbitrarily on the basis of a child's poor performance in one or more academic areas. In fact, some school districts adopt their own standards for making the determination.

The result is that a child who is labeled learning disabled and condemned to a slow learning track in Connecticut might well have emerged as a genius in Georgia or Kansas. There simply is no way for a parent to know because the special-education process is not standardized. Indeed, in many schools, school districts, and states, the special-education process is a trap that can put your child's educational and professional future at risk.

The Individual
Educational Program

After evaluation is complete, the study team makes its recommendation to a school district committee on special education (cse), which is made up of the members of the team and one or more administrators of special education—usually an administrator or assistant district superintendent.

By law, the cse must invite you to all its meetings, including its initial meeting to develop a recommendation for an iep to meet your child's needs. Remember that, in addition to the cse report and recommendation, you are entitled at all times to review any and all school documents and files relating specifically to your child.

Under the federal Family Educational Rights and Privacy Act of 1974—the Buckley Amendment, as it is often called—parents have the right to examine even the most confidential school records concerning their children. The school must not only give you access to such records, it must allow you to correct errors, and after a reasonable period of time, you may demand that the school remove a report of some misconduct that might blot an otherwise perfect record. Poor academic grades or failures, of course, cannot be changed.

Understanding
cse Recommendations

The cse may, however, find that your child does not need special education, but only the routine remedial services available as part of the normal school routine. Unlike special education, which deals with retraining children who cannot learn because of possible neurological impairments, remedial education deals with perfectly normal, healthy children whose learning differences have left them behind the rest of the class.

Although the term can have different meanings in different schools, remedial instruction usually uses conventional teaching techniques to help children catch up. It also gives them learning strategies to help them learn at a rate that will let them keep up with their classmates. In effect, remedial instruction is closer to individual tutoring than to therapy or retraining.

Special Education

If the CSE decides your child needs special education, it must then develop an IEP that describes your child's specific disability in detail, along with your child's strengths, weaknesses, and special-educational needs. The IEP must spell out short-term instructional objectives and specific programs and services the school will provide, including regular education, to ensure your child reaches those goals.

The CSE must make annual reviews and assessments of your child's progress and the school's programs and services. The CSE must remain in continual touch, send you its reviews, and notify you about any plans to review or modify your child's IEP.

The IEP, however, can often turn into as much of a mess as the evaluation process because in working out an IEP, the CSE must determine the least restrictive educational setting (LRE) for your child. But there are eleven categories of educational settings prescribed by law, with the least restrictive being regular class placement. In this setting, your child is assigned to special education without ever getting special education.

This is not a joke, and there is no better explanation. It is special education designed for a Franz Kafka novel. The CSE determines that your child is indeed learning disabled, with a specific learning disability. But the special education it prescribes is a return to regular classes where there is no special education and where your child is to carry on as before with all the other children. Nothing more.

A parent can only hope the child's teacher took a course in special education when studying for the teaching certificate and will make allowances for the child's learning impediment—and perhaps even give the child some special exercises. But that's the best any parent can expect.

The worst is that the child will be transferred to a slower academic track in elementary school, or worse, dumped into the academic netherworld of general education, where he or she may eventually graduate, but without adequate academic education to qualify for college or vocational training to qualify for a job.

Retention

There is one other possible recommendation and course of action under the umbrella of least restrictive settings—dropping back or repeating a grade. Although humiliating and often counterproductive for older children, retention can be a wise decision if the way is prepared properly for a kindergartner or first-grader.

If, for example, your kindergartner or first-grader comes home in despair after the first few days of school and falls apart in fits of crying or rage, you may want to consider retention. If your child's distress continues night after night for a week or more and recurs each morning before school, your child is in obvious pain, and it is up to you to find out why. It may be that your child lacks the emotional maturity to cope with school or has a developmental learning impediment which he or she will need another year to outgrow.

In either case, the wise strategy may be to hold your child back or repeat a year. Besides your child's emotional outbursts at home, here are some other signs that your beginning first-grader may need to repeat kindergarten:

- ◆ a need to be dressed or fed by an adult in the morning and physically forced into the car, onto the school bus, or into the classroom

◆ school reports that your child bothers other children in school, hits them or throws things at them, and steals or destroys their work and toys

◆ inability to cooperate with others or participate in group situations or relate to other children and make friends

◆ inability to express feelings or make himself or herself understood

◆ inability to initiate or complete a task

◆ strikes out at others or talks or shouts impulsively

Other Least Restrictive Settings

The next least restrictive setting is a regular class setting with consulting teacher assistance. In this category of LRE, a special-education teacher helps your child in the regular classroom setting, sitting at his or her side at specific times during the week to help your child handle classwork appropriately.

The third LRE leaves a child in the regular classroom setting most of the day, but requires that he or she report to a special resource room for one or more periods—but less than half the school day—of individual or group work with a special-education teacher

The next level of LRE sends a child to special-education classes 50 percent of the day. Such classes can include no more than five students per teacher.

The degree of restriction increases at the next LRE level, with students spending most of the day in special education and, at the next level, with them spending the entire day in special education.

Sometimes, if the school cannot provide adequate services, a child may have to remain at home to receive special education or be sent to a different school district or a facility operated by cooperative educational services for several districts. The most restrictive levels send children to special day or residential schools.

Recognizing Dangers of Special Education

Now if this sounds like an academic and emotional disaster for most children, it is.

First, there are no national special-education standards and both the type of education and the quality varies widely from school to school. Generally, the quality of public-school special education is as suspect as the quality of regular education—if not more so.

Second, there is almost no way to enforce the confidentiality requirements of the law. Too many people in each district are privy to the child's and the family's personal history. The cse evaluation amounts to a humiliating public airing of a child's learning difficulties. Every child in the class knows immediately which students are assigned to special education.

Perhaps the greatest danger of the special-education process is the lack of ways for you to authenticate before the fact the cse evaluation, the appropriateness of the placement, and the effectiveness of the school's program. You'll only know whether your child's iep is effective after the fact, but by then it will be a year or more too late to turn back the clock and try again with a better program. (The cse of course, will blame your child or you for failing to cooperate.)

The other danger of public-school special education is failure to identify some children who have critical learning disabilities and, without support services, will fail in regular classes with teachers who cannot cope with learning differences.

Evaluating Special Education

Does special education in public school work for some kids? Of course it does, but there is no way to guarantee it works for all kids at all schools. To make it work for your child, you must spend more than a few days investigating the programs at each LRE level.

Use all the school-evaluation methods outlined in Chapter 3, applying all the methods used to assess teacher quality and the school's regular classrooms and curriculum. Visit the special-education resource classrooms to see the type equipment the school uses and exactly how it works. Interview the special-education teachers who will work with your child. Investigate their training and experience. When did they start in special education and why? Was it because there were no jobs for English teachers?

Interview the director of special education for the school or school district to learn more about the program, its evaluators and teachers, their training and experience, and the director's background.

Above all, ask the director to explain the philosophy underlying the program. It is important for you to determine whether the school's program will teach your child essential skills for academic and intellectual independence or simply help your child get through the work, get passing grades, and get a diploma.

There are three broad approaches to special education:

1. *Total education.* These programs will not modify their curriculum to accommodate children with learning impediments, although they may provide temporary special tutoring to help a youngster overcome specific learning problems in a specific course. Children with long-term learning problems must complete the cur-

riculum or transfer to other schools. This is seldom appropriate for children with critical learning impediments such as dyslexia.

2. *Demanding curriculum with short-term modification.* Schools in this category modify the curriculum initially to allow children with learning problems to learn essential skills that will, after a year or two, permit re-entry into the curricular mainstream of the school. Curricular modifications include waiving foreign language requirements, for example, for ninth and tenth graders with dyslexia. For most bright children with critical learning impediments, this type of program is usually the best.

Here's how one such program works: An academically prestigious all-boys boarding school admits about fifty dyslexic ninth graders a year into its two-year language retraining program. During their first year, these students work in pairs with tutors in specially equipped classrooms, studying elements of phonetics, sequencing of ideas, handwriting, memorization techniques, and other language skills while attending regular history, mathematics, and science courses with nondyslexic students.

In the second year (tenth grade), the dyslexic boys, who constitute about 20 percent of the student body, join a language-skills class and a tutorial class, each of which meets four times a week. When they finish, they join the rest of the student body in the academic mainstream—i.e., the eleventh-grade college preparatory curriculum—and go on to graduate and enroll at some of America's finest, most academically demanding colleges and universities.

3. *Total modification.* Schools in this category modify the curriculum according to each child's ability. Usually

ungraded, such schools reduce the amount of materials covered in each course and give each child as long as he or she needs to finish the material. Aides serve as scribes, readers, and note-takers for the students. Students routinely use "talking books" and take untimed tests. Few students ever graduate or go on to college. Most simply earn a certificate of attendance when they leave. This program is designed for severely learning handicapped children with little potential for academic success.

The Decision for Your Child

If your child has a critical learning impediment, it is essential that you decide on the philosophical approach to his or her education. Do you want a program that will teach your child independence or one that will simply make school life easier? For a bright child, the second choice is the easiest way out. But it can be the worst of the many special-education traps because it never forces the child to discover his or her potential—to find out just how much he or she is capable of learning and accomplishing. It is the easy way out for parents, too, because it is far easier to modify their expectations for a child with learning impediments than to struggle to help that child succeed against often difficult odds.

Asking Questions

In addition to determining the broad type of program, ask for specifics—something more than vague terms such as *remedial reading* or *resource rooms*. Ask about specific techniques, such as method of special-education instruction (phonic tutoring, for example), class size (five or fewer in special-education resource rooms), individualized instruction, curricular modification. Ask what staff members are involved in the program. Is it limited to just special-education teachers or does everybody at the school know how to help kids and complement the work of the special-education teachers? Ask about available diagnostic and other services. How many students go on to college? Does the school provide any services to its students when they go to college?

Ask when the program began. Many private schools started remedial and special-education programs to attract additional students and offset a decline in enrollment and revenues from students without learning problems.

Ask if you can visit classes. If you can, here's what to look for:

◆ a regular teacher who moves from child to child, giving each student a share of individual instruction, picking up individual learning problems, showing different ways to solve the same problems, and allowing each student to contribute to class discussion

◆ a class in which children are not working on the same thing at the same time—not learning in lockstep

◆ a wide variety of learning materials, with each child or small group using different materials designed for different skill levels.

◆ a well-prepared teacher who answers student questions directly, informatively, constructively—and never evasively, as in, "We'll get to that later" or "You're getting ahead of yourself"

◆ enthusiastic students, absorbed in classroom activities, eagerly questioning and participating in discussions with the teacher

◆ one or more "invisible" special-education teachers who mix with and help all students but focus unobtrusively on the student or students with critical learning impediments and help them cope with specific learning tasks; the process is smoothly integrated into the general class atmosphere

Making Choices

If, after evaluating your local public school's special-education program, you decide against publicly supported special education, there are a host of alternatives for helping your child overcome one or more critical learning disorders.

The first step before deciding on any of them is a private evaluation of your child. Limit its scope to the smallest number of tests, interviews, and physical examinations that will still give you an accurate picture of the type impediment your child is facing. Remember that any evaluation should give you a whole picture of your child—his or her strengths as well as weaknesses—so you and your child can focus on building the positives, and as much as possible, bypassing instead of concentrating on the negatives.

Keep the process as casual and upbeat for your child as possible. Point out that no one is perfect, everyone has something that goes wrong. Point out some things that don't work for you, and promise your child you'll get to the bottom of the problem and fix it as quickly as possible.

Once you have an evaluation and an idea of the extent and type of remediation or retraining that's needed, you first may want to consult your child's regular teacher. He or she may have had experience working with children like yours in the regular classroom situation. If the learning impediment is not serious or is a short-term developmental impediment, such a teacher might, with your help, be able to handle your child routinely, with no special intervention by school authorities and without disclosing your child's problems to anyone else.

In any event, it's a good idea for your teacher to know of your child's impediment so he or she can make appropriate allowances when grading papers and evaluating classroom performance.

If your child's teacher cannot help, turn to a service organization or professional who will work with your child outside of the school setting, either at home or at special facilities, with minimum disruption of your child's normal school routine. Appendix C lists educational service organizations that can help you find accredited in-school special-education programs at both public and private schools across the United States. Appendix C also lists out-of-school programs and private assistance programs.

Taking the Private-School Option

Still another course of action you can take is to send your child to any of the hundreds of private schools and summer camps that offer remedial and special-education programs for students with special needs, in an atmosphere of warm acceptance, concern, and respect.

These schools stretch across the gamut of private education. Among them are day schools and boarding schools and combined day and boarding schools. Some are single sex; others are coeducational. Some offer minimal programs with only a part-time remedial reading or mathematics teacher or special-education consultant. Others offer extensive programs with specially equipped classes and highly trained, full-time teachers who work with students daily on an intensive, one-to-one basis and in small groups. All of the schools respect a family's right to privacy.

Appendix E is a directory of private schools, listed by state and divided into categories of remedial and special-education services, including a small group accredited for work with exceptional children with serious handicaps or emotional problems. Be sure to do a careful evaluation of the depth of each school's program because some financially shaky schools often exaggerate the extent of their offerings to lure additional paying students to their campuses.

Your school district must, under federal law, pay all costs of special education if an evaluation, either one you have had done privately or one that has been administered by the public-school district, has determined that your child is learning disabled and requires a specific type of education that your public school cannot or will not provide.

There are many private schools that are renowned for successful programs and effective teachers. Given a choice between any of these and the public-education system, there is absolutely no question the best choice is the private school—even if it means a difficult daily commute or actually moving to a new community.

Your child's intellectual future is at stake, and if you have taken the time to find and read this book, you are undoubtedly already looking for the right answers for your child. These answers lie with the best-trained special-education and regular-education teachers at academically demanding schools with national and even international reputations. Like your own child, the children these schools teach are bright and are trying hard, but they are facing learning impediments that stand in their way.

As I said at the beginning of this book, most children need good education, not special education. But even those who do need special education also need good education, and there is no reason for them not to receive both if they attend the right schools. Almost any accredited private school will help you find an appropriate remedial-reading or remedial-mathematics teacher.

Summary

The special-education process includes the following six steps:

1. evaluation, with parental consent, by child-study team consisting of a physician, psychologist, social worker, regular classroom teacher, special-education teacher

2. examinations, interviews and tests focusing on physical health; mental health; family history; reading, writing, speaking, listening, comprehension, reasoning, and calculation skills; broad academic skills; classroom behavior

3. determination of impediment or impediments

4. proposal of individual educational program (IEP), with short- and long-term education goals and timetable for meeting them; parental consent required

5. placement of student, with parental consent, in one of eleven least restrictive educational settings (LRE) that include return to regular class with or without special education; return to regular class with varying degrees of part-time work in special-education resource classes; removal from regular class in favor of full-time special education in the same school, in another educational facility, or at home

6. annual review by committee on special education of student's progress and effectiveness of IEP; parental consent required to continue IEP

Parents have the legal right:

◆ to review all confidential school documents about their child

◆ to approve or reject any or all elements of special education, including initial testing, evaluation, recommendations, formulation and design of individual educational program, placement of their child in a particular special-education program or least-restrictive educational setting, annual review and assessments

◆ to discontinue special education at any time

◆ to appeal the school efforts to override their rejection of a school IEP at a hearing before an impartial arbitrator

◆ to appeal the decision of the impartial hearing officer to the review officer of the state education department

◆ to obtain full reimbursement for the cost of sending their child to special education at a separate facility, either state-operated or private, if the local public school cannot provide the special education in the proper setting the child requires, as determined by an evaluation team

◆ to withdraw their child from the public-school sector in favor of a private facility or home education, at their cost

PART II

Chapter 7

A Guide to Infant Education and Intellectual Development

Since the dawn of civilization, educators from Plato to John Dewey have recognized the critical importance of an infant's first years of education in determining intellectual development and the kind of adult that child will become. Infant education is the key to preventing almost all critical and noncritical learning impediments that do not have a genetic or physiological basis. Inadequate or neglectful infant education is the most dangerous learning disability trap because it can produce learning disabilities in otherwise intelligent, intellectually healthy children.

Infant education must begin the moment baby arrives home for the first time. It's at that moment parents become their child's first and most important teachers. It's at that moment, too, that the home becomes child's first and most important school—the learning environment in which the child will reach his or her potential or develop learning impediments that may interfere with intellectual functioning.

Regardless of your child's age, it's important to have a good understanding of the entire educational development process and appropriate teaching techniques for children from birth. Here is a month-by-month synopsis of the infant education process, which you can apply to your own baby or use as a basis for understanding how your older child's learning skills developed. As you'll quickly see, many of the techniques for infant education can be adapted for improving learning skills of older children. Don't worry if you didn't apply some of the techniques when your child was an infant. You can begin now.

Infant Education: From the Beginning

Intellectual growth begins the moment a child is born. It's not enough just to be with one's child, to hold it and love it. Parents must be a baby's teachers and mentors, remembering at all times, during every stage of the child's development, that the child will learn and acquire almost all its parents' emotional and intellectual habits and those of the rest of the family. Being a parent is not an easy job. It is hard work, and it carries enormous physical, emotional, and intellectual responsibilities—and most parents make many mistakes. It's impossible not to. It's never too late, however, to correct some mistakes of the past.

Remember, for example, that if you tend to be nervous or sullen, your child, regardless of age, will sense your disposition and tension. If you fret, your child will be fretful; if you're friendly and outgoing, your baby will sense that, too, and reflect your cheer and warmth. Eventually, your child will adapt to the environment you create and reflect that environment with a tense and sullen or sunny and friendly disposition. In other words, you are constantly teaching your child, passively or actively, whether you realize it or not and whether you want to or not. Your child is constantly learning from you.

Communicating with Your Child

The same holds true for the language skills essential to learning. If you are silent around your child, your child will not learn to communicate. A child with whom no one communicates is likely to grow up with serious and perhaps irreversible language deficits—receptive and expressive language disorders—that leave the child unable to speak and understand and make learning difficult in every area of intellectual life.

That doesn't mean talking nonstop. Talking too much or leaving the television or radio on does not help your child learn to communicate any better than silence. Such one-way, conversational overload never allows a child to respond and leaves a youngster feeling that what he or she has to say is unimportant and not worth saying.

Television and radio are dangerous ways to build a child's vocabulary because the words are not associated with any objects or facial expressions the child can see. The words project no human values. Children raised by TV or radio "baby-sitters" invariably grow up bonding more to electronic than human voices and learn to communicate in electronic cliches. Moreover, much of the language they learn is grammatically incorrect and often includes gutter talk.

The conversational environment you create will determine one of your child's most important linguistic skills: speaking. In teaching this and other skills, remember that extreme approaches—too much talk or too little—will tend to be self-defeating and can produce serious learning impediments that will interfere with intellectual growth.

Two-way conversation is one of the keys to enhancing that growth—even with newborns. Talk to your child frequently, regardless of his or her age, but make it a two-way conversation, much like you would have with a friend. Talk to, not at, your child. Look at your child when you talk, and give your child a chance to respond.

Stop and listen while your child responds—with coos if your child is still an infant—and let your child finish cooing before responding. Don't interrupt your child with what you think are responsive or comforting words, and don't let others interrupt. Don't respond with disinterested monosyllables such as *yes* or *right*. Respond with meaningful words—complete sentences that indicate to your child that words and feelings elicit significant, caring responses from others.

And read and sing to and touch and hug your child, the way no radio or television can. Remember, when any window of learning opportunity is open, if you don't take full advantage, you will effectively reduce your child's ability to learn in the future.

It's important to remember that babies are not pets that will simply sleep or watch their parents contentedly without attention and conversation for indefinite periods. Your interaction with your baby should not be too different from your interaction with your closest friend—namely, warm and loving, alertly listening to responses, replying affectionately and understandingly. If an adult friend were in your kitchen, for example, you would not work silently and ignore your friend. Don't work silently in the presence of your child—even if your child is a baby who can only coo and is too young to understand or respond.

At birth, crying is a baby's only form of communication, but that will quickly change. From one to three months, most babies begin making friendly and cheerful oral responses by cooing and gurgling. Babies spend a lot of time sleeping but, when awake, they invariably react to many of the movements and noises of those around them. Baby's eyes follow and stare at the people nearby. At times, a baby demands attention with grunts and whines; it smiles instinctively during play.

A child needs as much contact with his or her parents as possible during early infancy—as they do with their child. For a baby, it's getting-to-know-you time, when the emotional ties a parent establishes will determine the strength of their relationship for the rest of their lives. It's important to gesture and to look in a baby's eyes when talking with a child and to show and tell a baby what you're doing so the child learns the joys of communicating and exercising linguistic skills.

Making Your Baby Your Friend

Parents should carry their baby from room to room to allow him or her to share family activities. When baby shuts his or her eyes and dozes, a parent should hum or sing softly (even off-key, if that's the case) so that baby senses the parent's presence and feels secure.

Once again, it's essential for any child's emotional as well as intellectual development that parents treat their child as they would a friend and not ignore the child or remain silent and uncommunicative for extended periods of time. Try never to be too busy to talk to your child—or your child will soon grow too busy to talk to you.

Apart from providing essential infant education, warm linguistic and physical contacts with a baby minimize the development of psychological and emotional problems that can also interfere with learning.

Even if a superior preschool or elementary school is able to compensate for deficient infant education, any psychological and emotional wounds suffered during infancy can evolve into serious learning impediments. Children cannot learn effectively when they're hurting and in tears, and it makes little difference whether the tears are flowing on the outside or the inside.

Practicing Conversational Skills

From the moment a child is born, a parent's words, phrases, and sentences begin laying the foundation for the baby's eventual verbal, or linguistic, skills. Linguistic skills are the most important intellectual skills in the learning process and the basis of all learning throughout life.

Linguistic skills differentiate humans from other animals and differentiate each of us from our fellow humans. They eventually permit us to read, write, and calculate and to communicate in complex ways with others. That is why it is so important for parents to talk *with* rather than *at* their children, regardless of their ages, if they are to avoid developing learning impediments.

It is also important to use real words when you speak to your child—not baby talk or popular street talk—and to speak in complete sentences. There is no reason real words and complete sentences cannot be uttered to a newborn, with as much joy, warmth, and love as gibberish.

Every principle of learning and child-rearing substantiates that frequency of exposure relates directly to learning, and the longer a baby hears gibberish, the older it will be before it learns to speak English. Surely, no loving parent can possibly have any serious objection to using real words. Exactly who benefits when mature adults utter incomprehensible, preliterate coos and grunts that mean nothing to either the baby or the adult? The practice is ludicrous and can delay a baby's ability to learn critical linguistic skills—possibly beyond the time when the baby is most able to acquire those skills.

Now that doesn't mean words don't sound like gibberish to the baby. Its undeveloped comprehension probably only hears the *b* or *ba* sound when you say *bottle*, and its limited linguistic skills only permit it to respond with a coo at first, and as it matures, with the *ba* or even *ba-ba* sound. Most infants normally respond to all adult utterances—gibberish as well as complex words—with the only sounds they can make, namely, baby talk.

Such sounds are the baby's efforts to practice saying what it hears and have a conversation with you. Initially, there is usually no way for most parents to know what their baby is trying to say, but it usually is not what they think. The baby word *ba-ba* might be *bottle*, *banana*, *baby*, or any other word that begins with the letter *b*. It may be nothing at all—just an imitation of a sound.

The best thing is not even to try to guess and certainly not to repeat any baby talk. Nor is it helpful to listen anxiously for that first word. In doing so, parents transmit their anxiety to their baby, who has no idea why they seem so anxious.

If you have a child who is still a baby, just enjoy baby's cooing for what it is: talking to you in baby language. Simply listen and respond in real words, as you would to any friend. Give your baby your attention, interest, praise, and love. Keep the conversation going—even though your infant may not understand a word and you feel a bit silly talking to yourself.

Your baby is learning, and it is important for you to keep talking and teaching. Point things out to your child as you stroll outdoors and describe what you see and what is happening. Do the same in the house as you dress your child, cook, do the laundry, or clean. When you shop together, describe the things you buy, count apples aloud. Build your child's vocabulary at every opportunity, naming each thing you see, defining its color, size, and texture and its purpose, or if it's an animal or person, what it is doing.

Know when to stop, however. Like adults, babies can get bored with too much talk and need some quiet moments of solitary contemplation or dozing.

Gradually, the baby's hearing and linguistic abilities will develop and begin to be capable of comprehending and uttering more complex sounds. If the only sound it ever hears when caregivers provide water, though, is *wa-wa*, it stands to reason that baby's language development will be slowed unnecessarily by forcing it to learn *water*—and the name of every other object—twice. It's always easier to learn things the right way the first time. It delays language development to spend two years learning to say things one way, then without a word of explanation, have to learn an entirely new vocabulary.

Building Baby's Vocabulary

Continue using adult words and phrases and conversing intelligently with your baby. Your child will learn more quickly and efficiently—and with less confusion—if you call a banana by its real name. Imagine, for a moment, the chaotic learning environment a teacher would create if she forced every child to learn every new word twice. That's exactly what parents who use baby talk do. It's important that the learning process be as clear and simple—and as free of chaos and confusion—as possible. If you don't use the word in adult conversation, don't teach it to your child.

Later, when baby's words do start flowing, don't worry about mispronunciations. Not every child's lips, palate, tongue, and facial soft tissues develop at the same rate. When your youngster begins talking, he or she will mispronounce many and perhaps most words. Most normal infants do. Chronic mispronunciations of one or more words may go on for weeks or months.

Such mispronunciations, along with a host of developmental problems such as lisping, are no cause for concern if your child is well adjusted and developing at a normal rate in every other respect. An occasional, friendly correction of a child's mispronunciation can be helpful, but constant corrections and interruptions discourage most children from learning conversational skills by instilling a fear that whatever they say is apt to be wrong.

Spotting Impediments

It's one thing if your child's speech is still too garbled to understand at five or six. Then you would almost certainly need to take your child for a diagnostic workup by a specialist. Before then, however, let your pediatrician be the judge of whether your child has a speech problem or not.

Well-trained pediatricians (with an M.D. from an accredited medical school in the United States) are well aware of the wide range in the rates of child development and will tell you after every examination how your child is progressing in skill development essential to learning.

True intelligence, which involves reasoning and memory, does not become evident until your baby is about two years old, by which time he or she may be talking nonstop. Remember, though, that some children start talking earlier than two, while others with superior intelligence may not show any language facility until they're thirty months old.

During the first three months, baby will be alert to the sounds a parent makes, and the small sounds it is able to utter in response will gradually evolve from crying—the baby's first means of communication after birth—into coos, often accompanied by smiles.

It's important *not* to coo back—but to talk in real words, unless you want to raise a child who coos and has expressive language deficits and learning impediments. Parents should talk to children of all ages in adult language every moment they are with their children, whether the latter are babies or older children.

A baby's eyes and head usually follow other people's movements by the second month, so it sees as well as hears what you're doing. Careful, teaching parents should always describe what they are doing in complete detail. It's immaterial that a baby can't understand the words the parent is saying. If you don't start speaking to a baby right away, it will never understand words or will be so late in its development it will already have language deficits and learning impediments that will affect learning skills.

Infancy is the only time in a baby's life that it can learn a maximum number of language skills. Babies that fail to learn those skills in early infancy may never have a chance to catch up.

By talking, you're teaching baby to listen, to understand that words mean something important: specific actions, specific objects, someone has something to say, and above all, they mean the parent cares and loves the child.

It's important then to talk to baby every moment you are together, describing what you're doing when you bathe, dry, powder, and dress baby, naming each item and saying what you are going to do with the item—unbutton, fasten, tie, etc. A basic teaching technique is to repeat each new word three times. Most experienced teachers believe three is the magic number for repeating new words to assure maximum learning, with two being too few and four producing boredom and disinterest.

So, just as you feed your baby food for bodily nourishment, you should also feed it a lot of language, the essential nourishment for baby's growing intellect.

When baby begins reaching for objects at around three months, name each object and say what it's for. An effective parent-teacher maintains a running description, like a sports commentator, but never forgets to let the baby reply with a few coos that will gradually evolve into gurgling and cries of pleasure. And good parent-teachers never forget to add some smiles, tickles, kisses, hugs, and love when they respond to their baby's efforts at conversation.

Asking Questions

Asking questions and offering choices is another wonderfully effective teaching technique in infancy or at any age. For an infant, the technique teaches the difference that tone of voice makes in speaking—the tone in a declarative sentence, the questioning tone when offering a choice, and the emphatic tone when saying no.

Regardless of what you say and how you say it, however, it's essential to keep giving baby a chance to answer with a coo, gurgle, or smile. It's essential also never to talk to baby in a loud, high-pitched voice. A terrible mistake many parents and teachers make is talking to babies or young children as if they're deaf, or worse, mentally retarded. The loudness of a parent or teacher's voice or the pitch doesn't help an infant or older child understand any better than a calm, soft, gentle voice. The louder a parent talks to its baby, the louder the baby will talk when it eventually does speak. A loud voice remains a lifelong disadvantage to learning because it drowns out other voices and is often offensive and even repulsive to others.

Adding Music to the Words

In addition to training in conversation, an integral part of infant education includes aesthetic experiences. It's important to sing and read to your baby from the day you return from the hospital. Sounds are a baby's primary entertainment. All rhymes are fun, and nursery rhymes are particularly wonderful because they repeat related sounds in a related tale over and over again and usually can be sung or spoken.

By starting early, you can facilitate your child's ability to learn words, say them correctly, and recite them in complete sentences. Having heard them since early infancy, your baby will know most of the rhymes when it's time to begin talking and singing independently. Suddenly, to your surprise, your baby will begin spontaneously reciting and singing with you. By then, baby will also have seen you handling and reading books and begin doing the same thing on its own, to look at the colorful pictures.

Infant Education: Three to Six Months

Although babies advance as much as a month or more earlier or later than the averages discussed here, after about twelve to fifteen weeks, the cooing sounds evolve into a variety of unintelligible squeals and grunts—*ee*, *ich*, etc.—and smiles occasionally erupt into giggles and laughter. Baby also begins making different sounds for different needs and babbles streams of meaningless sounds that pediatricians call "jargon." Its voice will rise and fall in imitation of the adult voices it hears. If your voice is expressionless, baby's will be equally expressionless.

Baby also begins recognizing the differences in parental moods, whether you are in a good or bad mood, pleased or angry. It will associate some of the words and language you use with those moods.

Playing and Talking with Baby

Babies of three to six months normally respond eagerly when playing with adults, and such play serves as a good opportunity to teach the names of various objects. Babies of this age also start looking for toys that drop out of sight and look forward eagerly to feeding time. Both developments offer wonderful opportunities to practice question-and-answer play.

In conversing with a baby, remember the analogy of conversing with a friend—smile when baby smiles, laugh when baby laughs, and praise baby's utterances, repeating them in conjunction with an appropriate word rather than meaningless sounds. If baby says *ba*, respond with a happy "Here's a banana," or depending on the circumstances, "Baa, Baa, black sheep, Have you any wool?"

Timely praise is always more effective for teaching than oppressive, inappropriate, and excessively effusive responses to normal development. There is nothing extraordinary about a baby's first utterance of the sound *ba*, although it's understandable that any parent would be—and should be—pleased and perhaps overcome with joy.

Nevertheless, it is a disservice to any baby and will almost certainly undermine the baby's motivation to learn if it is showered with rewards for doing what comes naturally or what is perfectly ordinary.

The principle of avoiding inappropriate praise applies to all ages. Later, inappropriate parental praise for ordinary work can seriously interfere with academic achievement at school because the child learns to expect rewards for doing the expected. It becomes difficult, if not impossible, to provide a child with enough rewards for extra effort in school if throughout its infancy its family overcompensated for perfectly normal, developmental learning.

Offering Praise

There is an appropriate time to say, "That's very good" or "That's wonderful" or to sweep a child up in ones arms to share the joy of an exceptional learning triumph. Despite understandable parental joy, a baby's first utterance of the syllable *ba* belongs in the first category.

Your conversations with baby can and should grow more complex from three to six months. As the baby begins to reach for and touch objects, you should name them and explain and demonstrate their purposes. Give your baby a variety of small but safe objects to feel, touch, and hold.

If, however, a baby has yet to make a sound or suddenly stops making sounds at the end of six months, contact your pediatrician. Rigid adherence to the pediatrician's recommended schedule of checkups is essential. Unless you are a physician, it can be dangerous to rely solely on personal observations to evaluate a baby's health and development.

Infant Education: Six to Nine Months

At six to nine months, baby's little grunts will become more wordlike, though no less unintelligible for the most part. The baby is beginning to assimilate the basic sounds of language—*ba*, *be*, *bi*, *bo*, *bu*, etc.—and occasionally putting them together into accidental words, such as *goo-goo*, and yes, *da-da* and *ma-ma*.

A child of this age may begin responding appropriately when it hears its own name and also to the word *no*. Unfortunately, many parents make the understandable error of turning their child into a trained seal after it starts responding properly or begins imitating others by saying *ma-ma* and other sounds and words. The baby still has no idea what it is saying, and it is detrimental to a child's learning skills for it to begin associating new knowledge with having to perform.

The key teaching technique at this stage is to encourage the use of such new word-sounds by repeating them as parts of words or sentences—either in songs or nursery rhymes or in phrases that demonstrate what you are doing. Such repetition should be distinct and a bit slower (not unnaturally so, though) so the baby can distinguish each word you say. Emphasize and repeat key words and show baby the objects they symbolize, as in, "Here is your milk."

Initially, your baby may not know what you are saying, but it will nevertheless begin imitating some of the word sounds you make and eventually recognize familiar words and the objects they symbolize.

Feeding the Intellect

It's important to feed a baby as many words and as much language as possible during these critical months by conversing, singing, and reading from oversized, colorfully illustrated children's books. Rhyming is a wonderful teaching tool that delights children, especially if you make a different face with each rhyme.

Show your baby the drawings and huge lettering as you read. Readings should not be too long. Baby simply doesn't have the attention span. Short sessions—one short nursery rhyme or song with pictures—are best. Stop immediately when baby shows a loss of interest.

Playing Games with Baby

It's important to wait for responses when talking with a baby— that is, to give it a chance to talk the only way it knows how, with squeals or laughs or grunts. And never forget that play is usually the most effective teaching tool in intellectual development. Games such as peek-a-boo are great techniques for stimulating both vocabulary and basic intellectual skills such as observation and problem-solving. Peek-a-boo, for example, teaches some rudiments of a wide range of intellectual skills, especially the appreciation of humor and the ability to recognize disappearance as a not necessarily permanent phenomenon. "One, Two, Buckle My Shoe" teaches counting skills and sound coordination. "So Big" teaches concepts of size, and so on.

Folk songs and nursery rhymes such as "Pop Goes the Weasel," "Jack and Jill," and "Hickory Dickory Dock," teach the baby the joy of melody, rhyming, and eventually, social interaction. Be sure to use games such as This Little Piggy to allow you to interact physically with your child while evoking peals of laughter as you tickle your baby and run your fingers up your baby's tummy. Be sure to teach the names of body parts at the same time.

Every sound is an opportunity to build an infant's vocabulary: a dog barking, a fire-engine siren, the roar of an overhead airplane, the ring of the doorbell or telephone. Parents should teach colors, textures, sizes, speeds, positioning, and other intellectual concepts such as soft, hard, hot, warm, cold, wet, dry, loud, quiet, light, dark, day, night, on, over, under, above, below, and many, many others.

When he or she is able, encourage your baby to explore as much as possible rather than keeping him or her confined, so you can explain every object the baby discovers. Questions are most effective for teaching decision-making concepts: "Are you ready for your bottle?" Commands should also be taught: "Wave good-bye," "Give Aunt Sally a kiss."

Baby will also begin understanding words essential to good manners, such as *thank-you* and *please*, if they are taught routinely and used in everyday family conversation. If good manners and courtesy are not integrated into your family's behavior, your baby will not learn courteous behavior on its own.

Learning Offstage

Again, it's important to avoid at all costs the dangerous association of learning with performing for others. Few children grow up with a love of learning and free of learning impediments if they are pushed onstage to display publicly every new thing they learn. Although parents are certainly entitled to feel reassured, happy, and proud that their baby is on the right learning track, there is nothing unusual about any baby learning to say *mama* or *dada* by nine or ten months.

Although you should praise your baby appropriately and reinforce the acquisition of new knowledge, it is not in the baby's best intellectual or emotional interests to lift the event to the extraordinary or to make the baby perform for others all the time. There's nothing more fun than two-way communication with one's own baby. But endless demands to "say it again for . . ." or "say ma-ma" or "say da-da" only lead to disappointment and unnecessary emotional stress for the baby—and to a certain degree, for the parent. Often, the baby simply doesn't understand a word you're saying or demanding.

Indeed, excessive demands to perform often provoke babies to conclude the opposite—that you're upset by the sound it made and that he or she had best not repeat it. In any case, the first time a baby does indeed say *ma-ma*, it usually is as meaningless a sound to the baby as saying *goo-goo*.

Infant Education: Nine to Twelve Months

By the tenth month, most babies happily wave hello and goodbye on command and actually say—and mean—*mama* when they utter those syllables. By twelve months, vocabulary will have expanded to several specific words, depending on how skilled and diligent a teacher the caregiver has been during the child's first year at home.

As mentioned earlier, it's unimportant if a child is a late-talker or not, especially if he or she is developing normally in every other respect. Although most babies begin uttering their first words at about twelve months, many normal, healthy children are late-talkers—boys more often than girls. If, however, a baby is not talking at all by eighteen months or has suddenly turned silent, take the child to the pediatrician for an evaluation.

The important thing is not to badger or get angry at your child for not talking or for not talking well. All children's soft tissues—lips, tongue, palate, throats—develop at different rates, just as bones do, and the ability to enunciate consonants evolves over several years. Some children may speak clearly at age two; others may not be intelligible until they're four, five, or six. Above all, never correct or punish or imitate your baby when it mispronounces words—*wa-wa* for water, for example, or *ba-ba* or *na-na* for *banana*.

Avoiding Overcorrection

Constant correction of mispronunciations intimidates most children and actually teaches them *not* to speak or develop a vocabulary. Constant correction creates learning impediments where there might have been none. To punish a child for mispronunciation by refusing, say, a banana until the child pronounces the word correctly all but assures learning impediments.

To imitate a baby's mispronunciations, on the other hand, implies that it is speaking correctly and assures that it will continue speaking that way and will have to relearn the correct pronunciations later. Making a baby learn English twice—first the wrong way, then the right way—will all but guarantee some learning impediments in school and perhaps all its life.

Parents who are enchanted by baby talk should tape their baby's voice, by all means, but to repeat, imitate, or use baby talk almost certainly retards the baby's language development. Often, by the time baby begins to learn to speak properly, it is too late to develop the rich language skills that should have been learned during infancy.

One simple and effective way to respond to the normal mispronunciations of one-year-olds is to learn to understand what your baby is trying to say, then to respond in a warm, loving voice, with appropriate praise, using the correct pronunciations in your own speech. It's best to show neither disappointment nor effusive, inappropriate joy when a baby asks for a *na-na*, but to respond appropriately by giving the baby a banana and saying, "Here's a banana." The baby will eventually learn to say the word correctly—when it is ready developmentally.

Playing with Sounds

This is one of the key vocabulary-building periods in a child's life—a moment when the window of learning opportunity is open widest and the baby will learn those basic language skills that will prevent most learning impediments later on. Parents of one-year-olds should double and redouble every effort to encourage baby's language development.

Interestingly, all primary schools once taught children to read from primers whose first page presented the alphabet and whose second page was a syllabarium with a list of all two-letter syllables that sounded like baby words from *ba* to *zu*.

With little or no effort, children progressed to single-syllable words and easily read many of the same words they had accidentally pronounced during their preliterate infancy—one-syllable words such as *be*, *by*, and *go* and two-syllable words such as *ma-ma* or *pa-pa*.

The old-fashioned syllabication method of reading instruction recognized that learning to read does not begin with instruction in letters. To learn to read, infants and young children must first hear language, associate meanings to sounds and words, and gradually intuit that words are composed of sounds represented by printed symbols or letters.

Playing with sounds, words, and rhymes is an essential element in acquiring reading readiness skills by focusing a child's attention on word sounds as well as meaning. Obviously, babies can't learn to read when they first begin uttering phonemes, but a parent can repeat those sounds and put them into words, rhymes, and sentences. Rhyming, with or without song, is the most wonderful way for a child of any age to play with, enjoy, and learn words.

Teaching and Teaching Again

During this period of the language-development months, give every person, animal, plant, place, or thing your baby sees a name and describe what it does—in the house, the car or store, the garden or park, and everywhere you go. Even though you may have repeated them a dozen or a hundred or a thousand times, it's important to keep repeating the names of body parts, objects in the bedroom, bathroom, kitchen, living room, and everywhere else.

Children need to be exposed to sights, sounds, feelings—sunshine, light, dark, bell, music, pretty, warm, sad, happy, angry. Everything they see should carry a description—hot, cold, soft, hard, etc.—and a purpose. In providing infant education, the cardinal rule for parents is simple: Teach. Teach. Teach.

Try to help baby use all its faculties. Baby is at the reaching and touching stage, so it should be helped to feel what is wet, cold, dry, warm, soft; to hear what is quiet and loud; to see what is big and little, light and dark, red and yellow, up or down. Seize every opportunity to name and describe things for a baby—and give your baby plenty of time to absorb the concept of the moment and to respond.

Teaching Baby to Count

You can also begin counting and telling your child how many objects or things you see together. Encourage baby to respond verbally by asking questions and offering choices: "Are you thirsty?" "Do you want some milk or some orange juice?" "Where's your doll?"

Again, always talk in adult language, using complete sentences. Many parents allow their baby to seduce them into talking in single syllables. It's easy to get into that habit, especially when you're tired and just don't feel like talking to anyone, let alone a baby who only speaks in monosyllables and doesn't seem to understand a word you say. To talk to your baby in baby language, however, can seriously undermine infant education and provoke learning impediments later.

Showing Joy

When baby responds correctly, by all means respond with appropriate oral or physical praise. Suddenly, after you give a baby a choice of milk or orange juice for the ninety-ninth time, one day the baby may say *ra-shh*, or perhaps a clearer baby term for orange juice—and wow! What a thrill you'll have. It's the moment that marks the true beginning of two-way conversation between you and your child, and your baby absolutely deserves a warm hug and kiss.

When the response is incorrect, however, simply respond with a smile and a pleasant word: "No, that's not your doll; that's your ball. See? It's round. That's your ball. Now, let's try to find your doll."

When baby does not understand, there is no point persisting. Good teachers know when to move on to another subject the child does understand and return to the original question another time when the baby has matured a bit more. Language-development skills mature on a daily, sometimes hourly, basis, and children often astound parents by clearly and suddenly understanding or saying what they did not or could not understand they day before.

A key to good infant education is never to criticize a baby's efforts to speak. A good parent-teacher tries to understand the baby's language, but continues speaking normally, always using adult language to respond. Remember: Most babies become adults, and your child will eventually learn how to speak as adults do.

Teaching Baby About Books

In addition to conversing, it's essential to good infant education to expand your baby's reading experiences with large, colorful, illustrated books, nursery rhymes, and short stories that don't exceed baby's attention span. Explore the illustrations together with baby and ask questions, pointing to each word or to people, animals, and objects in a picture, asking what it is or how many there are.

After baby coos an answer, praise your baby and provide the correct answer in correct English. It's more fun for baby and enhances learning to use words and sounds (animal sounds, for example) your baby can imitate. Reading to children helps teach new words and meanings, provide contact with letters and words, and generate awareness that printed words tell stories, provide information, entertain, and affect emotions.

Infant education begins to pay off by nine to twelve months with real language development. Suddenly out of the blue, your baby will say, *mama* or *dada*—and mean it. Or your baby will say the last word or words of nursery rhymes you've been singing or reading for months.

Some parents respond initially as if it were an accident—a simple extension of the goo-goo talk to include a new sound. That can be the case, but never for very long. The first evidence that your baby knows what it's saying comes when it utters "Mama"—and reaches out to you for love.

Building Vocabulary

When your baby utters its first real words, it will actually understand far more words than it can say. This is a key period for vocabulary building. Baby will understand the meanings of an increasingly wide range of words—its own name, *mama*, *daddy*, *dog* (or whatever the dog's name happens to be), the names of siblings, live-in relatives or caregivers, the names of frequent visitors, *good-bye*, and *hello*.

By this time, healthy babies develop a sense of and need to play and a distinct understanding of emotions and the difference between happiness and sadness, contentedness and distress. At this age, too, your baby should be quite skilled at and enjoy playing peek-a-boo and playing with toys. Your child should have a lot of safe toys, preferably toys of different sizes, colors, and textures you should describe, along with toys that make musical or other sounds you can sing or talk about.

In addition to toys, give your child a wide range of safe household objects to handle—plastic cups, plates, jar lids, containers, and other nonbreakable items to play with, drop, and pick up. These give you an opportunity to teach baby the names of common household objects. It's extremely effective to ask a baby to hand things to you, rewarding with appropriate levels of praise and love after the proper response. Don't worry about handedness. It is of no consequence, and every baby should be allowed to use whichever hand it chooses.

Teaching Through Play

It's important to use play as an opportunity to teach. The talking, singing, touching, manipulating, and loving that accompany play teach important language skills. Give everything a name and a description—toes, fingers, nose, doll, game, cracker, banana, lunch, dinner, sleep, kiss, hug, love, blue, black, white, high, low, pretty, and hundreds, even thousands of other words.

As every educator since Plato in ancient Greece has noted, play is the most effective teaching tool for children. Play teaches and allows children to improve motor skills, vocabulary and language skills, and social skills. It is a means of discovery because the toys children play with show them how things work.

It's seldom of any consequence if a child's motor development is slower than his or her intellectual development. More than 90 percent of babies with slow motor development develop normal intelligence. If you are concerned about your child's physical growth rate or motor development, take your child to the pediatrician for an examination.

Learning Yes and No

Between nine and twelve months, your baby will also know and recognize two words that are often essential to the conduct of everyday life—*yes* and *no*. Those two words, however, have nuances that can be most difficult to teach and can be the most complex concepts any child will ever learn.

Initially, parents use the word *no* to proscribe various types of behavior, and the tone with which they use the word will indicate a wide range of emotions from thoughtfulness to rage.

In saying no and teaching its meaning to a child, it's important to do so as carefully as possible because each action that you prohibit with the word *no* automatically assumes a value. The way you say no will affect the value of every other *no* you utter thereafter. If too many are rage-filled or emotion-free, you diminish the value of every *no*.

If you display equal rage over spilled milk as you do when your child smashes a plate over the puppy's head—or if you express no emotion over either action—you give your baby no way of differentiating which behavior pattern is more or less acceptable. In the end, you will have failed to help your child develop values to rely on.

The words you teach your children must teach the range of values they carry as well as the literal meanings. Spilling milk accidentally is simply not as heinous an act as injuring a defenseless animal—just as failure to brush one's teeth will not be as important as telling a lie or stealing. In other words, the way you say no must carry—and teach—an appropriate emotional priority.

Avoiding Electronic Sitters

Every parent tires of and needs a break from child care. Unfortunately, many turn to television or radio as a sitter or surrogate parent. Television and radio, however, can produce some of the most insurmountable learning impediments.

The use of radio and television as substitute caregivers teaches children the language of television and deprives them of the opportunity to learn essential speaking and language skills. Children can only learn those skills if they are given the chance to respond. Television and radio are substitute parents that give babies no opportunity to respond or receive any rewards for doing so. Indeed, as it tries to respond, the radio or television voice continues to talk, ignoring the baby's voice and ultimately teaching that no one cares what it has to say. It will soon stop trying to say anything.

Most infants find any number of manipulatives endlessly stimulating and entertaining, and these can provide you with a break from child care without interrupting infant education. Instead of TV, you can give your child entertaining toys that will teach some independence and self-sufficiency.

Good infant education is all but impossible, however, in families whose primary leisure activity is television and whose children, from earliest infancy, hear electronic voices as much as or more than human voices. Inevitably, television—not reading—becomes the child's closest friend and primary leisure activity. No amount of scolding or threatening will make reading or homework important when school begins.

Infant Education:
One to Two Years

Late infancy usually sees intellectual growth parallel physical growth. As baby begins to walk and climb, feed itself, turn pages, build and stack things, respond, and come when called by name, it will also begin talking endlessly. Much of the time, the words will be nonsensical—noisy gibberish mixed with real words and strings of non sequiturs. It's all healthy practice talk, and with increasing frequency, baby will gradually incorporate actual words in its imitation of grown-up sounds.

Sometimes a baby says things so grown-up that a parent often responds in disbelief—"What did you say?"—and the poor child won't be able to remember. That's nothing to fret about, of course. Baby is simply practicing the linguistic skills that are keys to all future learning skills and the chief preventive to learning impediments. Let your baby practice as much and as often as it wants, without interruption. A lot of the time, babies simply play-talk and do not want anyone to listen or respond—rather like our own occasional talking to ourselves.

When your baby talks to you, however, it's important to listen attentively. Parents who ignore efforts of a baby to communicate are sewing the seeds of learning impediments. When a baby wants to talk, stop reading, turn down or turn off the television or radio and pay attention. It is emotionally and intellectually damaging to a child to have its efforts to talk treated rudely by parents who walk away or pick up a telephone or start talking to someone else while the child is in mid-sentence. Parents owe their child—and its efforts to converse—the respect they demand when they talk to someone.

Teaching Manners Now

Parents should not, of course, allow their children to interrupt or be rude, but when talking, every child deserves the chance to be heard so it knows its language skills and knowledge command respect. What is the use, after all, of learning language or acquiring knowledge if it serves no purpose in the wider world? Parents are their children's wider world. They should teach their child how much they value learning and knowledge and what others have to say.

Again, many children are late-talkers, and it usually is of no consequence. Babies utter their first words anywhere from eight to eighteen months. It makes little difference to their ultimate language-development skills so long as they grow up in a language-rich environment where they hear words all the time.

It's well to remember that every baby and growing child is developing a lot of other skills that are competing with language skills for attention. Assuming there are no congenital or physical impairments, words will eventually begin to pour out of every healthy baby's mouth at an unimaginable rate if its parents have provided the right kind of infant education.

Understanding Baby Talk

One problem almost all parents have to face is the inability to understand what their baby is trying to tell them. It's frustrating for them, but even more so for their baby, and it's not healthy to allow a child's frustration to build up to explosive levels. The best way to handle such situations is to look at the child responsively when it speaks and obviously wants something. Even when it's difficult to understand a child's words, sometimes facial expression or body language will reveal the child's meaning.

If not, a technique that's far better than random guessing or expressions of frustration is to give the child a kiss to show love, understanding, and confidence, then calmly ask the child to "show me what you want" or "take me where you want to go."

The technique turns a frustrating situation into a learning experience because it teaches the baby alternative ways of solving interpersonal problems that avoid conflict. The baby will eventually learn to say what he or she wants, but in the meantime, a little parental imagination can teach the child other ways of self-expression. The same principle applies to older children.

Expanding Worlds

As every child begins walking and exploring its home, parents need to expand the scope of the child's education and vocabulary. They should expand their conversations even when their child's responses don't make sense—and they should keep talking, listening, reading, singing, naming, and describing everything in sight, even things they've already named. Parents must repeat and repeat, until baby starts repeating what they've said and has obviously learned what its parents have tried to teach.

Once again, the most traditional and effective technique of good teachers since Socrates remains the question. Sometimes a child's demand can be an opportunity to teach valuable linguistic skills. The question, "What is it, Sweetheart?" can prove more effective for infant education at times than simply handing a child what it wants. Even if a child just grunts with a finger pointed tentatively at a stuffed bear, the parent can find the right words for the child with another question: "Do you want your bear?"

Although parents can often use such opportunities to enhance their children's infant education, it can be detrimental to become obsessive and demand more than a child can give. No child can learn in a day what normally takes a year or more. It may be appropriate at times to respond to a child's whimper by simply giving it what it obviously wants—without an English language lesson. Lessons do not have to be nonstop, but they should and must be a routine part of daily family life interwoven throughout all activities.

Ignoring Timetables

Just as there's no need for concern if a child is a late-talker, there is usually no need for concern if a child suddenly stops learning new words for a few days or even seems to forget some words. It's normal for a child to make enormous progress—learn a dozen words or more in a few days—then either stop learning or even forget.

Children are continually learning motor and sensory skills as well as intellectual skills, and each skill competes for attention. It's an enormous effort and truly hard work for a toddler taking those first steps to try to stay upright and concentrate on learning new words. That's as difficult for a baby as it would be for you or me to try learning handstands while memorizing the "Gettysburg Address."

And remember: after a baby has learned to walk steadily and climb stairs, there's an enormous amount of exploring to do—things to touch and grab and throw, all of which can be far more interesting than learning words.

That's no excuse to stop feeding your baby new and old words or to stop talking, but it's unrealistic to expect immediate feedback at all times. Children in a language-rich home nevertheless absorb much of what they hear and eventually reap the rewards at school as literate youngsters, superbly skilled with words.

If your baby's language skills deteriorate noticeably over a period of three or four weeks and there is no progress in any other skill area, it is best to give your child a holiday from learning.

Such language setbacks often result from emotional upsets—separation anxieties or an unhappy relationship with a caregiver. A child whose mood changes noticeably or who shows physical or emotional symptoms, such as prolonged sleep or eating disturbances or aggressive behavior, should be checked by a pediatrician immediately.

Developing the Love of Learning

In addition to being a prime time for language development, one or two years old is also prime time for development of a love of learning, as children explore and discover their universe—their homes. Such exploration can be a source of huge family upsets unless parents take pains to childproof their homes—for the child's protection as much as for that of their prized treasures.

Curiosity is every infant's instinctive and primary learning tool and good parents and teachers must nurture and encourage it enthusiastically as it develops. An infant's curiosity can, however, drive some parents to distraction. It is essential to your child's future intellectual and academic health, however, that you come to terms with your child's curiosity and do nothing to discourage it—even with what would seem to be a perfectly loving admonition not to touch something.

Every healthy infant of this age will absolutely try to touch everything within reach. Rather than admonish your child for trying to learn by satisfying his or her curiosity, put objects you don't want touched out of reach and out of sight before your child takes its first steps. Crushing an infant's curiosity is the most certain way of producing a lifelong learning impediment.

Instead, give your child a lot of safe outlets—toys and books to play with and areas to explore alone or hand in hand to prevent too many falls. Here are other learning programs essential to infant education:

- visiting parks and playgrounds, zoos and puppet shows together

- teaching sensory skills: seeing, hearing, smelling, tasting, and feeling—and talking about and explaining every sensory experience

- reading as many books together as possible

- singing together

- using numbers and counting in front of and with a child; stores that carry instructional toys usually stock sets of colored manipulatives—cubes and rods—that help teach young children to count, add, and subtract

As your child begins walking, safety education becomes a new priority. Children must be taught what is safe and what is not and what they should and should not do. Parental realism is just as essential, however. Every baby spills and spills and spills again, and anger won't stop it.

Expanding Your Child's Horizons

The teaching process expands as the child reaches fifteen to eighteen months and can walk and climb stairs alone, scribble with crayons, and push and pull toys through the house. It's at this age, too, that children consciously begin to copy the things they see parents do, pretending to cook, clean house, read, write, and do every other activity parents engage in.

Ultimately, the heart and soul of good infant education—or education of children of any age—is the willingness of parents to share their lives with their children. Whether your child is a toddler or well into elementary or middle school, sharing your life, explaining what you do and how you do it, can have an enormous impact on your child's learning skills—not to mention its emotional bonds to you as a parent.

Whether your child is a toddler or a third-grader, you can improve your child's understanding of mathematics by preparing meals together. When you cook, use numbers and perform simple calculations slowly and out loud to teach your child mathematical concepts. For example, emphasize these words as you hold up the items and demonstrate the procedures: *one egg*, then *two eggs*, *separate* the *yolk* from the *white* and *add one teaspoon* or a *cup*. Let your child help whenever possible. Even when it's not possible, find something for your child to do that is helpful.

Use every activity—preparing meals, setting the table, and so on—to explain numbers. Color books together, play games naming objects and their uses, increase your reading activities. Go on interesting excursions. I always called them adventures. And I read to my son and read and read some more. Do the same if you want your child to be a reader and an eager, active learner.

Infant Education: Two to Three Years Old

From one to two years old, every healthy child's speaking ability increases substantially. By the time a child is two, so will his or her motor skills and levels of physical as well as intellectual activity. At two, he or she will be speaking in complete, although short, sentences, identifying the quality of objects it sees, and telling simple stories.

Parent participation in a two-year-old's activities must increase substantially to keep pace. A child of two will touch and examine every object in reach. Put precious things away!

Encouraging Natural Curiosity

Two-year-olds also begin to pepper grown-ups with endless questions—and parents must try to answer every one of them or search for the answers with the child. It's a terrific learning experience for a child to watch as Dad or Mom explores the dictionary or encyclopedia. To become a learner, your child must know and see that curiosity and learning are your top priorities, too. If they are, they will remain your child's top priorities.

To discourage a young child's curiosity is to assure that the child will develop learning impediments that will affect its academic future. It makes little difference how much knowledge your child retains at this age. What is important is to encourage curiosity and love of learning.

Think back for a moment to a teacher or class you loved. Surely you don't remember everything you learned from that teacher in that class. The key memory is the joy of learning the teacher imparted.

It's well to remember, however, that some questions are attention-getting devices, and you have to develop an eye and an ear to distinguish when your child's question is based on curiosity or the need for a little love. If you're not sure about the answer, one way to find out is to smile and ask, "Do you really want to know or do you want some love?" The answer may be both.

Making the "Terrible" Two's Terrific

The extraordinary energy of a two-year-old may mean participating in more physical games—playing catch or soccer, for example. Two-year-olds need more running, jumping, dancing, and more excursions and adventures to dissipate their enormous supplies of physical and intellectual energy.

Many two-year-olds begin to enjoy certain kinds of puzzles, which are great ways to settle a child down for a little while and give yourself a breather. (Parents who are out of breath and near distraction at times might imagine what it must be like handling twenty or thirty children—then keep that picture in mind when they consider preschools and kindergartens and talk to teachers.)

From two years to thirty months, a child's physical skills and dexterity will continue improving. Intellectual skills will mature dramatically. Physically, your child will begin jumping nicely, kicking a ball, walking up and down stairs, and turning pages of a book comfortably, one at a time.

Intellectually, a thirty-month-old child will easily name objects pictured in books, along with colors, relative size (bigger than, smaller than, etc.), and some single-digit numbers. Counting may still be a bit of a mess, but the child will certainly be experimenting with complete sentences and thoughts, using many new words, understanding suggestions, and remaining focused on single activities for longer periods.

The child will also become a real talker—a conversationalist—and begin telling stories. Most will be tales from his or her imagination, but wonderful nonetheless, with colors, plurals, clearly pronounced consonant sounds, and a real sense of language.

At mealtime, a healthy thirty-month-old will ask questions and participate in conversations. It's important not to dismiss these efforts or let other family members do so. The window of learning opportunity is open wider than it will ever be again, and you must take full advantage of the opportunity. A child of this age should join in the family conversation, ask questions, and express opinions as if it were the last chance to do so. It may well be.

Remember: interpersonal communication is a practiced skill that develops into a habit. Like any broken habit, once a parent and child stop talking, they may never start again.

Making It Fun to Read

Parents should step up their reading activities, using many different books and magazines, pointing out various objects, and letting the child point them out and tell stories about them.

Provide your child with a library of bedtime stories, along with a variety of coloring books, art paper, paints, crayons, clay, and other materials with which the child can create. Work with your child, helping match the right colors to the appropriate objects in coloring books—green to trees, for example, and so on.

A healthy child in a language-rich home is ready to learn the alphabet and to read two- and three-letter words. Beware of converting the process into a boring, classroom routine. Teaching letters and words should be done in conjunction with an illustrated story your child obviously enjoys. There are many colorful books that portray *a* for *apple, b* for *boy,* and *c* for *cat* in entertaining ways.

After asking your child to point out a cat in a picture, you might name the letters in *cat* and ask your child to pick out and name each letter—and perhaps spell *cat,* if your child seems interested. Stop the minute you see a sign of disinterest, and get back to reading the story. Teaching should be secondary to reading and enjoying the story.

At every step, try to make it fun to learn new words by playing with rhymes and songs. Labeling objects throughout the house with big signs can also be an amusing way to expand a child's vocabulary. This is a technique you can continue to use well into the late childhood years. Use all the big printed words on packaged products, along with large signs on stores and restaurants, to help your child recognize words and letters. Singing the alphabet song is also fun and instructive.

Building Alphabet Skills

Depending on your child's interest and aptitude, it's perfectly appropriate to expand from the alphabet to a syllabarium and first speller, using only those books with truly fine illustrations or stories that will capture your child's interest and imagination.

Avoid getting trapped by the idiotic phonics–whole-language debate that is eroding the quality of reading and writing instruction in public elementary schools. Television advertisements are tempting parents across America to get *Hooked on Phonics* and other instant education packages. They are inappropriate for most children and can actually turn off an otherwise bright child's interest in learning.

Most children do not learn to read by one method; they learn by all methods, leaning more to one than another according to their individual learning differences.

Long before learning to read from books, the average child intuitively uses the whole-word method to recognize such words as *pizza*, *Eggo*, *corn flakes*, and other words that appear in big, bold letters on packages or roadside signs. At that point, the child knows nothing about the alphabet, let alone phonics and the sounding out of letters and syllables.

When children are developmentally ready to read and sound out the alphabet and letter combinations, they will combine that skill with the whole-word method and use them simultaneously to learn to read, spell, and write. They will use more or less of each method according to their genetic predisposition, previous learning experiences, and what proves to be the easiest, most efficient method for them.

Forcing a child to use one method exclusively will inevitably slow the learning process. So it's unwise for you to get hooked on phonics or any other teaching method. The right method is any and every approach that works for your child.

A multisensory approach is usually most effective in helping beginners learn the alphabet, and in turn, to read and write. By tracing each letter with a finger, while seeing, saying, and hearing the letter, a child actually feels each new letter of the alphabet and each new word.

Magnetic letters are fun and allow a child to create words on the refrigerator door. There are a variety of spelling kits parents can make or buy, including sand and sandpaper letters, felt stick-on letters, and sewing cards with which a child can use a big plastic sewing needle (unpointed) to thread holes that dot the outlines of individual letters.

It's not a good idea to dwell too long on spelling when reading a story to a child, however. Doing so risks making both the alphabet and the story slow and boring. After spelling one word, perhaps it's best to return to the story and make spelling and reading incidental to storytelling—until the day the child insists on reading you the story! As your child begins to memorize stories or nursery rhymes, a nice game is to pick out key mystery words he or she must point to and read aloud each time you stop reading. For example, in "Pop goes the Weasel," you would stop at the word *pop* and your child would read the word aloud.

Laying the Groundwork for School

As a child approaches thirty months, the time will come to explain the wonderful things there are to learn at school and what school is all about. Most children's bookshops carry illustrated storybooks to help explain such new concepts as school and make them interesting and exciting.

By thirty months, many a child is already telling its parents simple stories, identifying colors and textures, using language skills such as plurals, pronouncing consonants and word sounds clearly, asking questions, and conversing logically and rationally.

This is a particularly good time to let children begin to dictate original stories and books. You can write each word in big, bold letters and even produce outlines of illustrations your child can color. Although true reading won't begin then, your child will acquire word-recognition skills and soon memorize entire stories, reciting along, word by word.

The depth of your child's interests, learning differences, and conversational style should serve as a guide for selecting subjects to discuss and teach. Some books always prove less successful than others, but there is no such thing as buying too many books. It's far better to have too many than too few. You can always donate the excess to worthy children's organizations. Regardless of your child's age, it's always best to buy rather than borrow books, so they have not been marked by other children and are as up to date as possible. A new book allows you and your child to trace key words in colors—and lay the foundation for learning note-taking skills.

As parents begin teaching more complex concepts, children begin to demonstrate clearly their learning differences and aptitudes. It's important not to push a young child to try to learn what he or she either cannot learn or isn't interested in learning, if it is not a critical skill. The way to reinforce a child's interest in learning is to help build the child's strengths rather than focusing on its weaknesses.

Take your child as frequently as possible on visits to parks, gardens, zoos, and appropriate museums to learn the names of trees, flowers, plants, birds, and animals. Again, most children will at times produce a stream of endless questions, some of which seem silly. Some will obviously be simple attention-getting babble, while others will be born of curiosity.

The job of the parent-teacher is to provide the appropriate answers for a child's every question, without discouraging the child from asking questions and seeking answers. Sometimes the answer to an attention-getting question is nothing more than a big hug and expression of love. But whatever your child asks deserves a simple, honest, and direct answer.

From two-and-a-half to three years old, you'll see your child evolve into a boy or girl, copying simple shapes, brushing his or her teeth, and developing many complex physical and manual skills. Your child will know his or her first and last name without thinking, repeat nursery rhymes easily and sing many songs comfortably from beginning to end. This is an ideal time to teach your child his or her address and telephone number. A rhyming song makes it more fun and easier to remember such otherwise dry facts.

Counting skills will improve and reach into the low double digits, and your child should become completely comfortable with such concepts of comparison as *bigger than, smaller than,* and so on. A child's understanding of number concepts is ready to expand to simple addition and subtraction and the concepts of *whole, part, half* and *quarter.* Use numbers as much as possible in conjunction with normal everyday activities such as dressing, cooking, and shopping. Colored manipulatives can improve your child's counting and calculating skills.

As a child approaches three, parents should expand all previous teaching activities at home and away from home with more complex painting, coloring, puzzles, model construction, doll houses, dolls for dressing and feeding, storytelling, reading, and trips to parks, playgrounds, zoos, and museums. In addition to reading to your child, encourage your child to create original stories using pictures as a triggering mechanism. "What do you think the little girl is doing?" "Where is the boy going?"

Learning by Role-Playing

A wonderful teaching technique to introduce at this age is the use of stories with settings and circumstances that are not dissimilar to those of the child and its family.

The "Winnie the Pooh" stories come to mind immediately. The British author A. A. Milne wrote them for his little boy Christopher, who is a central character in each tale. In one, Christopher, like many boys his age, is extremely sad about having to begin school and end his summer-vacation adventures with Pooh-bear and his other animal-doll friends.

Although there are many stories of this type in famous books, parents can make up their own. They can be enormous fun. It is comforting to children—to all of us at any age—to know there are others with the same feelings, hurts, joys, expectations, and disappointments—even if they are fictional characters in a story.

The nice thing about using dolls or puppets is that they give a child a chance to use his or her close "friends" in original stories. Not only do they encourage a child's creativity, but they allow the child to express many feelings that might otherwise remain suppressed. It's essential to listen very carefully without interrupting to every story a child creates, making every effort to understand. Children often tell their parents far more than a fairy tale in the tales they invent.

One type of learning equipment that's absolutely essential and wonderful is the miniature model—the doll's house with furnishings, the log-house building kit, the garage with cars and trucks, the play kitchen, and so on. Considerable care has to be used in selecting the size of the models and their parts. As wonderful as they are for combining play and learning, there is always a risk of injury from certain types of toys and the danger that a child might swallow a part.

Learning Academic Skills

By three, many children are copying and writing capital letters and whole words and may be practicing a form of rudimentary reading of simple stories based on word-recognition skills. Many three-year-olds can count accurately to twenty or higher. Different children acquire these skills at different ages, however. For the child who is ready, there are now a host of wonderful computers—*Talking Teacher*, *Kids Laptop*, *Talking Tutor*, and so on—that serve as fantastically effective tools for teaching youngsters to read, write, and calculate, and create imaginative texts, designs, and pictures. Most have encouraging voices, music, and animation that make learning such exciting fun that children often have trouble getting the computer away from their parents. Oversized, color-coded keys make them easy for small fingers to manipulate and understand.

Books with accompanying taped texts are also effective teaching tools. Parents can and should tape the texts of many stories to allow their child to read alone, accompanied by the comfortable sound of its parent's voice. That's a far more wholesome independent activity than watching television.

It's quite normal for children to want to reread the same story over and over. Even though you may be bored, such rereading not only makes your child feel secure, it also serves as an incredibly practical way to increase reading speed.

Talking Constantly

At this age, your child will be talking constantly, telling real and imaginary experiences, making up stories, and endlessly asking "Why?" "Where is . . . ?" and "What's a . . . ?" Hand skills and manual dexterity have matured to the point where your child can draw circles, squares, recognizable stick figures, and outlines of houses and cars. Your child will also be able to cut out pictures and other forms from magazines and newspapers—and play a wider variety of games, including guessing games such as charades, riddles, and hide-and-seek. Let your children select the games you play together. It's a good risk-free exercise in decision-making.

It's also time to expand the variety of excursions to include adult museums—especially museums of natural history, planetaria, libraries, restored colonial villages, farm museums, and dramatic historical sites such as the Statue of Liberty. Each trip should be a chance to teach your child to read maps and navigate as well as learn history and the natural wonders of botany, astronomy, and other sciences.

Like every child with new skills, talkative three-year-olds may stumble over a lot of words, stutter, or occasionally begin a story or sentence and lose the way. Never forget that your youngster is a child, not a small adult, and that your function as a parent-teacher is to remain patient and interested. Listen intently so you can help your child begin again if he or she loses the way. Stutters, slurs, and mispronunciations will tend to disappear.

Encouraging children's curiosity is the key to learning skills. Try to answer every question and look up answers you don't know in home or library reference works, even calling an appropriate authority when necessary. The search for answers to a child's questions at the library can and should be an exciting adventure in learning for both parent and child.

Developing Imagination and Creativity

The development of language skills is one of the essential building blocks to the development of abstract thought, which most children first exhibit in the form of nonstop questions. The leap into abstract thinking begins the first time a child says "What if . . . ?" instead of simply "Why?" or "What's a . . . ?"

The window of learning opportunity for abstract thinking skills, which are the basis of creativity and imagination, open wide during a child's third year, from twenty-four to thirty-six months, and it's incumbent for parents to encourage those skills. Abstractions are simply ideas conceived in the imagination and converted into visible, concrete form by individual creativity. As with every other skill, now is the time for parents to teach their child. The child may never have a chance to learn the same skill as well again.

There are endless materials to encourage your child's creativity. Chalk, crayons, finger and brush paints, clay, charcoal, pencils, pens, markers, paper maché, scissors and paper, paper and paste, foods for cooking—the list is endless.

It's foolish to worry about the mess. Just learn to live with it, cleaning up as best you can and encouraging your child to help. All parents can and probably should limit practice of the creative arts to a specific space where you can make clean-up easier and protect the walls and floor. Be sure to provide adequate shelving for the child's things.

Learning to Create

Aside from providing a wealth of materials, parents can encourage their child's imagination and creativity by taking advantage of the normal instinct to imitate and copy.

It doesn't make any difference at this age whether a child draws, sculpts, colors, or shapes cookies the way Mom or Dad thinks is right. At two to three years old, there is no right way. A child has only this one chance to learn to love—or to hate—creating, and that will depend on its parents.

The key to learning creativity is to try to create. A three-year-old does not have to do it well. Success lies in the effort, not the finished product.

By all means show your child how to use creative materials—how to hold a crayon, draw a circle, use a cookie cutter, and so on—and how to create with those instruments. Then give your child complete freedom to create with the materials you've provided.

If your child asks for help, provide it, but limit it to the specific assistance your child asks for and just enough to get started on the next step without anymore help.

The good parent-teacher gives her or his child the tools of creativity but does not take over the creative process. Individual creativity exalts the differences that make each child unique. Parents must try to do the same by letting their child "step to the music which he [or she] hears," rather than the music the parents hear.

Withholding Judgments

It is unimportant whether a child abandons or finishes the project. Each child is simply not going to enjoy every project, anymore than you or I enjoy all forms of art. When a child has finished and gives you the finished work, you should praise your child for having finished the work but be extremely careful about expressing any value judgments. At two or three, a child should not have to compare his or her creative skills to norms established by the world outside the confines of the playroom.

Parents should avoid being critics or suggesting corrections. To do so is to discourage their child's creativity—and differentness. Negative criticism disguised in the form of helpful suggestions automatically sets up an unnecessary learning impediment that can last a lifetime.

Before responding to a work of art, look into your child's eyes and ask how your child feels about it—then reflect those feelings in your own response. It's just as important not to go overboard with inappropriately effusive praise for an ordinary stick drawing as it is to criticize it. Inappropriate criticism or praise discourages effort and retards intellectual development and the development of values and judgment. Why bother learning or improving if every smear on a piece of paper or noise on the piano wins a Nobel Prize?

By now most children know what a good drawing looks like. They've seen them in picture books and can decide whether their own work is good or bad. In the end, whether a child's—or indeed any artist's—work is good or bad only depends on the child's judgment.

Encouraging Creativity

Regardless of age, when your child believes the work he or she has created is awful, it is not helpful to disagree and say it's wonderful. Of course, it's not helpful to agree either. In terms of supporting your child and his or her learning experience, the best thing is to withhold all judgments. The primary roll of the parent-teacher is to encourage creativity, not necessarily artistic skill. Unless you're an artist yourself, you probably cannot teach art anyway. But you can teach the love of trying to create something all your own in your own way.

When your child is happy with a drawing, share the happiness and display the work, either in your child's room or in a family area where others can see it. Collecting a child's best works in a portfolio the family can share is also a way of encouraging a child's creativity without covering every wall of the house with the child's pictures.

And when your child is unhappy with a painting, it's well to empathize instead of paying undeserved, insincere compliments. A child knows whether he or she has done a good job. A good teacher explains that no one is ever happy with everything one does but that it's important to learn from failures and to try again. You, too, should express sincere hopes that your child will continue to try to create. One good tack is to ask what he or she doesn't like about the creation. "What do you think is the best part?" and "What's your favorite part?"

Don't force yourself into the creative process unless your child asks for some specific help and you have specific skills to contribute. It's best to determine what your child wants and needs specifically to further his or her imagination and creative skills. Then limit your help to the minimum required to get your child restarted.

Getting Ready for Preschool

As a child approaches preschool age, parents should expand the teaching activities of earlier years, elevating them to levels appropriate for a three- to four-year-old—regardless of whether or not the child is actually attending preschool. It's also wise to expand decision-making skills by letting your child choose excursions on the basis of personal interest and aptitude.

By now, your child should have acquired the ability to think in abstract terms, and you can begin telling your child about appropriate events in the outside world—a world your child has already visited on excursions with you. These current events can vary from the neighbor's new cat, Aunt Nelly's move to a new house, or the president of the United States visiting your city.

The extension of your child's education to events in the outside world is significant in that it marks the end of formal infant education. From this point, parents gradually cede many of their educational responsibilities to schools, to the child's peer groups, and ultimately to the child. If they've done a good job of infant education, the child will thrive at school and eventually take full control of his or her own education.

Summary

Infant education is the most important segment of any individual's overall education—far more important than elementary, high-school or college education. Infant education teaches the basic language and calculation skills that permit children and adults to acquire all other knowledge. Without those skills, learning in school becomes difficult at best, and often impossible. Here are the milestones of normal intellectual development around which a parent should construct a carefully planned program of infant education:

- *Birth to six months.* Crying evolves into cooing, gurgling, and babbling, with pronounced vowel sounds.

- *Six to twelve months.* Baby understands first words, including own name, *mommy, daddy,* and names of key caregivers, some body parts, meaning of *no;* says first words, voice rises and falls, imitates word sounds.

- *Twelve to eighteen months.* Baby follows simple commands and points to familiar persons, animals, toys, and objects; can say first verbs and use at least three words to express a thought; can point to things it wants.

- *Eighteen to twenty-four months.* Linguistic ability expands to sentences of at least six words; responds to simple commands; comfortably expresses most basic needs in words;

uses pronouns such as *you* and *me*; speaking vocabulary expands to about 200 words, comprehension vocabulary to twice that number or more; uses plurals comfortably; knows own full name; knows most key body parts; can point to and name common objects.

- *Two to three years.* Vocabulary expands in explosive proportions to at least 800 words and perhaps 1,000 or more; understands concepts of descriptive adjectives such as *big, little, soft, loud,* etc.; enunciation clearly distinguishes vowels and consonants and is 75 percent to 80 percent understandable to a stranger; child can tell simple stories, relate own experiences, describe people and objects by variety of qualities such as colors, texture, size, and so on; child asks questions, participates comfortably in conversations.

- *Three to four years.* Vocabulary doubles; child uses three- and four-syllable words in six- to eight-word sentences; speech now clearly intelligible to strangers; concepts expand to include basics of reading, writing, calculating; sentences become longer, more complex, questions more abstract.

- *Four to five years* (before beginning kindergarten). Vocabulary doubles; able to cite age, birthday, and address; about 70 percent of girls and 56 percent of boys can write their first names; some can recite and write numerals to 20 (usually with some errors); knows left from right; expresses opinions, discusses family, pets, toys, uses conjunctions, and forms complex sentences; can comfortably recite poems and sing songs from memory; can match like objects and letters; reproduces patterns with blocks and simple shapes with pencil and paper; can recall and repeat series of numbers and follow a series of directions from memory (touch the top of your head, open and shut the door, return to your seat, and sit down).

Appendix A

Child-Care Options

American Council of Nanny Schools, Delta College, University Center, MI 48710. Tel: 517-686-9417. Association of fourteen schools that operate training programs, establish standards, and conduct competency tests for nannies.

American Nanny Agency Ratings Service, 220 West 19th Street, New York, NY 10011. Tel: 212-886-1840. Provides listing of nanny agencies and guide to hiring nannies in any area of the United States ($50 fee).

International Nanny Association, 125 S. 4th Street, Norfolk, NE 68701. Tel: 402-691-9628. Lists affiliated local nanny agencies.

National Academy of Nannies, Inc., 1681 S. Dayton Street, Denver, CO 80231. Tel: 303-333-6264. Private training school for nannies.

National Association for Childcare Resource and Referral Agencies. Tel: 507-287-2220. Group of three hundred local agencies that each provide further referrals at the local level.

National Association for Family Child Care. Tel: 800-359-3817. Accrediting agency for child-care organizations.

National Association for the Education of Young Children, 1509 16th Street NW, Washington, DC 20036. Tel: 800-424-2460. Study group with information on childcare options.

The Parent's League of New York, 115 East 82nd Street, New York, NY 10028. Tel: 212-737-7385. Provides listings of experienced caregivers and nursery schools.

Appendix B

School Accrediting Associations

Connecticut Association of Independent Schools, P.O. Box 159, Mystic, CT 06355. Tel: 860-729-6762. Private schools in Connecticut.

Middle States Association of Colleges and Schools, 3624 Market Street, Philadelphia, PA 19104. Tel: 215-662-5600. Public and private schools in New York, New Jersey, Pennsylvania, Delaware, Maryland, and the District of Columbia.

National Association of Independent Schools, 75 Federal Street, Boston, MA 02110. Tel: 617-451-2444. Private schools in North America and some foreign countries.

National Association of Private Schools for Exceptional Children, 1522 K Street NW, Washington, DC 20005. Tel: 202-408-3338. Private schools and programs for children with learning disabilities.

New England Association of Schools and Colleges, 15 High Street, Winchester, MA 01890. Tel: 617-729-6762. Public and private schools in Maine, New Hampshire, Vermont, Massachusetts, Rhode Island, and Connecticut.

North Central Association of Colleges and Schools, 15440 30th Street, Boulder, CO 80306. Tel: 800-525-9517. Public and private schools in North Dakota, South Dakota, Minnesota, Wisconsin, Michigan, Ohio, West Virginia, Indiana, Illinois, Iowa, Nebraska, Wyoming, Colorado, Kansas, Missouri, Arkansas, Oklahoma, New Mexico, and Arizona.

Northwest Association of Schools and Colleges, Education Building No. 528, Boise State University, Boise, ID 83725. Tel: 208-385-1596. Public and private schools in Alaska, Washington, Oregon, Idaho, Montana, Nevada, and Utah.

Southern Association of Colleges and Schools, 1866 Southern Lane, Decatur, GA 30033. Tel: 404-329-6500. Public and private schools in Kentucky, Virginia, Tennessee, North Carolina, South Carolina, Georgia, Florida, Alabama, Mississippi, Louisiana, and Texas.

Western Association of Schools and Colleges, 1606 Rollins Road, Burlingame, CA 94010. Tel: 415-697-7711. Public and private schools in California, Hawaii, Guam, and American Samoa.

Appendix C

Education Service Associations

American Association for Gifted Children, c/o Talent Identification Programs, Duke University, 1121 W. Main Street, Suite 100, Durham, NC 27701. Tel: 919-683-1400. Information on teaching and working with the gifted for parents, educators, others.

American Montessori Society, 150 Fifth Avenue, New York, NY 10011. Tel: 212-924-3209. Provides information about Montessori education and approved schools.

Association for Gifted and Talented Students, Northwestern State University, Natchitoches, LA 71497. Tel: 318-357-4572. Works with schools and parents to develop and implement extracurricular programs for gifted and talented students.

Association for the Gifted. See Council for Exceptional Children.

Children and Adults with Attention Deficit Disorder (CHADD), 499 NW 70th Avenue, Plantation, FL 33317. Tel: 800-233-4050. Provides information, conferences, support groups.

Council for Exceptional Children, Division for Learning Disabilities, 1920 Association Drive, Reston, VA 22091. Tel: 800-328-0272. Conducts, gathers, and distributes research relating to learning disabilities and giftedness for parents, teachers, and school administrators and professionals.

Independent Educational Counselors Association, 38 Cove Road, Forestdale, MA 02644. Tel: 508-477-2127. Professional association of counselors who aid in selection of appropriate schools.

Learning Disabilities Association of America, 4156 Library Road, Pittsburgh, PA 15234. Tel: 412-341-1515. Provides information, resources, and referrals to affiliated groups and serves as an advocate for individuals with learning disabilities, their families, and professionals.

National Association for Gifted Children, 1707 L Street NW, Washington, DC 20036. Tel: 202-785-4268. Offers guides to education and schools for gifted students.

National Association of Independent Schools, 1620 L Street NW, Washington, DC 20036. Tel: 202-973-9700. Accredits and provides listing of private schools.

National Association of Private Schools for Exceptional Children, 1522 K Street NW, Washington, DC 20005. Tel: 202-408-3338. Accredits schools and programs for children with learning disabilities; provides directory and referral service.

National Center for Learning Disabilities, 381 Park Avenue South, Suite 1420, New York, NY 10016. Tel: 212-545-7510. Provides information, referrals, and educational programs to benefit people with learning disabilities, their families, educators, and other helping professionals. Call for free lists in your state (or neighboring states) of schools specializing in teaching children with learning disabilities. Also conducts public educational and advocacy campaigns.

Orton Dyslexia Society, 8600 LaSalle Road, Chester Building, Suite 382, Baltimore, MD 21286-2044. Tel: 410-296-0232. Messages: 800-ABCD123. International, scientific, and educational organization dedicated to the study and treatment of dyslexia. Helps individuals with dyslexia, their families, teachers, and physicians by providing information, referrals, and educational programs.

Parents' Educational Resource Center, 1660 South Amphlett Boulevard, Suite 200, San Mateo, CA 94402-2508. Tel: 415-655-2410. Provides information and guidance for parents of children with learning differences.

Parent Training and Information Project, Federation for Children with Special Needs, 95 Berkeley Street, Boston, MA 02116. Tel: 617-482-2915. Federally funded program that provides local resources and advocacy training for parents taking legal action to force their school districts to provide special-education facilities.

Program for the Education of the Gifted and Talented, U.S. Department of Education, Washington, DC 20208. Tel: 202-645-3200. Provides listings of public schools with programs for the gifted and talented and information for helping schools and school districts establish such programs.

School and Student Service for Financial Aid, P.O. Box 6657, Princeton, NJ 08541. Tel: 609-951-1021. Provides information about financial aid to students attending primary and secondary schools.

Secondary School Admission Test Board, Educational Testing Service, P.O. Box 6451, Princeton, NJ 08541. Tel: 609-951-1060. Provides materials for preparing and taking the Secondary School Admission Test and for untimed testing of dyslexic students and learning-disadvantaged students.

Appendix D

A Core Curriculum for Elementary, Middle, and High Schools

(Source: U.S. Department of Education)

Subject	Kindergarten through Grade 3
English	Introduction to reading and writing: phonics, silent and oral reading, basic rules of grammar and spelling, vocabulary, writing and penmanship, elementary composition, and library skills
Social studies	Introduction to history, geography, and civics: significant Americans; explorers; native Americans; American holidays, customs, and symbols; citizenship; and landscape, climate, and map work

Mathematics	Introduction to mathematics: numbers; basic operations; fractions and decimals; rounding; geometric shapes; measurement of length, area, and volume; bar graphs; and estimation and elementary statistics
Science	Introduction to science: plants and animals, the food chain, the solar system, rocks and minerals, weather, magnets, energy and motion, properties of matter, and simple experiments
Foreign language	Optional
Fine arts	Music and visual art: songs, recordings, musical sounds and instruments, painting, craftmaking, and visual effects
Physical education and health	Physical education and health: body control, fitness, sports, games, exercises, sportsmanship, safety, hygiene, nutrition, and drug-prevention education

Subject	*Grades 4 Through 6*
English	Introduction to critical reading: children's literature; independent reading and book reports; more advanced grammar, spelling, and vocabulary; and composition skills
Social studies	Grade 4: U.S. history to Civil War Grade 5: U.S. history since 1865 Grade 6: world history to the Middle Ages

Mathematics	Intermediate arithmetic and geometry: number theory, negative numbers, percentages, exponents, line graphs, the Pythagorean theorem, and basic probability
Foreign language	Introduction to foreign language: basic vocabulary, grammar, reading, writing, conversation, and cultural material
Fine arts	Music and visual art: great composers, musical styles and forms, elementary music theory, great painters, interpretation of art, and creative projects
Physical education and health	Physical education and health: team and individual sports, first aid, drug-prevention education, and appropriate sex education
Subject	*Grades 7 and 8*
English	Grade 7: survey of elementary grammar and composition Grade 8: survey of elementary literary analysis
Social studies	Grade 7: world history from Middle Ages to 1900 Grade 8: world geography and Asian history and civilization
Mathematics	Grade 7: pre-algebra Grade 8: algebra
Science	Grade 7: biology Grade 8: chemistry and physics

Foreign language	Introduction to foreign language: vocabulary, grammar, reading, writing, conversation, and cultural material
Fine arts	Music appreciation and art appreciation (one semester of each): history and development of music and art, analysis of style
Physical education and health	Physical education and health: strategy in team sports, gymnastics, aerobics, self-assessment for health, drug-prevention education, and appropriate sex education
Subject	***High School: Grades 9 Through 12***
English	Grade 9: grammar and composition, literary analysis Grade 10: grammar and composition, English literature Grade 11: composition, literary analysis, English or American literature Grade 12: advanced composition, world literature
Social studies	Grade 9: anthropology, ancient history Grade 10: history—ancient, medieval, or modern European Grade 11: American history, American government, the Constitution Grade 12: electives

Mathematics	Grades 9, 10, 11: three years required from among algebra I, plane and solid geometry, algebra II and trigonometry, statistics and probability (one semester), precalculus (one semester), and calculus
Science	Grades 9, 10, 11: three years required from among astronomy or geology, biology, chemistry, physics, and principles of technology
Foreign language	Grades 9, 10, 11: three years required in a single language
Fine arts	Grade 9: art history or music history Grade 10: art history or music history (depending on previous year's study)
Physical education and health	Grades 9 and 10: two years required

Appendix E

Directory of North American Private Schools for Children with Learning Impediments

Note: Schools are listed alphabetically in each category by state. Each listing includes city; whether the school is coed; day, boarding, or both; and the grade or age range of students. Combined day-boarding schools usually offer boarding facilities only for students of junior-high or high-school age. PG refers to post-graduate year for students who have completed high school and require additional or more advanced courses to qualify for college. Canadian schools are listed at the end of each directory.

Inclusion of a school in this directory does not represent an endorsement of that school by either the author or the publisher. It is the full responsibility of parents to evaluate the quality and suitability of a school for their children.

Remedial Education

State-by-state directory of schools with remedial reading and writing or mathematics programs. Schools that limit programs to remedial reading or math are grouped separately at the end of each state list.

Alabama

Marion Military Institute, Marion. Tel: 800-664-1842. Coed, day or boarding, 9–12.

St. Paul's Episcopal School, Mobile. Tel: 205-342-6700. Coed, day, preschool–12

UMS-Wright Preparatory School, Mobile. Tel: 334-479-9039. Coed, day, preschool–12

Remedial Reading or Writing Only

Lyman Ward Military Academy, Camp Hill. Tel: 205-896-4127. Boys, boarding, 6–12.

Arizona

The Fenster School of Southern Arizona, Tucson. Tel: 602-749-3340. Coed, day or boarding, 9–12.

The Judson School, Paradise Valley. Tel: 602-948-7731. Coed, day or boarding, K–PG.

Oak Creek Ranch School, West Sedona. Tel: 520-634-5571. Coed, boarding, 6–PG.

Salpointe Catholic High School, Tucson. Tel: 520-327-6581. Coed, day, 9–12.

Arkansas

Mount St. Mary Academy, Little Rock. Tel: 501-664-8006. Girls, day, 9–12.

California

Alemany High School, Mission Hills. Tel: 818-361-9714. Coed, day, 9–12.

Bishop Mora Salesian High School, Los Angeles. Tel: 213-261-7124. Boys, day, 9–12.

CEDU School, Running Springs. Tel: 800-884-2338. Coed, boarding, ungraded, ages 12–18.

Central Catholic High School, Modesto. Tel: 209-524-9611. Coed, day, 9–12.

Fresno Adventist Academy, Fresno. Tel: 209-251-5548. Coed, day, K–12.

Golden Gate Academy, Oakland. Tel: 510-531-0111. Coed, day, 1–12.

The Hebrew Academy, Westminster. Tel: 714-898-0633. Coed, day, preschool–12.

Landmark West, Encino, Tel: 818-986-5045. Coed, day, ungraded, ages 8–18.

Le Lycee Francais de Los Angeles, Los Angeles. Tel: 212-369-1400. Coed, day, K–12.

Ojai Valley School, Ojai. Tel: 805-646-1423. Coed, day or boarding, preschool–12.

Palma High School, Salinas. Tel: 408-422-6391. Boys, day, 7–12.

Rio Hondo Preparatory School, Arcadia. Tel: 818-444-9531. Coed, day, 4–12.

St. Augustine High School, San Diego. Tel: 619-282-2184. Boys, day, 9–12.

Squaw Valley Academy, Olympic Valley. Tel: 916-583-1558. Coed, day or boarding, 9–12.

Sterne School, San Francisco. Tel: 415-922-6081. Coed, day, 6–12.

University of San Diego High School, San Diego. Tel: 619-298-8277. Coed, day, 9–12.

Valley Christian High School, San Jose. Tel: 408-978-9955. Coed, day, K–12.

Remedial Reading or Writing Only

Sacramento Waldorf School, Fair Oaks. Tel: 916-961-3903. Coed, day, K–12.

Whittier Christian High School. Tel: 310-694-3803. Coed, day, 9–12.

Remedial Math Only

Don Bosco High School, Rosemead. Tel: 818-307-6514. Boys, day, 9–12.

Fairbanks Country Day, Rancho Santa Fe. Tel: 619-756-0500. Coed, day, preschool–12.

Newbridge School, Santa Monica. Tel: 310-315-3056. Coed, day, K–12.

Robert Louis Stevenson School, Pebble Beach. Tel: 408-624-5309. Coed, day or boarding, preschool–12.

Colorado

Accelerated Schools–Randell Moore Center, Denver. Tel: 303-758-2003. Coed, day or boarding, K–PG.

Crested Butte Academy, Crested Butte. Tel: 970-349-1805. Coed, day or boarding, 9–PG.

Denver Christian Schools, Denver. Tel: 303-733-2421. Coed, day, preschool–12.

Eagle Rock School, Estes Park. Tel: 970-586-0600. Coed, boarding, ungraded, ages 15–18.

Connecticut

Eagle Hill–Greenwich, Greenwich. Tel: 203-622-9240. Coed, day or boarding, ungraded, 6–16.

Eagle Hill–Southport, Southport. Tel: 203-254-2044. Coed, day, ungraded, ages 6–18.

Grove School, Madison. Tel: 203-245-2778. Coed, day or boarding, 7–12.

King & Low–Heywood Thomas School, Stamford. Tel: 203-461-9988. Coed, day, preschool–12.

The Marvelwood School, Kent. Tel: 860-927-0047. Coed, day or boarding, 9–12.

The Master's School, West Simsbury. Tel: 203-651-9361. Coed, day, 1–12.

Mercy High School, Middletown. Tel: 860-346-6659. Girls, day, 9–12.

Milford Academy, Milford. Tel: 203-878-5921. Coed, day or boarding, 9–PG.

The Oxford Academy, Westbrook. Tel: 860-399-6247. Boys, boarding, ungraded, ages 14–20.

The Rectory School, Pomfret. Tel: 860-928-1328. Coed-day, boys-boarding, 5–9.

Saint Thomas More School, Oakdale. Tel: 203-859-1900. Boys, boarding, 8–PG.

Trinity Catholic High School, Stamford. Tel: 203-322-3401. Coed, day, 9–12.

Watkinson School, Hartford. Tel: 203-236-5618. Coed, day, 6–PG.

The Woodhall School, Bethlehem. Tel: 203-266-7788. Boys, day or boarding, 8–PG.

Remedial Reading or Writing Only

Rumsey Hall School, Washington Depot. Tel: 860-868-0535. Coed, day or boarding, 3–9.

Remedial Math Only

Sacred Heart Academy, Stamford. Tel: 203-323-3173. Girls, day, 9–12.

Delaware

Salesianum School, Wilmington. Tel: 302-654-2495. Boys, day, 9–12

Remedial Math Only

Padua Academy, Wilmington. Tel: 302-421-3779. Girls, day, 9–12.

District of Columbia

The Lab School of Washington. Tel: 202-965-6600. Coed, day, 7–12.
Parkmont School. Tel: 202-726-0740. Coed, day, 6–12.
Washington Ethical High School. Tel: 202-829-0088. Coed, day, 9–PG.

Remedial Math Only

Edmund Burke School. Tel: 202-362-8882. Coed, day, 6–12.
The Field School. Tel: 202-232-0733. Coed, day, 7–12.

Florida

Chaminade–Madonna College Preparatory, Hollywood. Tel: 305-989-5150. Coed, day, 9–12.

Crossroads School, Fort Lauderdale. Tel: 407-584-1100.
  Coed-day, boys-boarding, K–12.
Florida Air Academy, Melbourne. Tel: 407-723-3211. Boys,
  day or boarding, 7–PG.
Glades Day School, Belle Glade. Tel: 407-996-6769. Coed,
  day, preschool–12.
Gulliver Preparatory School, Miami. Coed, day,
  preschool–12.
Miami Country Day School, Miami. Tel: 305-759-0155.
  Coed, day, preschool–12.
PACE Private School, Inc., Longwood. Tel: 407-869-8882.
  Coed, day, 9–12.
St. Johns Country Day School, Orange Park. Tel: 904-264-
  9572. Coed, day, preschool–12.
The University School of Nova University, Fort Lauderdale.
  Tel: 945-476-1906. Coed, day, preschool–12.
The Vanguard School, Lake Wales. Tel: 941-676-6091. Coed,
  day or boarding, ungraded, ages 10–20.

Remedial Math Only

Cardinal Mooney High School, Sarasota. Tel: 941-371-4917.
  Coed, day, 9–12.

Georgia

Brandon Hall High School, Atlanta. Tel: 404-394-8177.
  Coed-day, boys-boarding, 4–PG.
Gables Academy, Atlanta. Tel: 404-377-1721. Coed, day or
  boarding, 6–PG.
The Heritage School, Newman. Tel: 770-253-9898. Coed,
  day, preschool–12.
Hidden Lake Academy, Dahlonega. Tel: 800-394-0640. Coed,
  boarding, 8–12.

The Howard School, Atlanta. Tel: 404-642-9644. Coed, day, ungraded, ages 5–18.
Mount Vernon Christian Academy, Atlanta. Tel: 404-256-4057. Coed, day, 8–12.
Tallulah Falls School, Tallulah Falls. Tel: 706-754-3171. Coed, boarding, 6–12.
Woodward Academy, College Park. Tel: 404-765-8262. Coed, day, preschool–12.

Remedial Math Only

Aquinas High School, Augusta. Tel: 706-736-5516. Coed, day, 9–12.
Arlington Christian School, Fairburn. Tel: 770-964-9871. Coed, day, K–12.

Hawaii

Academy of the Pacific, Honolulu. Tel: 808-595-6359. Coed, day, 7–12.
Hawaiian Mission Academy, Honolulu. Tel: 808-536-2207. Coed, day or boarding, 9–12.
Iolani School, Honolulu. Tel: 808-943-1111. Coed, day, K–12.
La Pietra–Hawaii School for Girls, Honolulu. Tel: 808-922-2744. Girls, day, 6–12.
The Parker School, Kamuela. Tel: 808-885-7933. Coed, day, 7–12.
St. Andrew's Priory School for Girls, Honolulu. Tel: 808-532-2418. Girls, day, K–12.

Idaho

Boulder Creek Academy, Bonners Ferry. Tel: 800-858-1933. Day, boarding, 7–12.

Illinois

Archbishop Weber High School, Chicago. Tel: 773-637-7500. Boys, day, 9–12.

Brehm Preparatory School, Carbondale. Tel: 618-457-0371. Coed, day or boarding, 7–PG.

Chicago Junior School, Elgin. Tel: 847-888-7918. Coed, day or boarding, preschool–8.

Gordon Technical High School, Chicago. Tel: 773-539-3600. Boys, day, 9–12.

Governor French Academy, Belleville. Tel: 618-233-7542. Coed, day or boarding, ungraded, ages 5–18.

Ida Crown Jewish Academy, Chicago. Tel: 773-973-1450. Coed, day, 9–12.

Illiana Christian High School, Lansing. Tel: 708-474-0515. Coed, day, 9–12.

Immaculate Heart of Mary High School, Westchester. Tel: 708-562-3115. Girls, day, 9–12.

Keith Country Day School, Rockford. Tel: 815-399-8823. Coed, day, preschool–12.

Latin School of Chicago, Chicago. Tel: 312-573-4630. Coed, day, preschool–12.

Loyola Academy, Wilmette. Tel: 847-256-1100. Girls, day, 9–12.

Montini Catholic High School, Lombard. Tel: 630-627-6930. Coed, day, 9–12.

Notre Dame High School for Boys, Niles. Tel: 847-965-2900. Boys, day, 9–12.

Regina Dominican High School, Wilmette. Tel: 847-256-7660. Girls, day, 9–12.

St. Patrick High School, Chicago. Tel: 773-282-8844. Boys, day, 9–12.

Timothy Christian High School, Elmhurst. Tel: 630-833-7575. Coed, day, K–12.

Walther Lutheran High School, Melrose Park. Tel: 708-344-0404. Coed, day, 9–12.

Remedial Math Only

Saint Mary's Academy, Nauvoo. Tel: 800-742-3997. Girls, boarding, 9–12.

Wheaton Academy, West Chicago. Tel: 630-231-0727 Coed, day, 9–12.

Indiana

La Lumiere School, La Porte. Tel: 219-326-7450. Coed, day or boarding, 9–PG.

Le Mans Academy, Rolling Prairie. Tel: 219-778-2521. Boys, boarding, 5–9.

Kansas

Thomas More Prep–Marian, Hays. Tel: 913-625-6577. Coed, day or boarding, 9–12.

Kentucky

Kentucky Country Day School, Louisville. Tel: 502-423-0440. Coed, day, K–12.

Millersburg Military Institute, Millersburg. Tel: 606-484-3342. Coed-day, boys-boarding, 6–PG.

Oneida Baptist Institute, Oneida. Tel: 606-847-4111. Coed, day or boarding, 6–12.

Shedd Academy, Mayfield. Tel: 502-247-8007. Coed, day or boarding, ungraded, ages 7–19.

Louisiana

St. Augustine High School, New Orleans. Tel: 504-944-2424. Boys, day, 8–12.

Maine

Carrabassett Valley Academy, Carrabassett Valley. Tel: 207-237-2213. Coed, day or boarding, 8–PG.
Elan School, Poland Spring. Tel: 207-998-4666. Coed, boarding, 7–12.
Fryeburg Academy, Fryeburg. Tel: 207-935-2013. Coed, day or boarding, 9–12.
Maine Central Institute, Pittsfield. Tel: 207-487-2282. Coed, day or boarding, 9–12.

Maryland

Archbishop Spalding High School, Severn. Tel: 410-969-9105. Coed, day, 9–12.
The Boys' Latin School of Maryland, Baltimore. Tel: 410-433-2571. Boys, day, K–12.
The Catholic High School of Baltimore, Baltimore. Tel: 410-732-6200. Girls, day, 9–12.
Charles E. Smith Jewish Day School, Rockville. Tel: 301-881-1400. Coed, day, K–12.
Good Counsel High School, Wheaton. Tel: 301-942-1155. Coed, day, 9–12.
John Carroll School, Bel Air. Tel: 410-838-8333. Coed, day, 9–12.
New Dominion School, Oldtown. Tel: 301-478-5721. Boys, boarding, ungraded, ages 11–18.
Thornton Friends School, Silver Spring. Tel: 301-384-0320. Coed, day, 6–PG.

West Nottingham Academy, Colora. Tel: 410-658-5556. Coed, day or boarding, 9–PG.

Remedial Reading or Writing Only

The Gunston School, Centreville. Tel: 800-381-0077. Girls, day or boarding, 9–12.

Institute of Notre Dame, Baltimore. Tel: 410-522-7800. Girls, day, 9–12.

Massachusetts

Bishop Stang High School, North Dartmouth. Tel: 508-996-5602. Coed, day, 9–12.

The Carroll School, Lincoln. Tel: 617-259-8342. Coed, day, 1–12.

Cushing Academy, Ashburnham. Tel: 508-827-7300. Coed, day or boarding, 9–PG.

The DeSisto School, Stockbridge. Tel: 413-298-3776. Coed, boarding, ungraded, ages 13–21.

The Fessenden School, West Newton. Tel: 617-630-2300. Boys, day or boarding, K–9.

Hillside School, Marlboro. Tel: 508-485-2824. Boys, day or boarding, 5–9.

The John Dewey Academy, Great Barrington. Tel: 413-528-9800. Coed, boarding, 10–PG.

Landmark School, Prides Crossing. Tel: 508-927-4440. Coed, day or boarding, ungraded, ages 9–20.

Matignon High School, Cambridge. Tel: 617-491-7972. Coed, day, 9–12.

Milton Academy, Milton. Tel: 617-698-7800. Coed, day or boarding, K–12.

Miss Hall's School, Pittsfield. Tel: 800-233-5614. Girls, day or boarding, 9–12.

Saint Mark's School, Southborough. Tel: 508-485-0050.
Coed, day or boarding, 9–12.
Valley View School, North Brookfield. Tel: 508-867-6505.
Boys, boarding, ungraded, ages 12–17.
Wilbraham & Monson Academy, Wilbraham. Tel: 413-596-
6814. Coed, day or boarding, 7–PG.
Willow Hill School, Sudbury. Tel: 508-443-2581. Coed, day,
ungraded, ages 11–19.
The Winchendon School, Winchendon. Tel: 800-622-1119.
Coed, day or boarding, 8–PG.
Xaverian Brothers High School, Westwood. Tel: 617-326-
6392. Boys, day, 9–12.

Michigan

Eton Academy, Birmingham. Tel: 810-642-1150. Coed, day,
K–PG.

Remedial Reading or Writing Only

The Leelanau School, Glen Arbor. Tel: 616-334-5820. Coed,
day or boarding, 9–PG.

Minnesota

Breck School, Minneapolis. Tel: 612-347-9200. Coed, day,
preschool–12.
Concordia Academy, St. Paul. Tel: 612-484-8429. Coed, day,
9–12.
Cretin-Derham Hall, St. Paul. Tel: 612-690-2443. Coed, day,
9–12.

Remedial Math Only

International School of Minnesota, Eden Prairie. Tel: 612-941-3500. Coed, day, preschool–12.
Lutheran High School of Minneapolis, Bloomington. Tel: 612-854-0224. Coed, day, 9–12.

Mississippi

All Saints' Episcopal School, Vicksburg. Tel: 601-636-5266. Coed, day or boarding, 8–13.
Jackson Academy, Jackson. Tel: 601-362-9677. Coed, day, preschool–12.
The Piney Woods Country Life School, Piney Woods. Tel: 601-845-2214. Coed, day or boarding, preschool–12.
St. Stanislaus College Prep, Bay St. Louis. Tel: 800-517-6257. Boys, day or boarding, 6–12.

Missouri

Kemper Military School and Kemper Girls' Academy. Tel: 816-882-5623. Coed, boarding, 6–12.
The Principia, St. Louis. Tel: 314-434-2100. Coed, day or boarding, preschool–12.
Whitfield School, St. Louis. Tel: 314-434-5141. Coed, day, 7–12.

Remedial Math Only

Missouri Military Academy, Mexico. Tel: 573-581-1776. Boys, boarding, 4–PG.

New Hampshire

Brewster Academy, Wolfeboro. Tel: 603-569-7200. Coed, day or boarding, 9–PG.

Cardigan Mountain School, Canaan. Tel: 603-523-4321. Boys, day or boarding, 6–9.

New Hampton School, New Hampton. Tel: 603-744-5401. Coed, day or boarding, 9–PG.

Tilton School, Tilton. Tel: 603-286-1705. Coed, day or boarding, 9–PG.

White Mountain School, Littleton. Tel: 603-444-0513. Coed, day or boarding, 9–PG.

New Jersey

Blair Academy, Blairstown. Tel: 800-462-5247. Coed, day or boarding, 9–PG.

Community High School, Westwood. Tel: 201-358-6221. Coed, day, 9–PG.

Marylawn of the Oranges, South Orange. Tel: 201-762-9222. Girls, day, 9–12.

Morristown-Beard School, Morristown. Tel: 201-539-3032. Coed, day, 7–12.

Mt. Saint Dominic Academy, Caldwell. Tel: 201-226-0660. Girls, day, 9–12.

Newark Academy, Livingston. Tel: 201-992-7000. Coed, day, 6–12.

The Newgrange School, Trenton. Tel: 609-394-2255. Coed, day, ungraded, ages 8–18.

Saint Dominic Academy, Jersey City. Tel: 201-434-5938. Girls, day, 9–12.

The Wardlaw-Hartridge School, Edison. Tel: 908-754-1882. Coed, day, preschool–12.

Woodcliff Academy, Wall. Tel: 908-751-0240. Coed, day, ungraded, ages 10–21.

Remedial Reading or Writing Only

Saddle River Day School, Saddle River. Tel: 201-327-4050. Coed, day, 4–12.

New York

Academy of St. Joseph, Brentwood. Tel: 516-273-2406. Coed, day, preschool–12.

Adelphi Academy, Brooklyn. Tel: 718-238-3308. Coed, day, preschool–12.

All Hallows High School, Bronx. Tel: 718-293-4545. Boys, day, 9–12.

The Aquinas Institute of Rochester, Rochester. Tel: 716-254-2020. Coed, day, 9–12.

The Beekman School and the Tutoring School Learning Center, New York. Tel: 212-755-6666. Coed, day, 8–PG.

Bishop Ludden High School, Syracuse. Tel: 315-488-3237. Coed, day, 7–12.

Buffalo Academy of the Sacred Heart, Buffalo. Tel: 716-834-2101. Girls, day, 9–12.

Columbia Grammar and Preparatory School, New York. Tel: 212-749-6200. Coed, day, K–12.

The Fieldston School, Riverdale. Tel: 718-543-5000. Coed, day, preschool–12.

Green Meadow Waldorf School, Spring Valley. Tel: 914-356-2556. Coed, day, 1–12.

The Hewitt School, New York. Tel: 212-288-1919. Girls, day, K–12.

Hoosac School, Hoosick. Tel: 800-822-0159. Coed, day or boarding, 8–12.

The Karafin School, Mount Kisco. Tel: 914-666-9211. Coed, day, ungraded, ages 7–21.

Kildonan School, Amenia. Tel: 914-373-8111. Coed, day or boarding, 2–PG.

The Knox School, St. James. Tel: 516-584-5500. Coed, day
or boarding, 7–PG.
La Salle Center, Oakdale. Tel: 516-589-0900. Coed-day,
boys-boarding, preschool–12.
Lycee Francais de New York, New York. Tel: 212-369-1400.
Coed, day, preschool–PG.
Maplebrook School, Amenia. Tel: 914-373-8191. Coed, day or
boarding, ungraded, ages 11–23.
Martin Luther High School, Maspeth. Tel: 718-894-1000.
Coed, day, 9–12.
Nardin Academy, Buffalo. Tel: 716-881-6262. Coed, day,
preschool–12.
New York Military Academy, Cornwall-on-Hudson. Tel: 914-
534-3710. Coed, day or boarding, 5–PG.
Norman Howard School, Rochester. Tel: 716-334-8010.
Coed, day, 4–12.
Old Westbury School of the Holy Child, Old Westbury. Tel:
516-626-9300. Coed, day, preschool–12.
Redemption Christian Academy, Troy. Tel: 518-272-6679.
Coed, day or boarding, K–PG.
Robert Louis Stevenson School, New York. Tel: 212-787-
6400. Coed, day, 7–12.
Salesian High School, New Rochelle. Tel: 914-632-0248.
Boys, day, 9–12.
Winston Preparatory School, New York. Tel: 212-496-8400.
Coed, day, ungraded, ages 12–19.
York Preparatory School, New York. Tel: 212-628-1220.
Coed, day, 6–12.

Remedial Reading or Writing Only

The Ursuline School, New Rochelle. Tel: 914-636-3950.
Girls, day, 6–12.

North Carolina

The Charlotte Country Day School, Charlotte. Tel: 704-366-1241. Coed, day, preschool–12.

Gaston Day School, Gastonia. Tel: 704-864-7744. Coed, day, preschool–12.

Greenfield School, Wilson. Tel: 919-237-8046. Coed, day, preschool–12.

Hill Learning Development Center, Durham Academy, Durham. Tel: 919-489-7464. Coed, day, K–12.

Laurinburg Institute, Laurinburg. Tel: 910-276-0684. Coed, boarding, 9–PG.

The O'Neal School, Southern Pines. Tel: 910-692-6920. Coed, day, preschool–PG.

Remedial Reading or Writing Only

Forsyth Country Day School, Lewisville. Tel: 910-945-3151. Coed, day, preschool–12.

Remedial Math Only

Charlotte Christian School, Charlotte. Tel: 704-366-5657. Coed, day, K–12.

Ohio

Central Christian High School, Kidron. Tel: 216-857-7311. Coed, day, 7–12.

Lake Ridge Academy, North Ridgeville. Tel: 216-777-9434. Coed, day, K–12.

Lutheran High School West, Rocky River. Tel: 216-333-1660. Coed, day, 9–12.

Notre Dame–Cathedral Latin School, Chardon. Tel: 216-286-6226. Coed, day, 9–12.

Olney Friends School, Barnesville. Tel: 614-425-3655. Coed, day or boarding, 9–12.

Regina High School, South Euclid. Tel: 216-382-2110. Girls, day, 9–12.

St. John's Jesuit High School, Toledo. Tel: 419-865-5743. Boys, day, 9–12.

Stephen T. Badin High School, Hamilton. Tel: 513-867-0043. Coed, day, 9–12.

Oklahoma

Heritage Hall, Oklahoma City. Tel: 405-749-3000. Coed, preschool–12.

Oregon

The Catlin Gabel School, Portland. Tel: 503-203-5111. Coed, day, preschool–12.

Mount Bachelor Academy, Prineville. Tel: 800-462-3404. Coed, boarding, 7–12.

St. Mary's School, Medford. Tel: 541-773-7877. Coed, day, 6–12.

Remedial Math Only

Sunriver Preparatory, Sunriver. Tel: 503-593-1244. Coed, day or boarding, preschool–12.

Pennsylvania

Academy of the New Church Boys' School, Bryn Athyn. Tel: 215-947-4200. Boys, day or boarding, 9–12.

Academy of the New Church Girls' School, Bryn Athyn. Tel: 215-947-4200. Girls, day or boarding, 9–12.

Carson Long Military Institute, New Bloomfield. Tel: 717-582-8763. Boys, boarding, 6–12.

Christopher Dock Mennonite High School, Lansdale. Tel: 215-362-2675. Coed, day, 9–12.

The Concept School, Westtown. Tel: 610-399-1135. Coed, day, 2–12.

Germantown Academy, Fort Washington. Tel: 215-643-1331. Coed, day, preschool–12.

Girard College, Philadelphia. Tel: 215-787-2620. Coed, boarding, 1–12.

The Grier School, Tyrone. Tel: 814-684-3000. Girls, boarding, 7–PG.

The Hill Top Preparatory School, Rosemont. Tel: 610-527-3230. Coed, day, ungraded, ages 11–20.

Kimberton Waldorf School, Kimberton. Tel: 610-933-3635. Coed, day, preschool–12.

Lancaster Country Day School, Lancaster. Tel: 717-392-3673. Coed, day, K–12.

Merion Mercy Academy, Merion Station. Tel: 610-664-6655. Girls, day, 9–12.

Milton Hershey School, Hershey. Tel: 800-322-3248. Coed, boarding, K–12.

Moravian Academy, Bethlehem. Tel: 610-691-1600. Coed, day or boarding, preschool–PG.

The Oakland School, Pittsburgh. Tel: 412-621-7878. Coed, day, 9–PG.

The Phelps School, Malvern. Tel: 610-644-1754. Boys, boarding, 7–PG.

The University School, Pittsburgh. Tel: 412-361-7182. Coed, day, 7–PG.

Valley Forge Military Academy, Wayne. Tel: 610-989-1300. Boys, boarding, 7–PG.

Remedial Reading or Writing Only

St. Basil Academy, Philadelphia. Tel: 215-885-3771. Girls,
  day, 9–12.
Solebury School, New Hope. Tel: 215-862-5261. Coed, day
  or boarding, 7–PG.

Puerto Rico

Robinson School, Condado. Tel: 809-728-6767. Coed, day,
  preschool–12.

Rhode Island

La Salle Academy, Providence. Tel: 401-351-7750. Coed, day,
  9–12.
Rocky Hill School, East Greenwich. Tel: 401-884-9070.
  Coed, day, preschool–12.
St. Andrew's School, Barrington. Tel: 401-246-1310. Coed,
  day or boarding, 5–12.

South Carolina

Aiken Preparatory School, Aiken. Tel: 803-648-3223. Coed-
  day, boys-boarding, preschool–9.
Camden Military Academy, Camden. Tel: 803-432-6001.
  Boys, boarding, 7–PG.
Hilton Head Preparatory School, Hilton Head Island. Tel:
  803-671-2286. Coed, day or boarding, 1–PG.
Trident Academy, Mt. Pleasant. Tel: 803-884-7046. Coed,
  day or boarding, 1–12.

Remedial Math Only

Ashley Hall, Charleston. Tel: 803-722-4088. Girls, day, preschool–12.

Tennessee

The Bodine School, Germantown. Tel: 901-754-1800. Coed, day, 9–12.

Brentwood Academy, Brentwood. Tel: 615-373-0611. Coed, day, 7–12.

Collegedale Academy, Collegedale. Tel: 423-396-2124. Coed, day, 9–12.

First Assembly Christian School, Memphis. Tel: 901-458-5543. Coed, day, K–12.

St. Andrew's–Sewanee School, St. Andrews. Tel: 615-598-5651. Coed, day or boarding, 7–12.

Washington College Academy, Washington College. Tel: 615-257-5156. Coed, day or boarding, 7–PG.

Remedial Reading Only

The Webb School of Knoxville, Knoxville. Tel: 423-693-0011. Coed, day, 5–12.

Texas

Gateway School, Fort Worth. Tel: 817-496-5066. Coed, day, 6–12.

Incarnate Word Academy, Corpus Christi. Tel: 512-883-0857. Coed, day, K–12.

San Marcos Baptist Academy, San Marcos. Tel: 800-428-5120. Coed, day or boarding, 6–8.

Steps of Faith Ranch, Uvalde. Tel: 210-232-6611. Boys, boarding, ungraded, ages 11–18.

Remedial Math Only

International Academy of Texas, Inc., El Paso. Tel: 915-544-0079. Coed, day, 7–12.

Utah

Cross Creek Manor, LaVerkin. Tel: 801-635-2300. Girls, boarding, 7–12.

Vermont

Burr and Burton Seminary, Manchester. Tel: 802-362-1775. Coed, day or boarding, 9–12.
Lyndon Institute, Lyndon Center. Tel: 802-626-3112. Coed, day, 9–12.
Pine Ridge School, Williston. Tel: 802-434-2161. Coed, boarding, ungraded, ages 13–18.
Rock Point School, Burlington. Tel: 802-863-1104. Coed, day or boarding, 9–12.
St. Johnsbury Academy, St. Johnsbury. Tel: 802-751-2131. Coed, day or boarding, 9–PG.

Virginia

Benedictine High School, Richmond. Tel: 804-342-1304. Boys, day, 9–12.
Blue Ridge School, Dyke. Tel: 804-985-2811. Boys, boarding, 9–12.

Eastern Mennonite High, Harrisonburg. Tel: 540-432-4521. Coed, day or boarding, 7–12.

Hargrave Military Academy, Chatham. Tel: 800-432-2480. Coed-day, boys-boarding, 9–PG.

Little Keswick School, Keswick. Tel: 804-295-0457. Boys, boarding, ungraded, ages 7–17.

The Miller School of Albemarle, Charlottesville. Tel: 804-823-4805. Coed, day or boarding, 5–PG.

New Dominion School Inc., Dillwyn. Tel: 804-983-2051. Boys, boarding, ungraded, ages 11–18.

Norfolk Collegiate School, Norfolk. Tel: 804-480-1495. Coed, day, K–12.

Oakland School, Keswick. Tel: 804-293-9059. Coed, day or boarding, ungraded, ages 8–14.

The Potomac School, McLean. Tel: 703-749-6313. Coed, day, preschool–12.

Remedial or Writing Only

Carlisle School, Martinsville. Tel: 540-632-7288. Coed, day, K–12.

Fork Union Military Academy, Fork Union. Tel: 804-842-3212. Boys, day or boarding, 6–PG.

Virgin Islands

The Antilles School, Saint Thomas. Tel: 809-776-1600. Coed, day, preschool–12.

Washington

Bellarmine Preparatory School, Tacoma. Tel: 408-294-9224. Coed, day, 9–12.

Wisconsin

Milwaukee Lutheran High School, Milwaukee. Tel: 414-461-6000. Coed, day, 9–12.

Wayland Academy, Beaver Dam. Tel: 414-885-3373. Coed, day or boarding, 9–12.

Remedial Reading or Writing Only

The Prairie School, Racine. Tel: 414-631-4393. Coed, day, preschool–12.

Canada

British Columbia

St. George's School, Vancouver. Tel: 602-224-1304. Boys, day or boarding, 2–12.

Remedial Math Only

Maxwell International Baha'i School, Shawnigan Lake. Tel: 604-743-7144. Coed, day or boarding, 7–12.

Manitoba

St. Paul's High School, Winnipeg. Tel: 204-831-2305. Boys, day, 9–12.

New Brunswick

R.C.S.-Netherwood, Rothesay, New Brunswick. Tel: 506-847-8224. Coed, day or boarding, 7–12.

Ontario

Havergal College, Toronto. Tel: 416-483-3519. Girls, day or boarding, preschool–13.

Robert Land Academy, Wellandport. Tel: 905-386-6203. Boys, boarding, 7–13.

St. Andrew's College, Aurora. Tel: 905-727-3178. Boys, day or boarding, 7–13.

Quebec

Lower Canada College, Montreal. Tel: 514-482-0951. Coed, day, K–12.

Sedbergh, Montebello. Tel: 819-423-5769. Coed, boarding, 5–12.

Weston School, Montreal. Tel: 514-488-9191. Coed, day, 1–11.

Dyslexia

Schools with special-education programs for dyslexic students.

Alabama

Bayside Academy, Daphne. Tel: 334-626-2840. Coed, day, preschool–12.

Arizona

The Fenster School of Southern Arizona, Tucson. Tel: 602-749-3340. Coed, day or boarding, 9–12.

The Judson School, Paradise Valley. Tel: 602-948-7731.
Coed, day or boarding, K–PG.
Oak Creek Ranch School, West Sedona. Tel: 520-634-5571.
Coed, boarding, 6–PG.

California

Arrowsmith Academy, Berkeley. Tel: 510-540-0440. Coed,
day, 7–12.
Dunn School, Los Olivos. Tel: 805-688-6471. Coed, day or
boarding, 6–12.
Landmark West, Encino. Tel: 818-986-5045. Coed, day,
ungraded, ages 8–18.
Sterne School, San Francisco. Tel: 415-922-6081. Coed, day,
6–12.
Valley Christian High School, San Jose. Tel: 408-978-9955.
Coed, day, K–12.
Whittier Christian High School, Whittier. Tel: 310-694-
3803. Coed, day, 9–12.

Colorado

Accelerated Schools–Randell Moore Center, Denver. Tel:
303-758-2003. Coed, day or boarding, K–PG.
Crested Butte Academy, Crested Butte. Tel: 970-349-1805.
Coed, day or boarding, 9–PG.
Denver Academy, Denver. Tel: 303-777-5870. Coed, day or
boarding, ungraded, ages 8–18.
Denver Christian Schools, Denver. Tel: 303-733-2421. Coed,
day, K–12.

Connecticut

Eagle Hill–Greenwich, Greenwich. Tel: 203-622-9240. Coed, day or boarding, ungraded, ages 6–16.

Eagle Hill–Southport, Southport. Tel: 203-254-2044. Coed, day, ungraded, ages 6–18.

The Forman School, Litchfield. Tel: 860-567-0140. Coed, day or boarding, 9–12.

King & Low–Heywood Thomas School, Stamford. Tel: 203-461-9988. Coed, day, preschool–12.

The Marvelwood School, Kent. Tel: 860-927-0047. Coed, day or boarding, 9–12.

The Oxford Academy, Westbrook. Tel: 860-399-6247. Boys, boarding, ungraded, ages 14–20.

St. Thomas More School, Oakdale. Tel: 203-859-1900. Boys, boarding, 8–PG.

Rumsey Hall School, Washington Depot. Tel: 860-868-0535. Coed, day or boarding, 3–9.

Watkinson School, Hartford. Tel: 203-236-5618. Coed, day, 6–PG.

The Woodhall School, Bethlehem. Tel: 203-266-7788. Boys, day or boarding, 8–PG.

Delaware

Archmere Academy, Claymont. Tel: 302-798-6632. Coed, day, 9–12.

District of Columbia

The Lab School of Washington. Tel: 202-965-6600. Coed, day, 7–12.

Washington Ethical High School. Tel: 202-829-0088. Coed, day, 9–PG.

Florida

Gulliver Preparatory School, Miami. Tel: 305-666-7937.
Coed, day, preschool–12.
PACE Private School, Inc., Longwood. Tel: 407-869-8882.
Coed, day, 9–12.
The Vanguard School, Lake Wales. Tel: 941-676-6091. Coed,
day or boarding, ungraded, ages 10–20.

Georgia

Brandon Hall School, Atlanta. Tel: 404-394-8177. Coed-day,
boys-boarding, 4–PG.
The Howard School, Atlanta. Tel: 404-642-9644. Coed, day,
ungraded, ages 5–18.
Lakeview Academy, Gainesville. Tel: 770-532-4383. Coed,
day, preschool–12.
Saint Andrew's School, Savannah. Tel: 912-897-4941. Coed,
day or boarding, preschool–12.

Idaho

The Community School, Sun Valley. Tel: 208-622-3955.
Coed, day, K–12.
Rocky Mountain Academy, Bonners Ferry. Tel: 808-858-
1933. Coed, boarding, 7–12.

Illinois

Ida Crown Jewish Academy, Chicago. Tel: 773-973-1450.
Coed, day, 9–12.
Keith Country Day School, Rockford. Tel: 815-399-8823.
Coed, day, preschool–12.

Roycemore School, Evanston. Tel: 847-866-6055. Coed, day, preschool–12.

Kansas

Thomas More Prep–Marian, Hays. Tel: 913-625-6577. Coed, day or boarding, 9–12.

Kentucky

Shedd Academy, Mayfield. Tel: 502-247-8007. Coed, day or boarding, ungraded, ages 7–19.

Louisiana

Metairie Park Country Day School, Metairie. Tel: 504-837-5204. Coed, day, K–12.

Maine

Kents Hill School, Kents Hill. Tel: 207-685-4914. Coed, boarding, 9–PG.

Maryland

Baltimore Lutheran Middle and Upper School, Baltimore. Tel: 410-825-2323. Coed, day, 6–12.
Calvert Hall College High School, Towson. Tel: 410-825-4266. Boys, day, 9–12.
Charles E. Smith Jewish Day School, Rockville. Tel: 301-881-1400. Coed, day, K–12.

The Gunston School, Centreville. Tel: 800-381-0077. Girls, day or boarding, 9–12.

St. Paul's School, Brooklandville. Tel: 410-821-3034. Coed, day, K–12.

West Nottingham Academy, Colora. Tel: 410-658-5556. Coed, day or boarding, 9–PG.

Massachusetts

The Carroll School, Lincoln. Tel: 617-259-8342. Coed, day, 1–12.

Cushing Academy, Ashburnham. Tel: 508-827-7300. Coed, day or boarding, 9–PG.

Eagle Hill School, Hardwick. Tel: 413-477-6087. Coed, day or boarding, ungraded, ages 6–16.

Fay School, Southborough. Tel: 508-485-0100. Coed, day or boarding, 1–9

F. L. Chamberlain Schools, Middleborough. Tel:508-947-7825. Coed, boarding, 8–12.

Landmark School, Prides Crossing. Tel: 508-927-4440. Coed, day or boarding, ungraded, ages 9–20.

Linden Hill School, Northfield. Tel: 413-498-2906. Boys, boarding, ungraded, ages 10–15.

Wilbraham & Monson Academy, Wilbraham. Tel: 413-596-6814. Coed, day or boarding, 7–PG.

Willow Hill School, Sudbury. Tel: 508-443-2581. Coed, day, ungraded, ages 11–19.

Michigan

Eton Academy, Birmingham. Tel: 810-642-1150. Coed, day, K–PG.

The Leelanau School, Glen Arbor. Tel: 616-334-5820. Coed, day or boarding, 8–12.

Minnesota

Convent of the Visitation School, Mendota Heights. Tel: 612-683-1705. Coed, day, preschool–12.

Mississippi

Jackson Academy, Jackson. Tel: 601-362-9677. Coed, day, preschool–12.

New Hampshire

Brewster Academy, Wolfeboro. Tel: 603-569-7200. Coed, day or boarding, 9–PG.

Dublin School, Dublin. Tel: 603-563-8584. Coed, day or boarding, 9–12.

New Hampton School, New Hampton. Tel: 603-744-5401. Coed, day or boarding, 9–PG.

Proctor Academy, Andover. Tel: 603-735-6000. Coed, day or boarding, 9–12.

New Jersey

Community High School, Westwood. Tel: 201-358-6221. Coed, day, 9–PG.

The Hun School of Princeton, Princeton. Tel: 609-921-7600. Coed, day or boarding, 6–PG.

The Morristown-Beard School, Morristown. Tel: 201-539-3032. Coed, day, 7–12.

Newgrange School, Trenton. Tel: 609-394-2255. Coed, day, ungraded, ages 8–18.

The Pennington School, Pennington. Tel: 609-737-1838. Coed, day or boarding, 7–12.

The Pingry School, Martinsville. Tel: 908-647-5555. Coed, day, K–12.

Woodcliff Academy, Wall. Tel: 908-751-0240. Coed, day, ungraded, ages 10–21.

New Mexico

Brush Ranch School, Santa Fe. Tel: 505-757-6114. Coed, boarding, 4–12.

New York

The Beekman School and the Tutoring School Learning Center, New York. Tel: 212-755-6666. Coed, day, 8–PG.

The Gow School, South Wales. Tel: 800-724-0138. Boys, boarding, 7–PG.

Hoosac School, Hoosick. Tel: 800-822-0159. Coed, day or boarding, 8–12.

The Karafin School, Mount Kisco. Tel: 914-666-9211. Coed, day, ungraded, 7–21.

Kildonan School, Amenia. Tel: 914-373-8111. Coed, day or boarding, 2–PG.

The Knox School, St. James. Tel: 516-584-5500. Coed, day or boarding, 10–PG.

Norman Howard School, Rochester. Tel: 716-334-8010. Coed, day, 4–12.

Robert Louis Stevenson School, New York. Tel: 212-787-6400. Coed, day, 7–12.

Trinity-Pawling School, Pawling. Tel: 914-855-3100. Boys, boarding, 9–PG.

Winston Preparatory School, New York. Tel: 212-496-8400. Coed, day, ungraded, ages 12–19.

York Preparatory School, New York. Tel: 212-628-1220. Coed, day, 6–12.

North Carolina

Forsyth Country Day School, Lewisville. Tel: 910-945-3151.
Coed, day, preschool–12.

Greenfield School, Wilson. Tel: 919-237-8046. Coed, day,
preschool–12.

Hill Learning Development Center, Durham Academy,
Durham. Tel: 919-489-7464. Coed, day, K–12.

The O'Neal School, Southern Pines. Tel: 910-692-6920.
Coed, day, preschool–PG.

Ohio

Regina High School, South Euclid. Tel: 216-382-2110. Girls,
day, 9–12.

Pennsylvania

Academy of the New Church Boys' School, Bryn Athyn. Tel:
215-947-4200. Boys, day or boarding, 9–12.

Academy of the New Church Girls' School, Bryn Athyn. Tel:
215-947-4200. Girls, day or boarding, 9–12.

The Grier School, Tyrone. Tel: 814-684-3000. Girls,
boarding, 7–PG.

The Hill Top Preparatory School, Rosemont. Tel: 610-527-
3230. Coed, day, ungraded, ages 11–20.

The Oakland School, Pittsburgh. Tel: 412-621-7878. Coed,
day, 9–PG.

Perkiomen School, Pennsburgh. Tel: 215-679-9511. Coed, day
or boarding, 5–PG.

The Phelps School, Malvern. Tel: 610-644-1754. Boys,
boarding, 7–PG.

St. Joseph's Preparatory School, Philadelphia. Tel: 215-978-
1012. Boys, day, 9–12.

Solebury School, New Hope. Tel: 215-862-5261. Coed, day or boarding, 7–PG.
The University School, Pittsburgh. Tel: 412-361-7182. Coed, day, 7–PG.

Puerto Rico

Caribbean Preparatory School, San Juan. Tel: 809-765-4411. Coed, day, preschool–12.

Rhode Island

Providence Country Day School, East Providence. Tel: 401-438-5170. Coed, day, 5–PG.
St. Andrew's School, Barrington. Tel: 401-246-1310. Coed, day or boarding, 5–12.

South Carolina

Trident Academy, Mt. Pleasant. Tel: 803-884-7046. Coed, day or boarding. 1–12.

Tennessee

The Bodine School, Germantown. Tel: 901-754-1800. Coed, day, 9–12.
Hutchison School, Memphis. Tel: 901-762-6672. Girls, day, preschool–12.

Texas

Cliffwood School, Houston. Tel: 713-667-4649. Coed, day, K–12.

Gateway School, Fort Worth. Tel: 817-496-5066. Coed, day, 6–12.

San Marcos Military Academy, San Marcos. Tel: 800-428-5120. Coed, day or boarding, 6–12.

The Winston School, Dallas. Tel: 214-691-6950. Coed, day, 1–12.

Vermont

The Greenwood School, Putney. Tel: 802-387-4545. Boys, boarding, ungraded, ages 8–15.

Long Trail School, Dorset. Tel: 802-867-5717. Coed, day, 7–12.

Pine Ridge School, Williston. Tel: 802-434-2161. Coed, boarding, ungraded, ages 13–18.

Virginia

Carlisle School, Martinsville. Tel: 540-632-7288. Coed, day, K–12.

Christchurch School, Christchurch. Tel: 804-758-2306. Coed-day, boys-boarding, 8–PG.

New Dominion School, Inc., Dillwyn. Tel: 804-983-2051. Boys, boarding, ungraded, ages 11–18.

Virgin Islands

The Antilles School, Saint Thomas. Tel: 809-776-1600. Coed, day, preschool–12.

Washington

Overlake School, Redmond. Tel: 206-868-1000. Coed, day,
   5–12.
University Prep, Seattle. Tel: 206-523-6407. Coed, day, 6–12.

Canada

Ontario

Hillfield Strathallan School, Hamilton. Tel: 905-389-1367.
   Coed, day, preschool–13.

Underachievers

Schools with special-education programs for underachievers.

Arizona

Oak Creek Ranch School, West Sedona. Tel: 530-634-5571.
   Coed, boarding, 6–PG.

California

The Cascade School, Whitmore. Tel: 916-472-3031. Coed,
   boarding, 7–PG.

Colorado

Denver Academy, Denver. Tel: 303-777-5870. Coed, day or boarding, ungraded, ages 8–18.

Connecticut

Eagle Hill–Greenwich, Greenwich. Tel: 203-622-9240. Coed, day or boarding, ungraded, ages 6–16.

Eagle Hill–Southport, Southport. Tel: 203-254-2044. Coed, day, 6–18.

Saint Thomas More School, Oakdale. Tel: 203-859-1900. Boys, boarding, 8–PG.

District of Columbia

Parkmont School. Tel: 202-726-0740. Coed, day, 6–12

Florida

Crossroads School, Fort Lauderdale. Tel: 407-584-1100. Coed-day, boys-boarding, K–12.

The Vanguard School, Lake Wales. Tel: 813-676-6091. Coed, day or boarding, 4–PG.

Georgia

Brandon Hall School, Atlanta. Tel: 404-394-8177. Coed-day, boys-boarding, 4–PG.

Gables Academy, Atlanta. Tel: 404-377-1721. Coed, day or boarding, ungraded, ages 12–19.

Hawaii

Academy of the Pacific, Honolulu. Tel: 808-595-6359. Coed, day, 7–12.

Kentucky

Shedd Academy, Mayfield. Tel: 502-247-8007. Coed, day or boarding, ungraded, ages 7–19.

Maine

Elan School, Poland Spring. Tel: 207-998-4666. Coed, boarding, 7–12.

Maryland

New Dominion, Inc., Oldtown. Tel: 301-478-5721. Boys, boarding, ungraded, ages 11–18.
Thornton Friends School, Silver Spring. Tel: 301-384-0320. Coed, day, 9–PG.

Massachusetts

The DeSisto School, Stockbridge. Tel: 413-298-3776. Coed, boarding, ungraded, ages 13–21.
Eagle Hill School, Hardwick. Tel: 413-477-6087. Coed, day or boarding, ungraded, ages 12–20.
Linden Hill School, Northfield. Tel: 413-498-2906. Boys, boarding, ungraded, ages 10–15.
The Winchendon School, Winchendon. Tel: 800-622-1119. Coed, day or boarding, 8–PG.

Missouri

LOGOS High School, St. Louis. Tel: 314-997-7002. Coed, day, ungraded, ages 12–18.

New Hampshire

New Hampton School, New Hampton. Tel: 603-744-5401. Coed, day or boarding, 9–PG.

New Jersey

Woodcliff Academy, Wall. Tel: 908-751-0240. Coed, day, ungraded, ages 10–21.

New Mexico

Brush Ranch School, Santa Fe. Tel: 505-757-6114. Coed, boarding, 4–12.

New York

All Hallows School, Bronx. Tel: 718-293-4545. Boys, day, 9–12.

Maplebrook School, Amenia. Tel: 914-373-8191. Coed, day or boarding, ungraded, ages 11–23.

Robert Louis Stevenson School, New York. Tel: 212-787-6400. Coed, day, 7–PG.

Storm King School, Cornwall-on-Hudson. Tel: 914-734-7892. Coed, day or boarding, 9–PG.

Pennsylvania

The Concept School, Westtown. Tel: 610-399-1135. Coed, day, 2–12.
The Phelps School, Malvern. Tel: 610-644-1754. Boys, boarding, 7–PG.

Tennessee

The Bodine School, Germantown. Tel: 901-754-1800. Coed, day, 9–12.

Texas

Steps of Faith Ranch, Uvalde. Tel: 210-232-6611. Boys, boarding, ungraded, ages 11–18.

Virginia

Little Keswick School, Keswick. Tel: 804-295-0457. Boys, boarding, ungraded, ages 7–17.
New Dominion School, Inc., Dillwyn. Tel: 804-983-2051. Boys, boarding, ungraded, ages 11–18.

Canada

Ontario

Robert Land Academy, Wellandport. Tel: 905-386-6203. Boys, boarding, 7–13.

Exceptional Children

The following schools concentrate on special-education programs for exceptional students with serious learning impediments, handicaps, and emotional problems who are achieving at levels considerably lower than children of the same age or intelligence. Because of the specialized nature of the academic programs offered, each listing cites the type of school, the grade range served, and in each school's own words, the type of students or learning impediments that are the focus of the school's programs. The grade level PG refers to a special academic program for post-graduate high-school students who are repeating the senior year.

Alabama

Three Springs, Huntsville. Tel: 205-880-3339. Coed, boarding, ungraded, ages 10–17. Emotional and behavioral problems.

Arizona

St. Paul's Academy, Phoenix. Tel: 602-956-9090. Boys, boarding, 9–12. Attention Deficit Disorder, emotional and behavioral problems.

California

CEDU School, Running Springs. Tel: 800-884-2338. Coed, boarding, ungraded, ages 12–18. Attention Deficit Disorder, emotional and behavioral problems, learning disabilities. Coordinates with Rocky Mountain Academy in Idaho (q.v.).

Landmark West School, Encino. Tel: 818-986-5045. Coed, day, 2–12. Dyslexia, learning disabilities.

Sterne School, San Francisco. Tel: 415-922-6081. Coed, day, 6–12. Emotional and behavioral problems, dyslexia, learning disabilities.

Colorado

Colorado Denver Academy, Denver. Tel: 303-777-5870. Coed, day or boarding, 1–12. Underachievers, Attention Deficit Disorder, dyslexia, learning differences, learning disabilities.

Eagle Rock School, Estes Park. Tel: 970-586-0600. Coed, boarding, ungraded, ages 15–18. Attention Deficit Disorder, dyslexia.

Connecticut

Eagle Hill-Greenwich, Greenwich. Tel: 203-622-9240. Coed, day or boarding, ungraded, ages 6–16. Underachievers, dyslexia, language disabilities, other learning disabilities.

Eagle Hill-Southport, Southport. Tel: 203-254-2044. Coed, day, ungraded, ages 6–18. Underachievers, Attention Deficit Disorder, other learning disabilities.

The Forman School, Litchfield. Tel: 860-567-0140. Coed, day or boarding, 9–PG. Learning disabilities.

Grove School, Madison. Tel: 203-245-2778. Coed, day or boarding, 6–12. Learning disabilities, Attention Deficit Disorder, emotional and behavioral problems, emotionally disturbed students with Attention Deficit Hyperactivity Disorder.

District of Columbia

The Lab School of Washington. Tel: 202-965-6600. Coed, day, Grades K–12. Attention Deficit Disorder, dyslexia, other learning disabilities.

Washington Ethical High School. Tel: 202-829-0088. Coed, day, 9–PG. Attention Deficit Disorder, learning disabilities, students who need small classes and individual attention.

Florida

Crossroads School, Fort Lauderdale. Tel: 407-584-1100. Coed-day, boys-boarding, K–12. Underachievers, Attention Deficit Disorder, emotional and behavioral problems.

PACE Private School, Inc., Longwood. Tel: 407-869-8882. Coed, day, 9–12. Attention Deficit Disorder, other learning disabilities.

The Vanguard School, Lake Wales. Tel: 941-676-6091. Coed, day or boarding, 9–PG. Underachievers, Attention Deficit Disorder, dyslexia, other learning disabilities.

Georgia

Brandon Hall School, Atlanta. Tel: 404-394-8177. Coed-day, boys-boarding, 6–PG. Underachievers and learning disabilities such as Attention Deficit Disorder and dyslexia.

Gables Academy, Atlanta. Tel: 404-377-1721. Coed, day or boarding, 6–PG. Underachievers, learning disabilities, Attention Deficit Disorders.

Hidden Lake Academy, Dahlonega. Tel: 800-394-0640. Coed, boarding, 8–12. Attention Deficit Disorder, emotional and behavioral problems, other learning disabilities.
The Howard School, Atlanta. Tel: 404-642-9644. Coed, day, 1–12. Learning disabilities.

Idaho

Boulder Creek Academy, Bonners Ferry. Tel: 800-858-1933. Coed, boarding, 7–12. Learning disabilities, emotional and behavioral problems.
Rocky Mountain Academy, Bonners Ferry. Tel: 808-858-1933. Coed, boarding, 7–12. Learning disabilities, emotional and behavioral problems.

Illinois

Brehm Preparatory School, Carbondale. Tel: 618-457-0371. Coed, day or boarding, 7–PG. Attention Deficit Disorder, dyslexia, speech or language disabilities.

Kentucky

Shedd Academy, Mayfield. Tel: 502-247-8007. Coed, day or boarding, ungraded, ages 7–19. Underachievers, Attention Deficit Disorder, dyslexia, other learning disabilities.

Maine

Elan School, Poland Spring. Tel: 207-998-4666. Coed, boarding, 7–12. Underachievers, Attention Deficit Disorder, emotional and behavioral problems, dyslexia, other learning disabilities.

Maryland

New Dominion School, Oldtown. Tel: 301-478-5721. Boys, boarding, ungraded, ages 11–18. Underachievers, learning disabilities, emotional and behavioral problems.

Massachusetts

Beacon High School, Brookline. Tel: 617-232-1958. Coed, day, ungraded, ages 15–22. Attention Deficit Disorder, emotional and behavioral problems.

The Carroll School, Lincoln. Tel: 617-259-8342. Coed, day, 1–12. Dyslexia, learning disabilities.

The DeSisto School, Stockbridge. Tel: 413-298-3776. Coed, boarding, 8–PG. Underachievers, emotional and behavioral problems.

Eagle Hill School, Hardwick. Tel: 413-477-6087. Coed, day or boarding, ungraded, ages 12–20. Underachievers, dyslexia, Attention Deficit Disorder, other learning disabilities.

F. L. Chamberlain Schools, Middleborough. Tel:508-947-7825. Coed, day or boarding, ungraded, ages 11–18. Learning disabilities, emotional and behavioral problems.

Landmark School, Prides Crossing. Tel: 508-927-4440. Coed, day or boarding, ungraded, ages 7–21. Dyslexia, other learning disabilities.

Valley View School, North Brookfield. Tel: 508-867-6505. Boys, boarding, ungraded, ages 12–17. Emotional and behavioral problems and difficulties adjusting to family and surroundings.

Willow Hill School, Sudbury. Tel: 508-443-2581. Coed, day, 6–PG. Attention Deficit Disorder, other learning disabilities.

Michigan

Eton Academy, Birmingham. Tel: 810-642-1150. Coed, day, 1–12. Attention Deficit Disorder, dyslexia, other learning disabilities.

Missouri

LOGOS High School, St. Louis. Tel: 314-997-7002. Coed, day, 7–12. Underachievers, Attention Deficit Disorder, Attention Deficit Hyperactivity Disorder, other learning disabilities.

New Hampshire

Crotched Mountain Preparatory School, Greenfield. Tel: 603-547-3311. Coed, day or boarding, ungraded, ages 6–22. Multiple handicaps.

New Jersey

Community High School, Westwood. Tel: 201-358-6221. Coed, day, ungraded, ages 14–21. Attention Deficit Disorder, dyslexia, other learning disabilities.

The Newgrange School, Trenton. Tel: 609-394-2255. Coed, day, ungraded, ages 8–18. Attention Deficit Disorder, dyslexia, other learning disabilities.

Woodcliff Academy, Wall. Tel: 908-751-0240. Coed, day, ungraded, ages 10–21. Underachievers, Attention Deficit Disorder, dyslexia, other learning disabilities.

New Mexico

Brush Ranch School, Santa Fe. Tel: 505-757-6114. Coed, boarding, ungraded, ages 10–19 and grades 4–12. Underachievers, dyslexia, other learning disabilities. College prep, general education, and vocational education.

New York

The Gow School, South Wales. Tel: 800-724-0138. Boys boarding, 7–PG. Dyslexia, learning differences.

The Karafin School, Mount Kisco. Tel: 914-666-9211. Coed, day, 1–12. Learning-disabled and emotionally disturbed students.

Kildonan School, Amenia. Tel: 914-373-8111. Coed, day or boarding, 2–PG. Dyslexia.

Maplebrook School, Amenia. Tel: 914-373-8191. Coed, day or boarding, ungraded, ages 11–23. Attention Deficit Disorder, dyslexia, learning disabilities, low average abilities (70–90 I.Q.).

Norman Howard School, Rochester. Tel: 716-334-8010. Coed, day, 5–12. Learning disabilities.

Robert Louis Stevenson School, New York. Tel: 212-787-6400. Coed, day, 7–PG. Underachievers, Attention Deficit Disorder, other learning disabilities.

Windward School, White Plains. Tel: 914-949-6968. Coed, day, 1–12. Learning disabilities.

Winston Preparatory School, New York. Tel: 212-496-8400. Coed, day, 6–12. Attention Deficit Disorder, dyslexia, other learning disabilities.

North Carolina

Hill Learning Development Center, Durham Academy, Durham. Tel: 919-489-7464. Coed, day, K–12. Attention Deficit Disorder, other learning disabilities.

Oregon

Mount Bachelor Academy, Prineville. Tel: 800-462-3404. Coed, boarding, 7–12. Learning disabilities, emotional and behavioral problems.

Pennsylvania

The Hill Top Preparatory School, Rosemont. Tel: 610-527-3230. Coed, day, ungraded, ages 11–20. Attention Deficit Disorder, dyslexia, other learning disabilities.

South Carolina

Trident Academy, Mt. Pleasant. Tel: 803-884-7046. Coed, boarding, 6–PG. Learning disabilities.

Tennessee

The Bodine School, Germantown. Tel: 901-754-1800. Coed, day, 1–12. Underachievers and learning disabled.

Texas

Cliffwood School, Houston. Tel: 713-667-4649. Coed, day, K–12. Attention Deficit Disorder, Attention Deficit Hyperactivity Disorder, Tourette Syndrome, Aspergers Syndrome, pervasive developmental disorder, other learning disabilities.

Gateway School, Fort Worth. Tel: 817-496-5066. Coed, day, 7–12. Attention Deficit Disorder, learning disabled.

Steps of Faith Ranch, Uvalde. Tel: 210-232-6611. Boys, boarding, ungraded, ages 11–18. Underachievers, emotional and behavioral problems, Attention Deficit Disorder, Attention Deficit Hyperactivity Disorder, dysgraphia, dyslexia, other learning disabilities. Episcopal Church school.

The Winston School, Dallas. Tel: 214-691-6950. Coed, day, 1–12. Attention Deficit Disorder, dyslexia, other learning disabilities.

Utah

Cross Creek Manor, LaVerkin. Tel: 801-635-2300. Girls, boarding, 7–12. Attention Deficit Disorder, emotional and behavioral problems, dyslexia, other learning disabilities.

Sorenson's Ranch School, Koosharem. Tel: 801-638-7318. Coed, boarding, 7–12. Learning disabilities.

Virginia

Little Keswick School, Keswick. Tel: 804-295-0457. Boys, boarding, ungraded, ages 7–17. Underachievers, Attention Deficit Disorder, emotional and behavioral problems, dyslexia, other learning disabilities.

New Dominion School, Dillwyn. Tel: 804-983-2051. Boys, boarding, ungraded, ages 11–18. Underachievers, Attention Deficit Disorder, emotional and behavioral problems, other learning disabilities.

Vermont

Pine Ridge School, Williston. Tel: 802-434-2161. Coed, day or boarding, ungraded, ages 13–18. Attention Deficit Disorder, dyslexia, other learning disabilities.

Canada

Robert Land Academy, Wellandport, Ontario. Tel: 905-386-6203. Boys, boarding (military), 7–13. Underachievers, emotional and behavioral problems, Attention Deficit Disorder, other learning disabilities.

Appendix F

Glossary

Glossary of Technical Terms Used in Special Education

agnosia A broad range of learning disabilities affecting sensory recognition of familiar objects. Usually associated with neurological damage, agnosias can be visual, auditory, and tactile and show up as an inability to identify, understand, or interpret information or objects with each of those senses. Autopagnosia is an inability to identify body parts, and form agnosia is an inability to identify familiar shapes.

Agnosias vary widely in degree, however, and unless supported by abnormal electroencephalogram or other diagnostic evidence, symptoms of agnosia can appear in perfectly normal children. Common children's games using blindfolds often demonstrate the frequency with which perfectly functional individuals are unable to identify familiar objects.

agraphia An extreme form of dysgraphia (q.v.) in which the individual has lost the ability to write because of a breakdown in neurological connections between the recognition of a number, letter, or word and the motor response needed to write it. Agraphia can occur without any muscular paralysis and have no effect on performance of other routine muscular tasks. Agraphics may have no difficulty reading, speaking, hearing, or understanding numbers, letters, or words, but their agraphia prevents translation into the muscular activities for writing.

alexia The inability to read because of brain damage. An extreme form of dyslexia (q.v.), alexia is a form of agnosia (q.v.) caused by irreversible neurological disruption such as a severe stroke.

anomia or dysnomia A learning disorder characterized by a consistent inability to recall names of common, well-known objects. Although not an uncommon phenomenon in normal individuals of all ages, occasional anomia is not a learning disorder unless it manifests itself as a persistent, long-term, all-encompassing symptom that obviously affects learning.

aphasia An inability to understand words and say them, even when the individual knows what he or she wants to say. Usually caused by neurological damage, aphasia may be limited to the inability to comprehend words (receptive aphasia) or the inability to express them (expressive aphasia). Once called adult-onset aphasia, it was believed to be the exclusive result of strokes suffered by adults until researchers found similar symptoms among learning-disabled children with either developmental or congenital aphasia.

apraxia An inability to perform specific voluntary muscular movements, such as speaking (verbal) or using classroom materials (nonverbal), even in the absence of any evidence of paralysis. Believed to be related to the neurological connections between the brain's thought center and muscle-control center, apraxia seldom causes muscle weakness, atrophy, or spasms and does not affect involuntary muscles or movement. Thus, a student unable to use his or her hand to pick up a pencil may involuntarily scratch a sudden itch—a movement that often provokes teacher or parent accusations of malingering. The degree of apraxia determines the ability of a student to adapt to conventional classroom conditions.

aptitude   The ability to learn a specific skill or group of skills. A child may have a high or low mathematical aptitude (specific) or scholastic aptitude (group of skills). Invariably affected by development, an aptitude may be genetically or environmentally determined and may or may not reflect overall intelligence or predict future performance.

articulation   For purposes of special education, limited to the process of speaking aloud. In regular education, it can also mean the coordination within overall school curriculum that permits a smooth transition from grade to grade in each course, with courses becoming progressively more difficult as students advance through the system.

Attention Deficit Disorder (ADD)   A persistent learning disorder that interferes with learning and acceptable behavior in the classroom setting. A puzzling, frustrating disorder, ADD shows up as an inability to pay attention, difficulty listening, daydreaming (or falling asleep), low frustration tolerance, argumentativeness, impulsive acts, frequent and unpredictable mood swings, avoidance of or withdrawal from group activities, and spending excessive time completing routine tasks. Children with ADD invariably fall further and further behind in their schoolwork.

A highly controversial disorder, ADD is probably the result of chemical imbalances and is often treated successfully with a combination of medication and special education. Although ADD symptoms can show up in almost any normal child, they are usually developmental and unrelated to true ADD. Because of the passive nature of its symptoms, true ADD is diagnosed more frequently among girls than boys, and indeed, goes largely undiagnosed in boys. The hypoactive behavior of boys with ADD is often mistakenly attributed to disinterest in learning.

Attention Deficit Hyperactivity Disorder (ADHD)   A chronic inability to concentrate, marked by excessive impulsivity and hyperactivity, including fidgeting, squirming, sudden impulsiveness such as darting around a room, low frustration tolerance, argumentativeness, fighting, bullying, and frequent and unpredictable mood swings. The causes are probably the same as Attention Deficit Disorder (q.v.)—that is, a chemical imbalance that provokes cerebral dysfunction.

Treatment and resolution depend on such factors as length and severity of ADHD episodes, their effects on the child's academic performance and social behavior, and adult response. The two most frequently recommended treatments for ADHD are special education, which does help most ADHD youngsters, and medication, which reduces hyperactivity and impulsivity but does not necessarily produce any improvement in academic performance.

Like the symptoms of ADD, the symptoms of ADHD may appear temporarily in almost any normal healthy child—most often in eight-to-ten-year-old boys. Although such symptoms are usually developmental and disappear with little or no treatment, they often provoke misdiagnoses of perfectly normal children.

True ADHD has a statistical correlation with dyslexia (q.v.) and dyscalculia (q.v.). One study found that 33 percent of children with dyslexia or dyscalculia also had ADHD.

attention span   The length of time an individual is able to focus exclusively on a particular subject.

autism   A multiple handicap affecting a child's mental, emotional, and physical processes by age five and sometimes from birth. Although its causes remain unknown, it is believed to involve some sort of physical damage to the brain or neurological system—or both. Broadly classified as both "emotionally disturbed" and "health impaired" by federal laws relating to education of handicapped children, autistic children are aloof, disinterested, withdrawn, occasionally impulsive, and display irrational fears at the sight of new objects. They respond only to certain sounds or voices and have extreme difficulty speaking and making coordinated body movements. They develop few social skills, cannot play with other children, and have difficulty understanding what is said to them. Massive, combined intervention of doctors, teachers, parents, and other family members has produced mixed results.

cerebral palsy A vague term for nonfatal and nonprogressive brain damage and a wide range of associated symptoms. Symptoms vary according to the extent of brain damage and may range from virtually imperceptible and undetectable to various degrees of limb paralysis, involuntary spasms, lack of coordination, muscle weakness, seizures, and mental insufficiencies. Educational potential varies just as widely, with some palsy sufferers able to blend completely into the mainstream of conventional education and others requiring special education and continuing physical treatment.

child-study team A group of professionals, usually including a pediatrician, psychologist, social worker, regular teacher, and special-education teacher who evaluate a child to determine the existence of a learning disorder and recommend an Individualized Education Program (q.v.) of combined regular and special education.

Committee for Special Education (CSE) A committee made up of a child-study team and appropriate school and school-district administrators who approve, modify, and implement Individualized Education Programs (q.v.) for students with learning disabilities.

communication disorder An impairment in speech or language that so interferes with a child's academic and social functioning as to require remediation or speech therapy. Communication disorders include stuttering, impaired articulation, voice impairment, or receptive or expressive verbal language impairment.

compensatory instruction Any form of instruction that teaches a child to compensate for a learning deficiency, either by bypassing learning impediments or using alternative methods of learning or performing. Among the most dramatic forms of compensatory instruction is the teaching of Braille and the use of touch to replace lost vision for reading by the blind. The use of word processors and calculators are forms of compensatory instruction for children with dysgraphia and dyscalculia.

corrective feedback   The immediate correction of a child's error by demonstrating the correct answer and method of obtaining it.

critical learning impediment   Any learning impediment that prevents individuals from learning the language and calculating skills essential for competent functioning in school, in the workplace, and in normal daily activities. Various critical learning impediments may prevent a child from learning to read (dyslexia), write (dysgraphia), speak (dysfluency), listen (distractibility or Attention Deficit Disorder), calculate (dyscalculia), or perform other language functions that are essential for learning almost all other intellectual skills.

curriculum compacting   A process whereby gifted children may demonstrate mastery of forthcoming elements of the curriculum and jump ahead to areas they need to learn, thus contracting, or compacting, the curricular materials they study in the course of the year. The extra time they acquire by compacting the curriculum may be used for supplementary educational activities inside or outside school.

curricular modification   The reduction or elimination in curricular requirements to adapt to the limitations of learning-disabled students.

direct services   Services that special-education personnel—teachers, therapists, and so on—provide directly to students. (*See also* indirect services.)

disability   Any impairment of normal bodily functions.

disruptiveness Any behavior by one or more students that interferes with the normal routine of the school, classroom, faculty, staff, or students.

distractibility The degree to which a child is unable to focus attention on a task.

Down Syndrome (Down's Syndrome) A genetic disorder caused by chromosomal abnormalities that produce varying degrees of mental retardation, physical deformities, and health problems, including heart defects and ear infections.

due process A constitutional right to fair treatment under the law by public authorities as guaranteed by the Fifth, Sixth, and Fourteenth Amendments. Due process as applied to education requires school authorities to provide adequate notice of decisions affecting students and open hearings at which the student or the student's guardians can argue decisions affecting the student's personal rights, including suspension or expulsion.

dyscalculia A critical learning impediment or disability that prevents a child from calculating, understanding mathematical functions, or reasoning mathematically.

dysfluency Any impairment such as stuttering that interferes with a person's ability to speak fluently and intelligibly.

dysgraphia A learning impediment of otherwise normal children characterized by an inability to write conventionally at the appropriate level for the child's age. Possibly the result of neurological damage, dysgraphia is characterized by letter reversals, incomplete letter formation, telescoping of letters, and inability to write along a straight line. A common developmental impediment, dysgraphia normally disappears as a child matures physically and eye-hand coordination improves. Word processors have proved helpful aids to dysgraphic children.

dyslexia A critical learning impediment of otherwise normal children characterized by an inability to read, write, and spell at an appropriate level for their age. A broad catchall term, dyslexia is often misused to include a variety of unrelated learning disorders. Indeed, as the meanings of dyslexia have multiplied, it has lost its specificity and become a reference to a broad category of reading problems. Often found in concert with other learning disabilities, dyslexia cannot be treated medically, but various methods of sophisticated special education can teach many dyslexics to overcome the most debilitating effects on their reading, writing, and spelling skills.

Although there is some evidence that dyslexia is associated with brain malformations, there is just as much evidence that it is developmental in some children and may appear and disappear. In a study of 400 Connecticut children at the Yale University School of Medicine, only one of six children who had dyslexia in first grade still had symptoms in the third grade. The study also found, however, that some children who showed no symptoms of dyslexia in first grade acquired them by the time they reached third grade.

dysorthographia   A critical learning impediment, characteristic of dyslexics, that blocks the ability to spell.

early intervention   Any educational or special-education program to prevent or correct intellectual, academic, emotional, psychological, or social dysfunction among preschool children and their families.

educational counselor   Any advisor in the field of education, but more commonly a specialist in learning disorders, who can test children for and diagnose specific learning disabilities and prescribe a course of special education. Counselors may provide special education themselves when the school is unable to do so. Although few states require any certification or licensing procedures, all competent educational counselors work closely with pediatricians and they are almost always members of the Independent Educational Counselors Association (see Appendix

C), a professional standards-setting organization in Forestdale, Massachusetts.

Education for All Handicapped Children Act A federal law passed in 1975 that reversed the long-standing practice of removing physically and mentally handicapped, unmanageable, and delinquent children from their homes and communities and placing them in isolated residential facilities. Renamed the Individual with Disabilities Education Act (IDEA) in 1988 and commonly called the Disabilities Education Act, the law asserted the right of all children, ages three to twenty-one, to the best possible education in the least restrictive environment, free of charge and free of discrimination of any kind. The law provides for the continual flow of federal funds to public schools to provide such education, which usually requires special-education teachers to supplement regular education in conventional classrooms.

When the law was passed, only 1.6 million of the eight million handicapped children in the United States attended public schools. Most of the rest were either languishing idly at home or incarcerated in residential facilities. In neither case did they receive any formal or special education that enhanced the possibility of eventual independence.

In addition to federal funding for special education, the law underwrites all necessary construction to make school facilities accessible to physically handicapped children. It also funds special transportation to carry children to and from whatever school they need to attend.

The high costs of the law have created a public backlash against special education. All taxpayers now share the costs of special education for the handicapped, while parents of the handicapped pay no more than any other taxpayers for their children's education. Although handicapped children represented only 7 percent to 12 percent of the student population during the first half of the 1990s, they absorbed 20 percent to

25 percent of funds spent on public-school education. Moreover, those costs soared uncontrollably in the wake of court decisions that expanded the concept of full inclusion (q.v.) in the public-school system to include even the most deeply retarded and autistic children.

etiology   The cause of any abnormal condition.

exceptional children   A term referring to handicapped children in need of special education; now expanded to include the gifted and talented.

full inclusion   The education of disabled children in their own district public schools, and as much as possible, in the same classrooms with nondisabled children; an element of the Education for All Handicapped Children Act (q.v.). The theory that generated full inclusion was the hope that the severely handicapped would benefit more in conventional classrooms than in segregated, special-education facilities and that their inclusion would teach tolerance to their more normal classmates.

Full inclusion, however, has so impeded teacher ability to pursue normal teaching activities and so interfered with education of nondisabled students in some classes that the American Federation of Teachers has called for a halt to the practice. One by one, state legislatures have responded by setting limits to full inclusion to prevent a deterioration of the quality of education to the nonhandicapped.

gifted   A quality of above-average intelligence, aptitude, learning ability, creativity, social skills, or talent, usually identified either by direct observation or standardized testing. Intellectually gifted children tend to read earlier, show greater curiosity, speak in more complex sentences, and recognize cause-and-effect relationships more quickly than most children. In school, gifted students have longer attention spans and learn faster than their peers. Gifted students master 35 percent to 50 percent of each year's elementary-school curriculum before the start of the school year and need special education to explore the limits of their own potential.

Children whom schools have identified as gifted constitute about 3 percent to 5 percent of the student population, although percentages vary widely from state to state, from as low as 1 percent to as high as 12 percent, with variations probably reflecting quality of education. One-third of all school districts in the United States deny special-education funds for the gifted. Only two cents of every dollar spent on K–12, public-school education supports special education for the gifted, compared to fifteen cents for the handicapped and nineteen cents for the economically disadvantaged. In 1978, when Congress enacted the Gifted and Talented Children's Act authorizing federal funds for specialized education for gifted children, fewer than forty states implemented such education. Most states that did so provide only two to three hours a week of special studies for gifted students.

hyperactivity-hyperkinesis Two equally applicable designations for a syndrome that includes excessive, impulse-driven activity, short attention span, high distractibility, social immaturity, inappropriate lack of inhibitions, and learning difficulties usually requiring special education. Most often the result of a chemical imbalance that produces brain dysfunction, hyperactivity-hyperkinesis may be developmental and, therefore, temporary. If permanent, it requires long-term, special education, and perhaps, medical intervention and long-term medication. Related to ADHD (q.v.), hyperactivity-hyperkinesis includes symptoms that appear as temporary, developmental behavior problems in almost every normal child at one time or another—especially eight-to-ten-year-old boys.

impulsivity The tendency to act or speak suddenly, often irrationally, without thinking, and as often as not, with no motive or goal. In the classroom, impulsivity shows up in a variety of both goal-oriented and nongoal-oriented forms:

speaking out before being recognized by the teacher, interrupting others, or behaving in a disruptive way.

inclusion *See* full inclusion.

indirect services Services that special-education personnel—teachers, therapists, and so on—provide regular classroom teachers and school staff to help them meet the needs of exceptional students.

Individualized Education Program (IEP) A plan of combined special and regular education tailored for an individual student with learning disabilities by a child-study team (q.v.) of professional evaluators operating under provisions of the Education for All Handicapped Children Act (q.v.).

Individualized Family Service Plan (IFSP) A plan of child and family evaluation, procedures, and infant education prepared by a team of professionals under an early intervention (q.v.) program.

intervention assistance team A group of special-education teachers and school administrators and professionals who help teachers solve problems with individual students.

itinerant teacher A special-education teacher who travels from school to school within a school district to provide remedial services to individual students or consult with teachers about students. School districts hire itinerant teachers when no school within the district requires a full-time special-education teacher.

language disorder Any disability that interferes with the ability to learn, use, or understand spoken or written language.

learning block Any basic, inexplicable, but remediable, interference in the learning process. Vaguely defined and little studied, learning blocks may be physical or psychological and due to fatigue, illness, or neurological injury. Unlike learning disabilities, learning blocks are puzzling to both student and teacher and often inconsistent with the student's usual learning skills—the inability of a good speller, for example, to learn to spell one particular word. Teachers generally develop specific mechanisms, such as mnemonics, word pictures, or other memory tricks, to help students overcome learning blocks—for example, remembering how to spell *Manhattan* by picturing a *man* in a *hat* that is *tan*.

learning disability   A broad spectrum of malfunctions of unknown causes that deter otherwise normal, healthy, intelligent individuals from understanding and acquiring language and mathematical skills. Learning disabilities, as they are usually defined, do not include learning problems resulting from visual, auditory, or motor handicaps, or from mental retardation or environmental, cultural, or economic deprivation. To be classified as a learning disability, the dysfunction must represent a stark discrepancy between a physically healthy and normal student's potential, as measured by I.Q. or comparable tests, and the student's actual achievement. Estimates of the number of learning-disabled students vary from 1 percent to 30 percent of the elementary- and secondary-school student population. Because of the vagueness of the definition, the term has been discarded in this book in favor of the more specific critical learning impediment (q.v.).

learning impediment   Any interference with the normal learning process.

least restrictive environment (LRE)   A legal requirement of the Education for All Handicapped Children Act of 1975 (q.v.) that all public schools and educative agencies provide a physical and educational environment that permits handicapped children "to the maximum extent appropriate" to be educated with nonhandicapped children. LRE requires handicapped children to receive as much of their education as possible in the same school and the same classrooms they would attend if they were not handicapped. Often confused with mainstreaming (q.v.),

LRE refers strictly to the site where special education takes place—that is, the regular classroom—whereas mainstreaming refers to the type of education.

mainstreaming The enrollment and participation of exceptional and learning-disabled children (q.v.) in the conventional curriculum of traditional schools and classrooms.

mental age A level of individual performance measured in years and months on a standardized test. Often called intellectual age, the mental age compares a child's performance with that of norms, or average scores, of children at every age—regardless of the child's own age. Thus, a child would have a mental age of ten if his or her score on a test matched the average scores of all ten-year-olds, regardless of whether the child's chronological age is eight, nine, ten, or fifteen.

mental retardation An irreversibly low level of intellectual functioning—at least 30 percent below the norm for the person's age group. Although mentally retarded children are too disabled to reach adult intellectual levels, they can often learn enough social and vocational skills to permit living and working in an unsupervised, noninstitutional setting.

mirror reading A visual-perception problem in which the individual sees the mirror image of letters—*d*, for example, instead of *b*.

noncritical learning impediment Any learning impediment that prevents individuals from learning nonessential skills. Noncritical learning impediments usually have little consequence to the kind of learning needed for academic, emotional, social, or economic success.

oppositional behavior The failure to fulfill requests or directions of teachers and other authorities; also noncompliance.

outcome-based education A primary and secondary school curriculum that ignores formal grades and ties student acade-

in irreversibly low level
f

RARIES

SED

SDAY

mic work to specific levels of competency appropriate for the individual student instead of norms for a specific age group.

paraprofessional Any school employee without a teaching certificate whose duties are tied directly to the teaching process. School paraprofessionals include teacher aides, educational assistants, and auxiliary school personnel who are not volunteers and are paid to work part- or full-time with regular teachers or administrators. They do not have the training to teach and should not be assigned to any academic supervisory functions in special or regular education.

precision teaching A teaching approach that pinpoints a student's specific weaknesses and adapts the child's classroom work and homework assignments to help the student improve in those areas; an alternative to special education that allows regular classroom teachers to deal with student learning problems.

prereferral intervention A form of intervention by a regular classroom teacher to help a student overcome learning impediments without referring the child to special education.

programmed instruction A teaching technique that presents new learning materials in small, sequential units, each of which the student must learn before progressing to the next unit. Programmed instruction divides each unit of instruction into subunits so small that their diminutive size makes them easier to learn. After each subunit is presented, the student must respond to a series of questions and be told immediately which answers were correct or incorrect. If incorrect, the student must restudy the subunit and cannot progress to the next without completing the previous one correctly. Individualized programmed instruction allows students to progress at their own pace. Computer-operated programmed instruction is now routine in teaching modern foreign languages.

pull-out program Any element of the curriculum or school activities that requires a student to be pulled out of conventional classroom activities. Tutoring, remedial programs, and special education are often pull-out programs in public schools.

pupil personnel services   A confusing term that is now misused to mean guidance services, including counseling, psychological services, social work, health services, speech and hearing therapy, and special education. Some schools designate pupil personnel teams to meet regularly to discuss student problems and propose resolutions.

Pupils with Special Educational Needs (PSEN)   Special-education jargon for children with reading levels in the bottom one-quarter of their classes, not considered disabled but in need of remediation.

Pupils with Handicapping Conditions (PHC)   Special-education jargon for any child who is disabled.

reading reversal   A visual perception problem in which the student sees letters, words, or even sentences transposed—for example, *was* for *saw* or *right makes might* instead of *might makes right*.

remediation   Specialized or additional tutoring or education to correct one or more student academic deficiencies not associated with any learning impediments. Remediation is generally aimed at correcting errors in specific learning areas, such as reading, writing, or calculating, in which the student simply learned to function the wrong way. The remedial specialist teaches the child the right way. Remediation is usually specialized by academic area—that is, remedial reading, remedial writing, remedial mathematics, and so on.

resource room   Any classroom equipped for the special education of students with learning disabilities. Staffed by resource, or special-education teachers, resource rooms are usually equipped to handle no more than five students, who meet for thirty minutes to two hours a day for individual instruction, either during free periods or in lieu of regular classroom work.

Although resource rooms in well-financed schools have a variety of special equipment designed for special education, such rooms in most public schools are simply conventional, unused classrooms.

resource teacher A teacher trained in special education to meet the instructional needs of the learning disabled. Resource teachers may test, evaluate, design, and teach individualized instructional programs for the learning disabled.

sensory disability Any impairment in vision, hearing, touch, or other senses that interferes with learning.

special education A form of education specifically designed to meet the needs of students with learning impediments by teaching them successful methods of learning basic skills, including reading, writing, speaking, and calculating, that they would not be able to learn on their own.

speech disorder Any impairment that interferes with speaking and controlling the rate and rhythm of speech.

strephosymbolia A word created by combining the Greek words meaning "twisted symbols." It was the original name given to what later became known as dyslexia, by Samuel T. Orton, M.D. (1879–1948). A pediatrician who pursued graduate studies in education, neurology, pathology, and psychiatry, Orton was the first to conduct research in dyslexia and identify it as a form of word-blindness, rather than feeblemindedness.

stuttering A speech impairment that blocks the smooth transition from one syllable to another. Stuttering can appear as either abnormally long pauses, prolongations of the previous sound, or repetition of the same sound. Some speech therapists differentiate between stuttering, which refers to speech repetition; stammering, which refers to speech blockage; and cluttering, which refers to garbling of syllables. The causes have yet to be found for any of the three types of impairment, and few therapies have proved universally successful.

supportive feedback   An immediate report to a student that he or she has performed a task successfully.

underachiever   A student who consistently performs academically at levels significantly below his or her potential, as indicated by standardized intelligence tests and other examinations.

zero-reject concept   A concept derived from the Education for All Handicapped Children Act of 1975 (q.v.) and subsequent court decisions requiring public-school districts to provide all handicapped children living in those districts with free, appropriate education. Often called full inclusion (q.v.), the zero-reject concept forced public schools to reduce rejection rates of handicapped children to zero.

Index

About the Author

A graduate of Yale University, with an M.A. from California State University, Harlow G. Unger is a veteran journalist and radio commentator and the author of six books on education. These include the three-volume *Encyclopedia of American Education* as well as works on public- and private-school education, vocational education, and college admissions.